FEMOCRACY, FEMALITY & PHOETICS™

"Rebecoming Our Authentic Selves...
...For a World of Female Centrality"

NANCY LLEWELLYN

BALBOA.PRESS
A DIVISION OF HAY HOUSE

Balboa Press books may be ordered through booksellers or by contacting:

Balboa Press
A Division of Hay House
1663 Liberty Drive
Bloomington, IN 47403
www.balboapress.com
844-682-1282

Because of the dynamic nature of the Internet, any web addresses or links contained in this book may have changed since publication and may no longer be valid. The views expressed in this work are solely those of the author and do not necessarily reflect the views of the publisher, and the publisher hereby disclaims any responsibility for them.

The author of this book does not dispense medical advice or prescribe the use of any technique as a form of treatment for physical, emotional, or medical problems without the advice of a physician, either directly or indirectly. The intent of the author is only to offer information of a general nature to help you in your quest for emotional and spiritual well-being. In the event you use any of the information in this book for yourself, which is your constitutional right, the author and the publisher assume no responsibility for your actions.

Any people depicted in stock imagery provided by Getty Images are models, and such images are being used for illustrative purposes only.
Certain stock imagery © Getty Images.

Print information available on the last page.

ISBN: 979-8-7652-5606-0 (sc)
ISBN: 979-8-7652-5605-3 (hc)
ISBN: 979-8-7652-5604-6 (e)

Library of Congress Control Number: 2024920748

Balboa Press rev. date: 02/18/2025

For DT

Many are called; few are chosen. Many have talent; few have the character to realize the talent. Character is the mystery, and it is individual.

—James Hillman, *The Soul's Code*

CONTENTS

PART 2: FEMALITY

PART 3: PHOETICS

PART 4: FEMALE GLOSSARY

FOREWORD 1

As someone who has known Nancy Llewellyn for thirty years, I have been a witness to her creativity, wisdom, and strong intuitive ability. Her creation of Phoetics© is an original concept. It is the culmination of her life's work in which she transforms the tragedy and abuse experienced in childhood into a method that brings lifechanging insights into past trauma, so the healing process can begin. Anyone who starts their journey with Phoetics will come away with new insights and self-awareness. It is, as it were, a window into the self. For the first time, you can read Nancy's deep dive into her own complex and abusive childhood, her years of recovery, and the method she has created toward the understanding and insights into our younger selves, so we may begin the process of healing and integration.

Nancy is a writer with gifts in the use of metaphor, mythology, and storytelling. Throughout this book, Nancy takes us through a personal journey to wholeness, integration, and healing and creates for all who are interested in Female Awakening, Authenticity, and empowerment a path as a means to get there.

I am sure that in reading her story, you will gain new insights into your own journey.

—Janice H

FOREWORD 2

In "Rhiannon," the legendary Stevie Nicks, lead singer of the band Fleetwood Mac, sang her brilliant and profound lyrics that capture Nancy Llewellyn to a tee. In her signature raspy style Nicks breaks out, "Once in a million years a lady like her rises." This is Nancy's leitmotif. Her ancient energy and unending dedication to the mission for this planet has arrived perfectly timed, when women and the future of society need it the most. What is the mission? *Returning this world back to its Original Female Cosmic and earthly nature.*

The universe is nothing more than energy that takes the shape of anything and everything. We all have the capacity to feel and experience energy and we often do without even realizing it. Some may be more tuned in than others. That doesn't make one better or worse, just different. The thing is, when you are tuned into energy, you have the opportunity to experience the frequency of something that's ancient, not of this world. You feel the energy of a force for truth and goodness so great, it can't be mistaken for anything else. It's raw. It's wise. It's powerful. Its purpose: to change the course of our existence in a way that benefits the whole. That's what I experienced the first time I met Nancy. *I had never felt this particular energy before. It was unmistakable and obvious.*

The level of insight and understanding of what needs to transpire to return the world to its original nature is the sole focus of Nancy's world. Against all seeming odds, and she has faced stiff and challenging odds over and over, nothing stops her. Nancy remains dedicated to the mission of bringing women back to their authentic female, powerful selves, that which was lost in childhood. That is her only purpose. Nothing else matters.

The energy of the planet needs to shift from its current, destructive, and unnatural state to its natural state of growth, cultivation, and healing. Turning this world back to its Original Female Cosmic and Earthly Nature means putting women in charge, which is natural and normal. But first, women must know who and what they truly are and how to take back their reins, the ones that have always belonged to them. The reason? Children first. Putting children first is the only way forward.

To put children first, women must re-learn how to think through their bodies. That's where the energies cycle, from the mind to the womb. No woman has ever taught this or been taught this critical element. Nancy teaches it. She teaches it through a never-before discovered technique, the ancient and cutting-edge process of Phoetics™; what Nancy calls, "The poetic truth in our childhood photographs." Nancy's genius of Phoetics is a serious game changer for all women and men who want to retake the Authenticity stolen from them.

Reclaiming our Authenticity unlocks and starts the launch sequence for this critical shift to take shape. Women taking their rightful and powerful place resets the balance of life and energy. Phoetics is the key to returning to that natural state down to its deepest roots.

It's time for women to assume their rightful place and exert their power filled with wisdom, compassion and problem solving the right way. Nancy is vital to this massive energetic movement. One only needs to spend a moment with this ancient, wise, game-changer to realize and feel within the depths of intuition that *she is the answer to the required shift of energy that is long overdue and of the utmost importance.*

Bo L. Arnold

PREFACE

This book came into being when I was having my third nervous breakdown at forty-one, when my younger daughter was turning eight. It was different this time. My old, "Get thee to a therapist" morphed into "Get thee to a Real-Deal Female Therapist" (RDFT). Finally, at long last, I was ready, willing, and able to brace myself to see a woman instead of the old, moldering Freudian psychiatrists in Beverly Hills, as my mother before me. In 1991 it was no mean feat to find a Female Therapist let alone the right one but I did. When the student is ready, the teacher will come.

Ladye Synchronicity was in full force that day. Pat, a child rights advocate, was exactly my age. Her first request would change the course of my life: "Bring in any family photographs."

That would set me on a path that was both my true Character and Calling, leading me to the creation of *Phoetics*: "The poetic truth in every childhood photograph," and eventually to the creation and publication of this book. That original request galvanized a process I had carried with me from Female Otherworld, ready to share with women *the authentic Great Sacred Girl we all begin as.*

What I discovered was that *to become a fully present mother, it would translate into becoming the mother I deserved all along for the girl I once was. It all connects and interweaves.* Sometimes what we catch ourselves saying— "Oh my, I sound just like my mother." On a deeper level our actions need a brand new awareness of healthy mother-daughter relationship. For that was the nitty-*gritty* of what would become my life's purpose.

FemaleLove is based on the earthly-cosmic MotherDaughtering of lead and follow, teach, and learn, our sacred symbiosis. Daughters teach their mothers; that is how this primal process flows. And this is how we grow and roll. Under the Death Culture (World Patriarchy), we lose pieces of our inborn authenticity awaiting in our Girlhood Photographs.

I pray all women and the men who love them, embark on the Phoetics journey-that pilgrimage to Rebecome the Great Authentic Sacred Girl who awaits to be embraced, supported, celebrated all days forward.

At forty-one, it became more and more obvious I had scattered behind me my most precious gifts, but here's the thing about Childhood Photographs. They remain where we left them, preserved with all our Female Truths, and they wait for us to return, reclaim, and Rebecome our authentic selves, with Phoetics.

Repression's Duality

Repression cuts both ways. Throughout youth, it acts as a shield though triggers and red flags often intrude. By and during teens and adulthood, those PTSD traumas metastasize. As a dysfunctional woman and mother, something was wrong. My daughters deserved a mom who was fully integrated and fully present. I remember asking Pat how long it would take to heal, learning the minimum average was seven years, yet the caveat takes in account; how early the abuse began, and how often. There was no guesstimating. So. Bring it. I pledged aloud, "Whatever it takes, no matter how long it takes." My daughters' souls hung in the balance.

Dedicating myself to healing from Child Sexual Abuse-Incest (CSAI) was natural, because my Authenticity is all. In those early sessions, I had to lie down afterwards in the side office. I could not safely drive. I would break the cycle of abuse that had rotted every generation on both sides of my biological family, the very least of what we all deserved.

The Phoetics Breakthrough: 'There is a photograph that is both my shame and salvation'

I never stopped interacting with my childhood photographs. Months, years passed. And then one day, I found my left hand begin to write with its own will. What had I been staring at? What had prompted some long-repressed truth to run through the inked truth and feel so accurate, yet undiscernible at the time?

Nancy As Kewpie Doll (Photo lost)

A tiny, faded Kodachrome shot of me—passed around to the grandmothers and aunts. My mother's first publicity shots of a pretty, adorable, "happy" daughter. Dressed like a baby doll from Uncle Bernie's, melting like a Hershey's Kiss in the searing Southern California rays, itchy organza bonnet bow under my chin, a Helen Fenton Easter dress of white organza with red velvet hearts, white Mary Janes and bobby socks, a poufy purse dangling from the crook of my toddler's arm. Illusion accomplished. I was almost three, and to say it was my shame and salvation makes total sense today. It made sense then too, but I had to dig, dig, dig to bring it up to full consciousness.

What I proffer to all souls:

> *We lock away our shame, we lock away our potential for a mentally, physically healthy life. Without normal memory reprocessing, we lock away our Authenticity with its accompanying gifts: Character and Calling.*

I used to hand over my dream notes to my Pat and in her signature India ink fountain pen, her last note read, "Nancy must tell her story, costumes or no costumes." A joking reference about how all I watched were BBC costume dramas, comedies, mysteries, and Brit faire.

And that is how, over the next twenty-five years with a new rare, wise, gifted, and sacred female therapist (RDFT), I continued interacting with my childhood photos, goddess culture, and the Female sacred reunion of our BodyPsyche that women know less than little about how we cycle in tandem with the cosmic-earthly moonpulse). As I began, one thing led to another, and "*connecting the Female Dots*" birthed a brand-new *Female Glossary of Terms* for our first female language go-tos. Phoetics itself took on a life of its own in workshops, private sessions, even a radio show. A broadcast to the world of women and the men who loved them who so desperately needed its wisdom and counsel.

No Mean Feat—Breaking down the teaching of Phoetics

What I did came naturally but would have to be broken down and reprocessed for women and men to receive and apply this life-changing intuitive counseling technique. They were entitled to reclaim and rebecome their original authentic selves preserved in their sacred childhood photos. I named Phoetics for "The poetic truth in every childhood photograph." The brave souls I worked with, either in private or publicly on the air sessions, have graciously permitted their jaw-dropping Phoetics in Part Three. They were my first test marketing both in workshops and one-on-one sessions, seeded in my native SoCal, watered, and blossomed in Ohio, garnering its own live radio show,[1] "Fun with Phoetics."

Time to Soar Home

On the Wing'd grace of Phoetics, I flew back to California to continue my Phoetics practice, which, in turn, fed, cultivated, and yielded many of the insights offered in this book.

It is my deepest desire these insights, Female Truths, commonalities of girl-loving MotherDaughtering, will open your Female Eyes to inspire *your own* unique journey to reclaim what was stolen from your Sacred State of Girlbeing supported by its twin pillars: Character and Calling.

---

[1] **WCRX-LP** (102.1 FM) was a low-power FM radio station licensed to serve Columbus, Ohio, United States. WCRX-LP was a not-for-profit, volunteer, non-commercial radio station whose broadcast license was held by the Bexley Public Radio Foundation, a registered 501(c)(3) non-profit corporation. Programming and broadcast operation assistance was provided by Sax Entertainment Music and Media. Its license was cancelled by the Federal Communications Commission (FCC) on October 2, 2020 for failure to file an application for license renewal. Wikipedia

ACKNOWLEDGEMENTS

Ladye Fate graced me with wise, selfless females who showed up when I needed assistance, creating a blog, website, and photograph, attending, and assisting in workshops, guest attendants on my radio show "Fun with Phoetics," sharing their Phoetics with me and to those who offered sharing theirs in this first book. Healing, reeling, and revealing—I was privy to their deepest Female Truths, granted the privilege and pleasure of dancing with each and every one, singing and sheer female energy exchanged. I have been validated, appreciated, complemented by each one's sacred presence. Dreams can come true.

It has been a journey, always was their inner girl who sparkles in their eyes—secretive, impish, fierce, and great—that kept me going.

Women alone are my muses, champions, and spirit carriers and above all, healers.

My long-term RDFTs—Real Deal Female Therapists—were my first trusted friends as an adult, and I followed their sound, wise, female advise as each was a child's-rights advocate. My Columbus, Ohio, peeps, some of whom chose to gift you with a courageous sharing of their personal Phoetics, are my teachers of uncommon courage, the Female Leadership Brain, Great Cosmic Mothers, and make me who I am today. They are my female spirit medicine as I pray I am theirs: Amanda Mia Mahelick, Susie Schiering, Lisa Noland Shalosky, Cindy Riggs, Marcia Reel, Carrie Sabba, April R., Sally K., Dara C., Julie M., Joetta P., JP H. and others.

To the talented and gracious Sandra U., who brought me back to brace myself and hold the guitar after forty years and whispered in my ear when I was learning Scottish folk dances to the fiddle and the pipes. And for following my lead in rounds of *Tender Shepherds,* serenading your sacred grandchildren to sleep. *Tapadh leat.*

To Kelly "Doc" Austin, who was there to bear witness with a kind and generous heart during my most critical healing as my long-term repression lifted. She was the epitome of a safe and sacred witness to Great Sacred Girl Truths, and for that I am forever grateful.

And endless hugs to a special woman whose glint of female masculinity takes me home whenever it flashes, a giving, savvy, strong, oh-so-human being. I can call on you for healthy female advice and counsel. Your insight and support were a game-changer even in its mid-stages, it catapulted the courage to draft the rest of the necessary pages. You are always there when I can say anything and not hesitate, while Dixie listens. I always wanted a best friend like you, so thank you, dear Sherrie Dean. Could not have completed this first book without you.

It is said we may find our true spirit family along our journey, and though I had no positive adult role models in my biological family, I found them in grammar school. They are the teachers, mothers, and girls of My Female Tales that I invite you to meet. Consider this a soiree, where I offer you the privilege of these great female souls from my past and present, alive on these pages. It is amazing what the sheer magical presence can do for a girl who is anorexic in MotherDaughter Love. Blessings to you, Barbara A., Carolyn Woodward, Harriet Williams and Molly, the unforgettable Jeanne Breedlove S., her blessed daughter Christine Lee S., and my precious, loving, sweet Madolyn S. (Other girls' and boys' names are fictionalized to honor their privacy.)

I am indebted to those Women's Women authors, especially Adrienne Rich, who hit upon the reason females belong together and why we are all so starving as "little girls lost" in the primacy of women's relationships: Motherhood and Daughterhood. She was able to see past the then-popular idea of Sisterhood. Bless you, Adrienne. And the Women's Women of Femality's Spirit, the late great Audre Lorde, Kathie Carlson, Monica Sjoo, Barbara Mor, Ellen Bass, Laura Davis, Judith Herman, Elinor Gadon, Marija Gimbutas, et al. Yet I would not and could not have integrated what and all I needed to without their pages of Female Truths, Female Love, Child Abuse Sexual Healing memoirs.

Gratitude to the male writers and their insightful visions....

My greatest gratitude goes to the great, sightful, wise James Hillman. Without his book, I do not know if I would have parsed together the pieces of my sanity, until he expressed it in *The Soul's Code: A Key to Character and Calling*. By the time I came to his last chapter, it felt like it left off where I pick up. I could quote him to eternity and kept the calendar of his 365 quotes. His last signed book to me—someone he did not know—resides in a safe deposit box (thank you, Kelly, for procuring this treasure, knowing what it meant to me).

Blessings to Melvin Konner MD, author of *Women after All*, who was inspired *by* Ashley Montague's *The Natural Superiority of Women (1955)*. Not all our treasured friends are those we know in the flesh. Most of my friends live in spirit on the written pages of their courageous, generous genius of inspiration and validation. Altogether they are a blessing to a girl who learned, by these authors and others, that there are much more than "just a few good men." There are many caring, smart, savvy men who look to the Great Sacred Girl and Woman for guidance, wisdom, and light. They honor the Great Sacred State of Childbeing. I doff my cap to them, one and all.

Throughout this book, I reveal and expose newly-unredacted Female Truths, like how the energies of MotherDaughtering cures us safely in FemaleLove. I have the honor of covering this primacy granted to me by Diana Cortès's riveting insights in her exclusive interview, *The Echo of the Other*. It was from viewing her leading in Female Tango, where I witnessed how MotherDaughtering goes back and forth between all females, from the sandbox to the dance floor to life itself. This is who we are and why our stories are critical to build world Femocracy and turn it back on its rightful axis, Female Centricity.

Finally, through RDFT (Real Deal Female Therapists) and my Ladye folk spirit guides—learned how to be a better mother; to listen and pay attention, to be fully present, because *kids out-wise us every time. Don't be a Stupid Adult. No excuses.*

Lastly, an Homage to My Lifesaving Childhood Photographs

Without my childhood photographs, I would not exist to myself. If I didn't have my childhood photographs, I would have no proof ever of my own, true existence. My early childhood was so bizarre, isolated, and suffocated by bizarre and crazy "grownups," trying to survive their insanity was impossible. The only way my female eyes and ears was an immediate vision of the Death Culture's archetypal characters.

Fortunately, I see through Female Archetypal Eyes, necessary to see Female Truths behind every hidden disguise. Adults are well-versed in this evil practice, as they learn in childhood from other adults. My given acronym for them is SA for Stupid Adults; but make no mistake, not all SAs are as stupid as they pretend, and many are evil by proxy.

Evil has its organizations, groups, cults, flags, symbols, propaganda, and clubs, which I call Isms. Isms are implemented by souls who refer to them as "families," but the concept of Family carries different yet similar meanings across the sphere. When I refer to our planet in a cosmic way, it is This Sphere. When earthly, it is Earth, Mother Earth, sometimes Global. All are relevant depending on the spirit context to which they relate.

Childhood photographs carry and resonate energies like nothing else. Whenever I ask, "What is the first childhood photo that pops into your mind?" The answers are very telling. Then, I ask, "What is the second? The third?" Eventually, we get around to how they are kept and where they are, equally as revealing to how we feel about the child we once were, what she survived, what she adored, the sacred states of Girlbeing alive within who awaits our return. If I sound too esoteric, it is because of what I saw on both sides of every which way in between Evil and Beauty, during my Sacred State of Girlbeing (SSGB).

What and all I tell, rewind, and project again on the written page is simply this, for it is every girl's story in this sphere, full stop: "The Sacred State of Girlbeing under the Death Culture." Since this sphere has been forever enslaved by the Death Culture, there is no other way to report it as a girl's early years. I call it as I saw it, what and all I saw, felt, heard, and intuited is documented in Part 1, Chapter 5: My Female Tales, which are selected Girls' Stories, courtesy of my childhood photos. I did not have actual photos of us. They existed only in my Great Female BodyPsyche, and it was the process of Phoetics that opened the portals to those particular times and sacred events that were safely remembered.

Without Phoetics, I could not have found the courage to revisit those times Trauma, and Joy. And yes, when one is treading the Toxic Waters of the Death Culture, even Joy can be unbearable to revisit.

With the magic of my childhood photos, safely witnessing, as my trusted Witness, I revisited the beauty and horror of those Sacred Girl times, with successful results of Rebecoming My Sacred Female Authentic Self.

Blessings. It's always about the Photographs.

Nancy Llewellyn, October 2024

INTRODUCTION

To All Great Sacred Girls and the Women They Inhabit

My story is captured and lives forever in my childhood photos. I am the one who carries the truths I had to figure out; how to hide from any adult retributions and retaliations when I was so little and just stood poker-faced for the camera:

- As a toddler in full pinafore-dissociation;
- As a sweet, loving five-year-old cradling Midnight the cat, hiding dark, disturbing secrets no child should ever have to lug inside her sacred psyche; and
- As the eight-year-old Great Sacred Girl in my first Mythographs, I was resolute and determined to figure out this place of insanity and to live to tell about it—no matter what it took, no matter how long. My eyes say it all.

We have nothing but our stories. It is why we arrive here. It is our Ultimate Female Power. Whether you volunteered for good or bad intentions, your story is your Character and Calling, lived, and reflected in your childhood photographs—your *Phoetics*. They may carry cartoon characters, or echo archetypal figures from books and films the child in you recognizes as the real-life scary and sacred background characters of your own true-life story.

Your story is not the one your parents plagiarized to you.

Your story is not what kids concocted about you.

Your story is not versions from Stupid Adults (SAs): parents, extended family, teachers, religious leaders, coaches, and others who project their low self-esteem self-images on to you.

> *Your story is all about the Authentic You. The Great Sacred*
> *Girl being you began as carry deep inside. Your story is*
> *captured in the* fullness of your *Phoetics.*

Only you own your true story. It belongs to you solely and *soul-ly*. Your childhood photos preserved all its truths, waiting to be blessed by your return and sacred reunion. Like all blessings, they are symbiotic and bless you for honoring your imaged truths. Your burning desire to Rebecome your Authentic Self—just as you were and appear in each and every one of them—answers their prayers.

How We Keep Our Childhood Photos Speaks Volumes

Our toxic secrets hide right under our noses. They are toxic. We are not.

They remain in frayed boxes scattered in piles of generational black and whites, pages falling away from their mother albums, shrinking away from a cardboard frame, faded color shots now anemic from sun exposure and, of course, the digitals. Not all childhood photos are toxic. Many capture goodness, joy, and hilarity that arrives on the wings of Lady Irony. These preserve a plethora of storied child wealth. These energy-truths clicked before Stupid Adults of the Death Culture stole our sacred Female Authenticity, and with it, the freedom and creative release of the Platinum of Natural Spontaneity.

The Seeding of Phoetics—1991

When I was facing forty-one, my youngest daughter was facing the same age I was in a photo I had avoided all my life. (See: You are looking at an image of a Great Sacred Girl. Page 15)

I hold my skirts out in an arc in front before a dank, dark, unforgiving fireplace. Snapped during my death wish times of my father's nightly abuse. I feared my melting down projected from the photo. I was to learn the greatest Phoetics lesson.

That which you may cringe over (in a particular childhood photo,) often turns out to be your most powerful Mythograph—the childhood photo that carries and projects one's Character and Calling. As I faced sharing it with my therapist, dying inside because of the tell-tale dark circles under my eyes, she leant back Gertrude Stein-ish. 'Oh, The Power Photo.' What?

Suddenly and as time went on, I gleaned from my photo anew. My eyes project a determination broadcasting, 'I will figure this all out and one future day, will spill all my Female Truths.' My lips, a Mona Lisa ambiguity. It would prove to guide me through Phoetics to infinite earthly and cosmic Female Otherworlds.

However, that age of eight was the main trigger—when my youngest daughter was approaching it—and really rocked what little I had in the world. I was in despair. Remembered nothing, so I believed. I was at the crossroads of losing my mind versus putting my children first. They deserved an integrated and fully present mother. I was sick of pretending as a pseudo-adult. Frantically seeking the rare female therapist—no mean feat in 1991—my spirit guides stepped in and gifted the perfect fit for me. *Bibbidi-Bobbidi-Boo*, Pat! Pat was like an empathetic surgeon. She detoxified all the poisons while giving me my first empathy experiences. I thank my loving guides every day for her presence at the time I had no one to help me make any sense of the world. Until then I had no understanding that empathy was a thing that existed—at least for me. I had never been a recipient.

A child's rights advocate, Pat had published a children's book. For that reason alone she was for me. My then husband and I came in ostensibly for marriage counseling. Yet, as I was in such a desperate way, she assessed I could start coming in for single sessions. Having found the first Real Deal Female Therapist (RDFT) I took the ball, ducked my head, and ran with it.

The First Thing Pat Requested-Bring in your family photographs.

Of whom? What? Whatever I wanted. I remember dragging boxes up her wiggly elevator; the ones we talked about that first day were my wedding album, but soon I zeroed in on those of me, from birth to age eight, where they abruptly curtailed.

In the early months, we were working on lifting a lifelong Repression. I distinctly recall asking her, "Why do you suspect abuse? If there were fifteen red flags to meet those requirements, I could check them all." Too many red flags of abuse had to be addressed. Too many Death Culture redactions that needed what was hidden beneath. Too many red flags. And a plethora of beautiful, exciting girlhood moments I had repressed along with the traumas.

How long does it take to heal from CSA, (Child Sexual Abuse)? "The earlier it happened, the longer it went on, the longer it takes," she added.

Since that was true for me, I decided to go with EMDR (eye movement desensitization and reprocessing) and hypnosis, to assist cracking open the vaults where I locked away my triple threats. We went over each and every photo with surprise after surprise coming and leading to more and more questions. A good therapist will ask you to ask whoever was around as an adult, the wherefores, and any whys. Sometimes it is like a magic wand—the false stories render you nearly numb, while the wand promises a better, more authentic life.

More time dragged on. At home, I practiced everything Pat taught me about being a fully present mom. She had no qualms with faking it till you make it. Until practice makes normal, in this case. Post sessions, I had to lie down in the next room until I was able to drive. Pat kept a trashcan next to the couch for clients who vomit with their toxic abuse-incest memories.

And then it happened.

Scene: Pat's office six months later

I stare blankly at the empty light socket when a voice from my throat announces:

'Uncle Al pretends to be Goofy, but he's really the Big Bad Wolf.'

Pregnant pause. Clock ticks. Bird pecks at the window. What happened?

Pat: 'I think little Nancy just came out.'

She was one thousand percent right. I had locked little Nancy away in Bluebeard's castle-keep; the tower door had a key for her to come and go. Since she was a target and kept getting attacked, this was my Female Creative hack to keep her safe from family and world predators—protecting my original, Authentic Identity.

Instead of being ashamed of three-year-old Nancy, we began to interact via the photos and beyond. Authentic Nancy's newly grown trust of the 'adult me' opened the door to *why the light socket was my trigger of the abuse-incest trauma*. It was something I had to dissociate after the abuse for hours as he did his carpet laying in my grandmother's apartment house. His knees kept whacking a Knee Kicker. My stomach stopped. I did not know if would ever see my grandma again. Traumatized, terrorized, I went into full-on dissociation and stared at the unplugged socket. Stared, because I had finally remembered and tapped into the ugly, scary truths of who my uncle really was, and no one saw but me, especially the SAs (stupid adults) in that Family of Dark Denial.

At least that is what I thought at the time and many decades forward. Then I would remember he took me to Felix Chevrolet while he played poker, with wads of cash. I was passed around from lap to lap of strange, grease-stinking, dirty men, and then ordered to stay in the back of the store. There I found a bunch of boys peeing on the wall. High above was Felix the Cat's evil smirk of coconspirator. I was Betty Boop again. Chased after. Abused. Abandoned. With no phone, no way to reach Grandma.

Know this: The Big Bad Wolf and Goofy Are Two Sides of the Same Being

Uncle Al preview

A tall, gangly, stooping creature like the hitchhiking ghosts in The Haunted Mansion ride; long snout, gravel voice, Rasputin air, ate Grandma's chopped liver sandwiches, pieces dropping like turds from the sides of his cramped palette. Right out of Central Casting. His bushy black tail protruded from his Big Bad Wolf overalls and high-top tennis shoes. Walt Disney created this duality. He did so because while making the character slow-witted, he could masque its flipside: evil. The Big Bad Wolf Child Predator. If Uncle Al fooled some, those whom he had already abused had grown up in a permanent state of PTSD. Grandma Mary blew up when I was crying my eyes out not to "take a ride" with Uncle Al, and she beat him on the chest, berating him, wailing, "Again? *Again?*"

Relieved, I expected her to take my hand and bring me with her back into the house. Instead, she turned her back on me, whirling on her Mandel pumps, and the front door slam-banged behind her. Safely hidden in her Kitchen Comfort Zone, brewing in her caldron on the burners for her "good family" of ghouls, ghosts, and goblins. When I first saw the Dining Room Scene in Disneyland's Haunted Mansion, it triggered a near panic attack. Right before me in 360 degrees was the phantom automaton-family of my early childhood. The only difference was unlike the ride, the figures of my family were not twirling in a waltz. No music ever played in that house, except in my head or on my mother's radio.

I was alone. All alone. Even though Grandma knew who and what the Big Bad Wolf was, she abandoned me to his pea-green '35 pickup, which had stopped idling. All because of my mother's sadistic suggestion: "Al, why not take Nancy for a ride? She's been all cooped up here."

To go for a ride meant torture in Grandma's apartment house basement. And not the first time. Not the only place. Before that when I was on the black cherry soda can and hid inside Grandpa's gigantic sunflowers' black fly-eyes where the seeds lived. (*See: Part One, My Female Tales 'If You Could Peer Back'*).

He throttled me on top of the tool table in Grandpa's garage. The door was barred so his evil was muffled in silence. He barked at me in that gravelly throat that if I didn't stop screaming, he'd saw me in half, holding the trembling saw over me to drive the point home. Betty Boop lashed onto a conveyer belt trapped in a cube of ice, headed toward my final dismembering. Terrorized, mournful pleas for mercy, I did what we all do in fight-flight-freeze mode: I left my body through the oil-smeared window next to the tool table, holding hands with The White Rock Fairy on the black cherry soda can and hid inside Grandpa's gigantic sunflowers' black fly-eyes where the seeds lived.

Sexual Abuse: The Ultimate Trespassing of One's Body and Soul

The transference between a predator and its child prey carries a *trespassing participation mystique*. Ignored, unexplored by child therapists let alone written and taught, it is this under-the-radar scenario that is the fodder of this book's contents. We hide the abuse—unbearable to bear the shock of such cruelty, let alone at three years old. I stuffed it into the trauma zones of our child memory bank, slammed shut like Fort Knox. In fight-flight-freeze, we have no choice but to leave our bodies, leaving the initial abuse—to even begin to get on with a life that is not a life. Yet, *the body always remembers what the Conscious Mind forgets*. The trauma remains unprocessed until or unless you are ready to address its intrusive, gnawing symptoms: Triggers. Triggers are tripped by any sights, scents, songs, sounds, smells, and other sensory memories linked to the trauma. *Make no mistake: a toxic secret is malignant psychic cancer. It metastasizes over a lifetime.* In gallows humor, those of us abused as children come from "Metastas City."

Phoetics—never-seen images of our Authentic Self

Hunting for more photos, I sought girls and boys I had known in grammar school. I found a girl who lived down the block and this is the story that ensued:

'Three Great Sacred Girls in Full Flight' (Photo Lost)

Phoetics is a journey of many roads that whip and wind, serpentine and drop us to life-altering events with which we would never otherwise have been gifted. These are the Sacred Sleuthing Female Truths. We become Nancy Drew—hot on the trail for our Sovereignty and Sanity. Trust me. Who would ever stop a treasure trove hunt? You may find yourself going forth detecting where long lost-relatives, teachers, or old friends if they have any old photos of you at that certain grammar school age. She did.

And what I saw, dazzled. She dug through what her mother had left behind and found one that her father had taken of us three girls when we were all seven. *I got to glimpse a side of me I'd never seen before, never reflected by any soul.* We met in person, and I wish I had made a copy.

Three Great Sacred Girls, leaping over a berm on the front lawn of one's house. He must have been practicing photography, because he took the worm's eye-view while lying on the grass, making us appear larger than life.

Me in the middle, Janey on the right, Sharon on the left. Milky charcoal grays, contrasted with the sunbeams projected behind us, were evocative of The Place with Only girls. I have never ever seen a photo of myself at any age where my energies flew out the frame.

I was fast, high-leaping, and triumphant, the leader in the trio, instead of the wilting violet my mother projected upon me. This time was my grand Phoetics' gift of truth. The me I never knew existed—beautiful, formidable, fierce, and fearless. So excited and grateful for this first positive spontaneous image of my true seven-year-old authenticity that I asked my old friend if she would be so kind as to copy and scan it for me.

Lesson learned. Hard. No matter how many times I reminded her, she said she could not find it. A cautionary tale: this often happens. For some unknown trigger reasons, they avoid it. Once is enough. To go home. I would have to accept and respect this mental block while at the same time be honest about no future possibility of picking up on a relationship we never really had. It is amazing how you can run into someone you broke up with or lost connection with fifty years ago, and in a nanosecond, remember why.

Then, there are past friends who give back full measure, everything you long to shower them with to make up for the times you were kids, juggling the Death Culture. I whipped on my Nancy Drew cloak, jumped in my blue roadster, sleuthing, all my childhood friends for validation, information, and reconnection with their photographs and stored memories, especially any with me I had never seen.

Reunion with Madolyn—Long lost slides of us third grade's May Festival.

Fifty years is a long time, but she proved faithful and was only too happy to send whatever slides she could scrounge up from the May festivals in our elementary school. Her daughter assisted with the digital part, and what do you know ...

It was 1957. Dancing the Wabash Cannonball on the blacktop. There were a few cute ones close up with Madolyn, looking like the little Dutch Girl; but the ones in bonnets and aprons, *dancing* to music (her dad was a violinist in the LA Philharmonic) were focused on me. It's that old energy physics thing: the camera lens is just pulled to where the energy is strongest. Too bad the brim of my bonnet hides my face, but it's my body language, and I wear a bracelet on my right hand. That's me. My dancer's concentration of getting the steps to perfection is baked into all those slide images.

I found Madolyn again in the early 2000s. A happy, fun, and warm outcome. Madolyn. I flew up to visit, met her adult daughter. She, played piano for me. I sniffled. No one played like Madolyn. She was a child protégé. We reunited, and so inspired, 'The Swan called Madolyn' (see: My Female Tales, The Girls.)

Ghosting My Way through Life

Under the Death Culture, we become less and less real to ourselves. That's how it was, *ghosting my way through life*. Seldom did I stare at a mirror. When I did it was as a vampire—no reflection. To me, I did not exist in Real Life. The biggest shock of all was that instead of my sacred childhood photos—crammed in the catacombs of my psyche, interred in faux brass frames, moldering in the mausoleums of my mind—the Real Me was vibrantly alive. Both in the photos and in Real Life.

This is why and how I owe my story of true existence, my body and soul's voice to those sacred photos of the girl I redacted. The camera does not lie. Snapped mostly by my father, on his haunches, the old Brownie swinging between his knees, peering down into the upside-down lens. These priceless gems—birthed as negatives, bathed in honest solutions, and developed into the finished positives at Kodak—assured me that yes, there was a time where I did exist as a child. I had really once existed—the real, authentic, spontaneous Great Sacred Girl Nancy—in those old photos my father took when my mother ordered him to.

Reentry into Real and Human

From that first time Nancy peeked around the corner and told the truth about her uncle she had to repress upon threat of death, I was free to ask questions of the little girl I once locked away. I could reassure her. Adore her. Sketch her. Sketch with her. Laugh at her wit. Cradle her in my arms and assure her she would never again be trapped in Al's truck, Dad's car, or Mom's presence. It was the beginning of a long, trying, rewarding time that continues to this day.

So, I owe my story's soul-voice and gift for true memoir to the first eight years, from ages two to eight. These photos and the Phoetics they gifted and continue to do whenever I choose to tap into them when The Great Sacred Girl calls. Something—only in the photos—saved me. And yet there was much more ...

That very first moment when I found my pen writing with will and force all its own: *There is a photograph that is both my shame and salvation* in which I intuited a rare and overreaching process. My Calling was finally tapped into, to invite every great sacred girl in her sacred childhood photographs, a voice. *Hers to, at last, speak her Female Truth aloud. With me her safe witness to validate those long-stuffed-down truths.* What was really going on when a particular photo was snapped, before, during, and after? The world she was trapped in, the souls orbiting around her. Her intuitive brilliance and seeing through female eyes, the evil all around, of what I would name The Death Culture (Patriarchy).

When a wise woman, seasoned editor, asked: "You mean you got all this prose and stories just from interacting with your childhood photos?" Yes, how else? She begged me to, "Please find a way to teach this to women. They are so creatively blocked and starved to open up their deepest voices. You have an innovative yet ancient way of tapping into these resources. It is a brand-new, freeing-up-major-healing process."

Phoetics to Teach? Piece of Cake

Within two weeks, Poetics came into being, ready to test out and observe the successful results. I had to work backward, disassembling how I naturally intuited making a safe place for their Female Truths to enter their consciousness. Mentally and spiritually I began to try my process for coaxing out our powerful, original Sacred Female Authenticity for women brave and resolved to put their trust in me and Phoetics, guiding and reuniting with the Great Sacred Girl they had abandoned so long ago.

I broke it down like colored building blocks. All the steps I so naturally did its creation, and named it *Phoetics, for the poetic truth in every childhood photograph. After years of workshops, what kept coming back at me,* "We want your book!"

I wanted my book. Intuiting it was time I explore that vast journey to find The Place with Only Girls, female centrality, governance, and essence. Nothing we girls, nor our grandmothers, great grandmothers and our ancestresses had ever been taught, but I had brought with me to birth into this world.

I realized I had to dive fathoms deeper to gather a vaster, understanding of what my PsycheBody had created to be receptive to new ideas, discoveries, growth, and opportunities for Phoetics's clients, all the while foreseeing a brand-new world of Female Centrality.

It is thirty-plus years in the making, for every Great Sacred Girl who ever lived and is alive today in every woman's eyes and those yet to grace this planet.

By Rebecoming Our Sacred Authentic Female Selves, we galvanize, organize, and release the Force of Sacred Femality to return this sphere back to its original, natural, central state: Female.

PART ONE

FEMOCRACY

1

MY FIRST TASTE OF FEMOCRACY

'The more this beast will eat, he wants more, more, more.'
Ukrainian President Volodymyr Zelensky, March 7, 2022

FEMOCRACY DEFINITION: "The female's inborn self-governing system from her uterine body & brain (PsycheBody). The Sovereign Female who listens, follows, respects her PsycheBody's directives, i.e. red flags, yellow warnings and greenlights. Female inner self-governance."

I got my first taste of Femocracy from a child's matinee. It was the perfect year. The perfect time. The perfect escort. The perfect theater just blocks from where I lived. Inside the El Rey Theatre, the perfect Otherworld darkness contrasted with the projector's overhead beam of light. It was a fifty-minute animation from France by a man and woman who knew quite well of the Dark Forces' hold on the world and gave their best to children viewers to give a triumphant victory.

Femocracy Found – 'Johnny the Giant Killer' on the Silver Screen

The Giant: Tyrant. Dictator. Reductionist. Mechanistic. Existential threat to the Natural Female Based world. Monster in human disguise.

Queenie: Embodiment of Female Life Centrality. Represents the sacred harmony of The Great Female Leadership Brain & Body. Creatress of the 'the stuff of Life,' No queen bees, no life.

What I recognized as Femocracy was really what I had always called "The Place with Only Girls."

Johnny the Giant Killer, French Animation, 1950 (Producer Jean Image)

Johnny the Giant Killer proved a controversial film in Europe; those adults who saw it recognized the symbolic truths—those who saw evil through the eyes of truth. This was no mere animation but a way to express what the postwar world had come to and had always been: a protest for those protesters who read nature's archetypal truths in the characters and plot.

The Giant's World: A slam dunk for man-as-machine, insatiable consumer, heralding a warning by pitting it against the Natural Female World.

Producer and writer Jean Image and his writer wife knew what they were doing. The giant's castle high atop the crooked hillside encompassed symbolically, a post-war world of the Giant's World of tyranny, domination, greed, entrapment, reductionism, and exploitation of all the world's natural female resources, be they animal, vegetable, or mineral, and the children who face the giant.

I knew this giant, intimately and symbolically, his MO, his psyche, and the archetypal nature of how the creators portrayed him. Queenie I recognized from where I hailed. She moved from a great Female Leadership Brain. Composed. Productive. Unflappable. Escorting Johnny through her domain with regal elegance, pastel pink, and blue eggs into their sacred hexagon incubators.

Way ahead of its time, we watch Queenie in a sheer peignoir as each egg slides from beneath her gossamer wings into each golden hexagon. The eros of the Great Mother Being. Her hive is the epitome of Femocracy in humming action. A microcosm of the Earthly Cosmic Female Principle. I watched in total enthrallment as her loyal nursemaids lovingly cradled and cared for the newly born bees. Through the screen they nodded at me. I smiled a secret smile back.

"JOHNNY THE GIANT KILLER, 1950"

JOHNNY AWAKENS QUEENIE   JOHNNY & QUEENIE "THE GREAT COSMIC DANCE"

Johnny & Queenie-The Cosmic Dance

Femocracy Is Built upon Women's Stories, Centered in the Sacred State of Girlbeing

> He who has the story has the power. She who has no story, not even her own, has no power.
> —Rebecca Solnit, "The Storykiller and His Sentence"

Femocracy is built upon the authentic female truths we lived during our Sacred State of Girl Being under the death culture. These sacred female stories are the stuff of true female governance and power and the essential task of every woman.

Woman: Know Thy Story

None of us truly know our sacred stories. We cannot. Millennia of gaslighting and indoctrination stand between us, doing what the Dark Force's dirty Death Culture did: Divide and Conquer: Keep women from women. Make them taboo to each other. Body and Soul. Brainwash girls via their mothers to believe what The Normal means to submit to Male Rule and Perception of their side of "Life."

Brainwash them to leave their father while he keeps the Rule of the Father alive. He gives her away to the Male-Created Death Culture. Those who play with the boys' stay with the boys, be it politics, sports, or life itself.

In other words, women will never come into power as their Authentic Female Selves (AFS) as witness to all the lies, manipulations, and redactions of what we knew—were even born knowing. Our psyches infiltrated by The Death Culture.

We cannot return fully and completely to our female selves, the great female *bodypsyche,* until we embrace that girl we had to abandon so many eons ago. She never leaves. Loyal. Smart. Savvy. And she has the patience of a saint for the day we realize and accept. There is no other way to be. It comes from our childhood photographs, sacred in their own right and rite. That is how I returned. I had the right and finest female therapists, and both understood the relevance and core meaning of the photos that never die.

I—the one who was forever seeking the place with only girls—started dictating what I had held back consciously at an early point in this therapy. Bolstered by the courage to heal, and later the books *The Great Cosmic Mother, The Soul's Code, In Her Image, Of Woman Born,* and *Women Who Run with the Wolves,* my neurons had the chance to fire into all the synapses they had waited forever for. One day, as I was looking at one with a particular photo, my pen started to write the RDF truth that had always been. A whole world I was suffering in at three, impossible to make sense of the senseless. Under the precious, sacred power of me in a party dress is scrawled, "There is a photograph that is both my shame and salvation." I had no conscious understanding, except that did not matter. It was spot on. I trusted the female truth pouring out, and I would be ready to go down that rabbit hole in my own time, place, and way.

I carried with me that the world on the other side of the looking glass was identical to the topside world. One did not go down a rabbit hole; one straddled both worlds, both of which were batshit crazy. My pen knew the female truth, and I let it tell me the truth through the girl in the photo, no matter her age. Even the baby. By eight she had it all in her kitbag in front of a fireplace, her father snapping away, and me refusing to smile.

Femocracy was solidly fixed within my being. From there, everything had a chance to be figured out and then shared with the women and the girls they once were—of this sphere.

2

MY ANNUNCIATION
STRUCK AT FOUR

> When a peculiar turn of events struck like an
> annunciation, this is what I must do; this is
> what I've got to have. This is who I am.
> —James Hillman, The Soul's Code

An annunciation means a higher consciousness or cosmic directive. Its image resonates in your character and calling. We are redacted from birth by the Death Culture, and make no mistake: it is World Death Culture. Always has been, since the male brain, male mindset, and its brawn took us over. All of us.

When first the reality of Femocracy struck at four, I took my lead. Until then, there was nothing in the world that verified, validated, and assured me it even existed. I may have been four, but that can be a lifetime under the Death Culture. We females (and males) are born into what is an intangible prison—the prisms of Isms. Isms are dogma. Cults. Institutional tirades. Isms are what women and girls suffer is never made visible in our full, accurate, and profound truths.

Our inborn female truths are redacted by The Death Culture, yet remain alive and waiting for us and well in our childhood photos and Great Female Leadership Brain. Isms' toxic testosterone has forever been the world's greatest existential threat. Women and girls have always intuited it. Men have forever known, fear and enact it. Boys play with them. Phoetics liberates and springs us out of its traps.

7

Isms are prisms of darkness
Impossible to surmise
They put on a show of sparkle and glow
But their traps are a rainbowed disguise
Their glass is stained for good reason, same as
that rainbowed disguise
So pure, so pure, they seduce and allure
In their cults of The Blindly Unwise

Reenacting the Alchemy of The Great Sacred Female Union

At four, I reenacted the truth of what female meant. With cousin Ellen, Grandma's Otherworld living room living room, the costumes we would create, with natural knowing (gnosis), I directed us in the alchemy of The Sacred Female Reunion of our Masculine and Feminine energies.

Creation and Reenacting with El was the one female rite of healing Female wounds and conjuring up at the Otherworld from which we hailed. That summer's eve saw us doing a promenade, thrice. A Regal March. My Annunciation consecrated that summer's eve under a thirty-foot, barrel-vaulted ceiling created just for our purpose.

Scene: Female Rebecoming: The Sacred Reunion of Female-Masculine and Feminine Energies

Musical Theme: Romance Music from *The Gadfly,* Dmitri Shostakovich, 1955

PRINCE ELLEN & QUEENIE ME

I was four. She was seven and a half. My big cousin Ellen, my heroine, female prince, and partner in Female Rites Unlimited. She was there to play the role I needed, for sacraments and sacred rites of female reunion, spending the night where I lived at Grandma's house. That evening, when all the grownups receded into their bedrooms, I would reenact Femality's reunion with her. That French matinee, the perfect timing of our ages, the perfect set of Grandma's castle-like living room were all set in motion by the Ladyefolke (my appointed spirit guardians).

My cousin would not recall the film, the day, or the evening's sacred reunion rite. I would go on to remember it, as a passport back to my

First Healing through the portals of Annunciation and The Great Sacred Girl. Not every girl would be willing to go along in creative partnership like my beloved cousin. Fun, free-wheeling and happy to do my bidding. Whenever I suggested something new, it would be an adventure. And that adventure was Female Healing.

As a RDND (Real Deal Nancy Drew), I was awed over her relationships with her "chums," Bess Marvin and George (Georgina) Fayne. Mildred Wirt wrote under the pen name Carolyn Keene. As a girl I soaked myself in those first 1929 to 1959 mysteries, most especially *The Tolling Bell*. Pure Triple Goddess.

I love you, Nancy Drew!
Bess and George and Hannah too.

I see now that this moment in Female Cosmic timelessness lead to all the others, few though they may have been. Age four Annunciation ceremonies would lead to my full-fledged Femocracy by eight and all that transpired with Chris (see: Chapter 4).

Background the fantasy streetscape where Grandma Lived:

Each house on that street had a Disneyland look before Disney ever broke ground in Anaheim. In fact, I believe it was the fantasy lands of art nouveau and deco of Los Angeles that influenced Disney and not the other way around. What I noticed about LA and its outgrowth sub-areas was that they fell into "lands." Beverly Hills and Westwood Village were Main Street. The San Fernando Valley, with its small horse ranches and dusty roads and giant western signs of cowgirl waitresses, Feed and Saddlery stores, were distinctly Frontierland. Olvera Street and its maize-tortilla sizzling smells, piñatas, and red-blue-yellow paper fans were the Mexican Village. And on my grandmother's street, Fantasy Land shot up from corner to corner.

These abodes, designed and built in the mid1920s, were theme homes. Hollywood trickled into its very streets. Some elevations were Spanish Colonial. Across the street was French Normandy with gray turrets. Three doors down stood the house of the Three Sisters, a shallow brook to cross over, and purple pansies up the path, straight out of Tudor fairytales. Not Shakespearean. More Vita and Violet.

I would knock on their door, peeking around for Snow White, and once they even let me in. These octogenarians lived a quiet, still life. I remember being told as I crossed the threshold, her sister was taking a nap. Apparently my brother was doing it every day for 'fun' and my mother was politely asked to have the children stop knocking on their door.

All around those neighborhood streetscapes, homes so whimsical they were named Witches House, Fairy House, just like the rest of this fantasy-surreal town. Grandma Mary's stood alone in that; it was more Alhambra Nights-meet-Blenheim secluded from curbside. Upon the long entry from the driveway, you arrived through the portal to Female Otherworld.

No one else felt it but make no mistake. The entry that led to the front door were like a cloistered mission. In my parent's wedding pictures, I always took it for granted that everyone had a setting like this. But it was unique, and specific. It became where I lived, played, danced, and belted out "Broadway Melody" on the wrought iron gate.

An open atrium patio lived across, with Grandpa's banyan trees and bird bath fountain. Sounds of birds—the oak titmouse, dark-eyed junco, and occasional lost seagull on the way back to Santa Monica heralded rare rainfall. Ladye Santa Ana blew her sensual breaths in May through searing Septembers, when the grownups watched *The Miss America Pageant* in the courtyard, with rabbit ears (an early day version of cable)and table fans blowing hot air in circulation.

I could not say when this auspicious occasion took place, but cousin Ellen would stay over once in a while, what Grandma called, "Once in a blue moon." Midsummer or early fall, because kids would be out of school. Madame Mythstery cloaked the air. Holding hands at the theater's doors, we were unaccompanied by adults. Kids were dropped off to matinees very young, watching the even younger. I lucked out and always felt a strange, timeless sense of pride to be accompanied by my big Cousin Ellen.

Three and a half years my senior, tall for her age, she foreshadowed Vita Sackville West to my Violet Keppel Trefusis. Ellen was female and androgynous and knew it. Her straight nutbrown hair, sheared in a medieval pageboy (popular in the 1950's) all the rage, gave her that Prince Val-[2]Renee Vivienne air.

By the time we came blinking back out into Wilshire's searing sunlight, I was transcending into my natural state—a thing I treasured, I would feel as *The Place with Only Girls*. Dinnertime, baths, nothing sticks except what I was able to orchestrate once Grandma and the grownups receded into the back bedroom of the house.

The living room was all ours, the scene set for the Great Female Union.

This was no mere living room. To me at four, it was Blenheim or Duntreath. There were shot silk European sofas and lounges, two sets. Lathe and plaster walls. A floor that, had it been wood, you could do at least twenty[3] chainè turns across. The Palladian windows that popped out over the lawns

---

[2] Renee Vivienne, born Pauline Tarn was an English pro-female poet circa the early 1900's
[3] Consecutive turns on point in a straight line

had Venetian blinds where dust specks climb upward like a backwards escalator; where Ellen's mother and mine could see us on the lawns playing, 'Here we go 'round the Mulberry bush.' The day Ellen told baby Davey it was okay to eat a mulberry we ran to our moms who went berserk. But that is what happens when The Sacred Cosmic World of Children clashes with the third dimension of SAs (Stupid Adults).

The Great Sacred Female Reunion.

Ellen gathered the costumes: capes, wreaths, crowns, and billowing gowns. She wore a cape (Grandma's champagne-colored silk comforter) slung over one shoulder, with long PJs and ballet satin slippers. I, in my nightgown looked down as she deftly tied a 1950's tulle slip round my waist with the proper royal drag behind me. I became Queenie.

Prince Ellen materialized. Backlit from the peach frosted art deco torchiere. From my throne on Grandma's seafoam green shot silk sofa, (having been rendered unconscious by the Giant's armies of wasps) I peeked to make sure she was on cue.

Our sacred ceremony was to dance, promenade into it. Ellen studied ballet, so she knew that toe-first regal walk. Following suit, I showed how to offer her arm as my escort. Female Otherworld was upon us. She tread softly. I could feel her nearby. My Queenie eyes fluttered. Then, as she approached me, with the forehead kiss from a butterfly, I rebecame my Authentic Female Self. She, the embodiment of our Female Masculine and Feminine energies, brought to me my other half. We needed to merge.

Before I knew it, we were in promenade. Once. Twice. Thrice. The magic number required for transformation and transcendence. What we did was every girl's due. We may not live in the "place with only girls," but we could do the dance, conjure up the feel. No one to interfere, judge, or call us away. Time stood still. The way females connect; earthly and cosmically. A moonpulse thing.

There would come a time when we would start our periods, and go through menopause and every phase in between. And for me, the future meant my first Great Sacred Girl loss. Ellen was my only connection. I was nine when I stayed the night with Rick Nelson and Elvis posters on her bedroom walls; I felt a new unbearable and unexpected Female Exile. She was unreachable at the level I so needed.

Still, for that magical coming together four and seven, came my fated, timeless eve at Grandma's house where I dwelt until I took advantage. The Ladyfolke had set all in motion—from the matinee, my awakening, and the opportunity to create the Great Female Reunion. For one future time, I connected the Female Dots and waved my wand for the magic of Phoetics.

An Annunciation Is Your Calling

An announcing of the spirits, the accompanying genius remembers for you in a particular image you are here for. When I watched *Johnny The Giant Killer,* my remembrance of what and why I was here switched on. I arrived there with its knowing. I watched it nod to me. *Go. With our blessing.* So, though I was only four, what I was enacting was the sacred union of the Female Masculine and Female Feminine. Not as we are lied to by patriarchy, the male mindset, and its dark force Death Culture, but *what is the Female Truth.* I was gifted with all the gnosis to carry this truth and recreate a ceremony that would seal its truth.

My Annunciation stayed with me in permanence. That holy eve would have to last me a lifetime, against all odds of the Death Culture heading me off at every pass, in every way.

Fully united by the will and love of my cousin's enactment of *The Reunion of the Great and Sacred Female Masculine and Great Sacred Female Feminine* merged and shared, I founded the Way Back to Full Female Integration, the one and only precursor to Full Female Femocracy.

3

THE GREAT SACRED GIRL

> I come from another place
> I hail from a different grace
> No soul can ever know my face
> Until they know my story

You are looking at an image of a Great Sacred Girl. There are no statues of Her Sacred Existence. As we begin to recognize Her/She as the root of all things, we stand an excellent chance for positive change—not mere survival but a brand-new Female-Centric world. That is what the girl in this sketch sought and never gave up—that somewhere, somehow there would exist a Female Centric World. This, then, is my Mythograph. I stand, one of legions of Great Sacred Girls, many of whom I knew when we lived back in the Sacred State of Girlbeing.

More than sixty linear years have passed, barely a drop in the bucket of Cosmic time. Although little has changed, it is Awakening Time for Femality's emergence within this corrupted sphere. We start. Then statis. We start again with a brand new advantage of Rebecoming our Authentic Selves using a technique that is both pre-ancient and cutting-edge visionary. *Each generation of Great Sacred Females is here to find her original Female Authenticity.* The movement of *Phoetics.*

The Most Feared Being on the Planet: The Great Sacred Girl

She has been called everything from "just a little girl" to a "pussy" and is parodied, satirized, trivialized, demonized, and mocked as the arrogance of laughter dilutes her innate potency.

Mocked and dismissed as trivial by her enemies, they are not considered enemies by her. Ironically, they are the ones who need her most—for leadership, empathy, and order and balance. But they have done all they can to destroy her before she gets too old, too smart, too real-deal female (RDF).

Taking a page from The Death Culture Playbook:

Control. Dominate. Indoctrinate. Before she gets too old. Gaslight. Brainwash. Hide your sneaking smirks behind the timeworn-time proven disguises. Before she takes her rightful place, shrink her down to a Little Girl. Just like *The Giant, 'miniaturize to terrorize' and then consume. Insatiable for the power we hold as girls.

Do not be duped. This Norman Rockwell-esque waif of a girl, confronting the ginormous Wall Street "macho" bronze bull, commissioned by the centuries-long, male-dominated Wall Street Bullies, is not the Great Sacred Girl. She is a placebo to placate well-meaning yet naive women who very much believe in the power of girls. "Fearless Girl," facing down the "big, bad, bullish market" anthropomorphized in solid brass, dwarfing her size and breadth, all animalistic male idealized snorting his smart-ass nostrils, while she—a wispy spirit inspired by Hillary White's illustration, hands on hips, skimpy pigtails, knobby knees, pretending a stance of "high girl spirits" she projects—nonetheless is no physical match.

This anti-girl, female-phobic propaganda, sculpted through the eye of the male ego, is one puny stab to placate the #MeToo-ers and all those dumb gals, broads, mommies, and women libbers. I can just picture the kings and princes of Wall Street commissioning the artist: Make her appear defiant but keep her dwarfed and no match for The Great Phallic Bull.

I was duly insulted and incited. How could so many be fooled by the obvious? Or were they? Women were snapping pictures and giving street interviews all agog. *No*, I wanted to tell them. *This is patronizing all of us, our Real-Deal Great Sacred Girl.*

Finally, I came across women in the news who did see through female eyes (TFE). They called out this "corporate feminism," while other agreed with me as projecting the empowered woman as a little girl. Still, other women warned that putting up these gender stereotypes is belittling, stressing these types of images are corporate sidelining of *women*.

Brava! We live on the same pages—Femocracy did exist! I just had to stay alert and connect with women who lived it.

The question was, Where were the true images of the Great Sacred Girl in terms of metaphor and Female Truth? Well, if you can't find her, look for her in your childhood photos. Find her in goddess images. And if you can't find her, draw her. How she really felt when the photo was taken.

Visitation Dream c. 1957- The Real Deal Great Sacred Girl (TGSG)

The aunts on my father's side are setting a table for Hitler, Stalin, and Mussolini. At the head, it is left empty. Where's Churchill's?

They ignore me. I leave the house. In my parakeet yellow China Boy's costume, worn in *The Nutcracker* at the park. At the ocean water's edge—I see something like a headstone. *Here lies Nancy, 1950–1957.* Keeping in mind there is no place of welcome for Winston, I recognize his body language is identical to my own during this age of seven. Just as goddess images echo our childhood body language in photographs, so do famous people's archetypal energies resonate with our psyche. In William Manchester's books *The Last Lion,* I learned how Churchill stood up warning Parliament of Hitler's evil existential threat. *For twelve long years he was laughed down.* All the while, Prime Minster Neville Chamberlain fawned over Hitler, visiting him in Germany carrying his infamous bumbershoot. Chamberlain was, in essence, the dark energies of the adults in my family: Denial. Appeasement. Pretense. Dismiss.

While Winnie (Sir Winston) was my Authenticity to speak truth to his colleagues, that they were, the whole world was facing its Darkest Threats. *Open your bloody eyes! Identical to all that's threatening our country and the world today.* The horror of the ignorance of evil's "isms" taking hold on conformist-tribal minds. I had come full circle having intuited the dark underbelly of anything, anyone.

My dream gravestone, lined up with the photo of me at seven at Highland Springs. I am strong, my masculine energies fully present, my natural self. While all the while the ugly truth appears behind me as the darkened bungalow window where my father takes me "for a nap" while my mother stays at the pool with my brother. The predator once again, seizing his opportunity to pounce.

By that year and those to follow, I was in a suicidal state of mind—or rather, I had a death wish, symbolized by the gravestone at the ocean's edge.

Nancy Llewellyn

Me   and   Winston

Once Upon a Time
I was the Smartest Girl in the World
I would sit like Winston
Facing down Hitler, Eichman, Stalin & Mussolini
When all my aunts set a table for them...

The Great Sacred Girl is in us from the start, in our Sacred Photographs of Girlbeing. Phoetics is the portal through and path back to our Sacred Female Authentic Self, awaiting our sacred return, to Recover, Resound, and Rebecome at One with Her—and We Are Ready.

1 The Last Lion: William Spencer Churchill by William Manchester 1983

4

MY STORY BELONGS TO…

My story belongs to the state and State of Southern California, to the eucs, the salt that clings from the Pacific Ocean on their delicate leaves, to the sands, dirty/filthy in my child's day to the silted way they shift and sift. To every globular pop of amber seaweed, every bit of tar washed up on the seaweed's twisted leaves, on the bottom of children's toes tracked back on to the very same hot, steamy asphalt it came from, wobbling on the sides of their little feet, plastic buckets of confused, wet sand crabs, carted off to their untimely deaths.

To the State of California, to every dying palm tree, the squatty old grandfather ones with the dirty gray beards, the ones that were never indigenous, to every stick of Beechnut gum spat out on the broken sidewalks from Beverly Hills through The Miracle Mile to downtown LA from past centuries to today. To the beautiful palms, Queen Palms, the Twenty-Nine. To Los Angeles in the 1950s, under a thick iron lung of smog, that scary ache you wheezed as the smog-alert bell warned you to return to your classroom. Coughing. That old familiar toxic tickle. And finally, to the schoolyard built on sacred grounds, it further sanctified a trillion times by the running, jumping, and pounding of little feet. Our steadfast blacktop, poured and rolled anew, making ready for our late September Return, and the May Festival Dances I longed for all year.

I was born smack dab in the middle of the last century, the last millennial, on the sacred female number in the most autumnal time of year. My birth certificate states just the facts, ma'am. I prefer to see it in poetic mindset: 'Twas smack dab in the middle of the last century in the last millennium, in its tenth month, ninth day, at 3:26 in the morning when my mother gave birth at my chosen time of entrance.

My story belongs to the many lands I grew up in for the first ten years where I intuit inspired Disney, consciously or subconsciously, to create a theme park that already existed. Beverly Hills: Main Street. The San Fernando Valley's dusty, horsey scents blown in by Ladye Santa Ana: Frontierland. Downtown and East LA became the Mexican Village. There was no Chinatown in those days, but the Mexican Village was kissin' cousins to Olvera Street. Even Angel's Flight, The Big Dog, Tail of the Pup, and The Brown Derby must have worked furiously in the background of Disney's psyche.

To the black void of evil in Knott's Ghost Town's *Old Livery* Stable, and Grandpa's garage. Like the inside of an open coffin. The dusty, late-Victorian hearse, its glass windows revealing a child-size coffin, black and gold mitered edges for any girl's fate. Giselle. Helen Burns. Betty Boop. Little Eva. Barb'ry Allen and the families who would never mourn them.

My Story belongs to my panic: *Where's Nancy? Find her, find her!*

I had not wandered away; more like I was left frozen in horror. That is how my classmates found me, in a total dissociative state. Having passed by the child-size graves with crude wooden crosses on Boot Hill. Only I knew it was no coincidence they were not made an adult scale.

After we panned for fool's gold at the Old Mill—and the boys won—we came upon half-naked Saloon Ladies perched on laps of creepy, unshaven, crazed-looking miners. My head hung in Femality's Shame. Every miner was every man in my family and in homes of girls I visited. These grownup-sized Saloon Gals, on grimy, leering laps, were the women of my family and the world. Fawning over these derelicts, just to stay alive.

Baked into the Death Culture were male fantasies everywhere. Guns, gunpowder, pistols and holsters, flintlock rifles … phallic symbols, ubiquitous. Female images what my father accused me of. Teases. Crazies. Just askin' for it. Doing their Hard-Hearted Hannah routine. Corsets and strapless gowns. While these thoughts shot through my psyche that day, my classmates laughed and enjoyed themselves, oblivious to the evil so thick in the air you could cut it with a machete. Knott's Berry Farm, a stone's throw from Disneyland. Mrs. Knott's fried chicken, mashed potatoes and gravy, and mouthwatering boysenberry jams and pies carried on the Santa Anas. Those same boysenberries were cross-pollinated by Mrs. Knott herself.

<https://www.youtube.com/watch?v=qjPtYw1VO7c>

My story belongs to the "bingity-bangity" school buses with no seatbelts and exhaust fumes that made us cough and sneeze relentlessly, those same Los Angeles school buses for YMCA camp. To the prying fingers of boys, just like Al and my father, poking, abusing, irritating the soft flesh inside seashells still half-alive, precious, defenseless sea creatures shrinking away from their filthy, brutish, boyish fingers. Another stupor as we swung around the block. In shock, I stumbled down the bus steps, with the sounds of little boys' fiendish glee mocking behind me.

My story belongs to every flapping, close-pinned newsprint papers to easels taller than us in second grade, rippling, tempera paint splattered, dried in caked green lollypop trees and gray paint slathered on to wooden airplanes (I cajoled the boys to "saw and sand" for me because I had more important things to attend to).

Thus, my story belongs to the sacred child souls of 1950 with whom I moved and shook and matriculated from 1956 until 1962. Bless you all. Hardly happy days for girls and some boys, preyed upon by Stupid Adults and older siblings. My story belongs to the billboards that projected, validated, celebrated, glamorized, and rewarded that Child Hell, from the Unholy God of anti-female messages in his fake Animation and Amusement Parks. My story belongs to the Peanut Gallery mentality that conscripted innocent children into laughing at the scary antics of Clarabell the clown. My story belongs to Captain Kangaroo, Sherriff John, and Engineer Bill—and yes, even to Miss Barbara on Romper Room, who never saw me through her Magic Mirror. And I know why.

My story belongs to my kindergarten teacher, Mrs. Wilson, who duly noted in private office files: "Has a nervous habit of rolling her eyes, mother seeing a psychiatrist, reflects what is happening at home." This was my deliberate distraction of 'look up, look down' was the how I dealt with repressing any remembrance of Uncle Al's threat: 'If you ever tell Grandma, no one will ever find you.' My coping method noted by my first grade teacher on an official LA School file.

My story belongs to the system that never investigated those notes and to my grandmother, who would have never complied with any investigation because her family reputation trumped my threatened life, limb, and psyche. She, a collapsed mother, went on to breed two more.

My story belongs to The Western Pest Exterminator on the billboard above the company's downtown building. You could see it from the Hollywood freeway. I shrank down in the backseat, hoping my parents would not see him. Mister Undertaker was Al in a mourning suit, concealing a mallet behind his coattails, pretending to be blind behind fake dark glasses. A long, Pinocchio nose. Al's mustache. Nineteen-thirties spats. That itsy-bitsy mouse pleading for the mercy that will never be meted out. I was that precious, innocent mouse. My story belongs to the obvious cartooned Evil slapped in front of that billboard. I knew the Moles of This World feigning friendliness, pretending to be blind while all the while, plotting your brutal murder.

My story belongs to Felix the Cat and all the evil behind his salacious grin and to the day my uncle abandoned me in the back of the tire shop to *teach me a lesson if I ever cried in front of my grandmother again about refusing to take a ride in his truck.* To his gangrene-green 1930s flatbed truck from early 1930s Disney and Fleischer characters plotting evil adult cartoons.

Today, it is known that these first, crude, rickety, jiggly animations were targeted toward adults before the main feature, not for children. I say it was both. That said, my story belongs to every defenseless little child, animal, flower, tree, nature herself, animated thing that was ever tortured, pummeled, beaten, laughed at, or torn asunder by the bully that is My First Mythograph-Stylized Death Culture, and penned as the heroes in Disney's arsenal of child weaponizing.

Above all, my story belongs to and is imbued with *My Sacred Childhood Photographs; the only validation and reflection that I actually once existed.* That it wasn't all a bad dream. It was a real child's life where my best moments were spent alone in song, dance, and reverie. No matter what they did to me, I was not the Victim. I was the Victorious.

Like Queen Boudica, (daughters by her sides), in a show of Female Sovereignty, burned Londinium to the ground rather than surrender to the invading Roman armies. When I behold Boudica's statue in its Golden Chariot Glory, I see me. That is what my childhood photographs preserved for me. My Authentic Sacred Queen Bee-Boudica Female Self.

In sum: my story is to what happens when women abandon Woman. Abdicating their duty to all Great Sacred Girls. As they were betrayed, generation to generation. It is time to break this deadly cycle and come together in the Great Sacred Female Family.

Lastly, My Story Belongs to My Sacred Childhood Photographs

If my story belongs to anything, it is to the childhood photographs that testify I ever existed at all. If there had never been an image of me as an infant, baby, toddler, at two, three, at four, five, at six, seven, and eight, I could not have remembered having existed. I could only have remembered the chaos of being.

My story could never have been told without the images of the first eight years I spent in this sphere, trying to make sense out of its relentlessly overwhelming insanity. My story belongs to the images for my childhood photographs, for they are my best friends, my staunchest supporters, my greatest allies, sacred witnesses to all I had struggled with and what every female child struggles with to try and survive in this hellhole we call planet Earth.

I grew up in the Death Culture, maniacally crafted and mechanized by the female-fearing, female body-envying Others who exist in an outer limits zone I left long ago. I grew slanted and twisted, an African violet leaning toward whatever light my being could instinctively soak up.

When one is born into a Death Culture, darkness *is* reality, darkness that exists in broad daylight, making it all the more crazy making. That is why childhood photographs serve so us perfectly. They and they alone capture, preserve, protect, and project the darkness that sets off the lit image of Child-being.

Child-being is not Childhood. Child-being is what sacred childhood photographs remember, revere, and call us back to.

My childhood photographs are not about the Death Culture. They capture and speak volumes about what it does to a female child. My childhood photographs are about my story and seeing through female eyes.

Reflections upon My Mythograph: The Great Sacred Girl and Force of Femality

The full-on Boadicea determination and resolve in my face and body, standing in front of the old unlit fireplace, holding the corners of my skirts as I was directed to do, a Sphinx smile playing on my lips projects the very image of the first stage of Femality.

Add my character, and you have the full, harmonious, holding the-tension-of-the-opposites, female at age eight. Inscrutable. Invincible. Unstoppable. Lilith has nothing on this cookie.

My story began with Female images invaded by the evils of the Death Culture. What looks to be a poised girl in a party dress, hairband of flowers crowning her long brunette hair, is not a family album Kodak moment. *It is my moment. My character and calling. It is the very image of the force of Femality, the story I live.*

By eight, I began to notice how many girls were coping with a thing so insidious, so prevalent, so all-fired crippling that *there was simply no known name for it. Nowhere* was this thing made real, named, identified. Not in any book, cartoon, magazine, TV show, film, painting, fresco, statue. Not in any temple, church, mosque, shrine; PTA minutes, classroom curriculum, AMA medical records. We, sacred female children, relying on our female elders to lead, guide, inform, and teach us who we were were left tumbling backward in some black hole, the black void with no language. And where there is no language, there is no consciousness.

But that is where our childhood photographs come in, for they are the consciousness waiting for us to name and claim it: our Original, Sacred State of Authenticity.

Woman, Know Thy Story—ongoing

Story—your story—is the most fundamental way to understand and become visible to yourself. There is simply no other way. Want to know thyself? Know thy story.

My story—which I curse, revile, shrink from, flee, resent, and hold at bay for all that happened still retains my essence, my character, my beauty, which is the poetic female eye. We go into therapy to find our story—make sense of our lives. And women's stories—our first nine or ten years as told through the long lens of adult objectivity—are the building bricks of Female Culture and our female spirit, female soul, its mortar.

Stories are medicine. Male stories carry male medicine. Female stories carry female medicine—the most potent of all. (Again why we find ourselves in such suffering today.) When I was a girl I searched for female tales, stories of other girls' lives told by them or in a library book. Nothing existed. I never bought into the crap they pushed on us. Nearly every last one was about a boy, a man, a male animal. Where were the girls? I felt some gargantuan betrayal was afoot that would take me another half century to deduce. And today I understand what and why it was.

The Dark Force Stole Our Stories

The darker your story, the more reluctant you will be to retrieve it. I was. *And that is precisely what the Dark Force counts on.* It has the skinny on every woman's story. Your fear seals its fate. Yet it doesn't have to stay that way. That is the reason we as women, as girls, suffer. And that is the reason the world is on its way to extinction. No female stories, no female connection. No female connection, no Female Culture. No Female Culture, no creation. No creation, no life.

My Story Belongs To … is an homage to the Great Sacred Female Being. To all she must suffer in the face of stupid adults and to her resilience and ability to keep on nurturing herself in every way she can. It is a revelation of the truth no one wants to acknowledge. Of the evils of organized religion. Of the hatred born of the envy of Stupid Adults for the bitterness they feel for the child they got to live and never got to be.

My Story Belongs To … was written in hopes that it would inspire all women to want to remember their own because we all suffered. Suffered fools. Suffered patriarchy. Suffered the stigma of having been born the sacred female principal in a world gone completely mad. My story belongs to, in the final analysis, every female whoever lived and ever will. In the spirit of saying once and for all, I love you. My Own. That is who I am. I love My Own. And I want them to know they were never alone and are not alone in their female sacrality while I am here and long after I am not.

My story belongs to … is a passionate plea, a bloodcurdling scream for children's bodies and souls and for My Own to rise up and tell their own stories so we can truly organize ourselves at long last.

My story is a litmus test, a barometer for the ingenious women who have contributed and continue to contribute to women's rights and children's rights. Yet it wants more from each of them, My Own. My story belongs to the fervent prayer that these women who would be leaders of us all to summon uncommon courage to retrieve and tell, publish their own. For without that, there can be no true female leadership. My story belongs to the Global Female Library, the Female Archives that start with its inception. Let it serve as a prototype for every woman's telling. Let it loosen tongues and melt hearts and steel backbones and attune uterine creation.

It's an offering. An exercise in telling what it was like through the longshot, the hawk's eye-view. And what it felt like from a worm's eye-view.

My story is every female's story, the story of what happens when female consciousness must try to make sense of an alternate and unnatural, a false, duplicitous consciousness called "universal."

Is a litany of what it was like to try to survive as a natural female in an unnatural, dark Death Culture. To grow up in Southern California in that first decade of the midway point of that last millennial was crazy making. A false pall of evil all around. Encountered it every day and night, up close and personal, afar, and distant My Story Belongs to captures all the evil I tapped into in the surrealism of a no-female-consciousness sphere.

It has been noted Los Angeles is a city without soul. I go one further. It is a zone where souls go to get lost, not found. A merciless town. Truly the eponymous town without pity, especially for its namesake angels, the children. A town that should go down in infamy for the crimes it perpetuates, rewards, manufactures, and profiteers from. We all have a story. Few cherish theirs. We would much rather hear someone else's, because it gives us a safe emotional distance while ironically inspires, influences, enlightens us consciously and subconsciously. As I shared, my respect for real-life stories was appalling. I demanded escape to beauty and people acting civilized, so whether it was loosely based on a real person or fictional, just keep it easy on the eyes and as far away from my life as possible. Nothing wrong with escapism, yet I learned the biggest lessons of all.

That scented, whooshed, and blew where I walked, the rare beach visits, the grammar school I attended, remembering safely that time when I observed what it was like to be a kid and got the rare moments away from The Death Culture from home and the world, to be a kid and cut loose, dance, and sing without SA's mocking, sexualizing, and minimizing.

<https://www.youtube.com/watch?v=qjPtYw1VO7c>

5

MY FEMALE TALES

Why I Wrote My Female Tales

We are surrounded by women from the day we are born. We do not get to choose. The kind of woman I would have chosen for my mother in a fantasy match is not the way of Story. Story demands contrast, which means conflict. While I would never have deliberately chosen the warped psyche of the woman in whose body I quickened and her reign of child hell in which I endured, her deficits and deficiencies did drive me to search for and seek qualities I prayed existed in other women—and on a deeper level, what Woman was.

When I was eighteen, I knew it was just a matter of years before I would have to self-refer using that word. Woman, as defined by my mother, was so misaligned, distorted, disturbing, creepy, and dark-mattered, I could not meet it even halfway between eighteen and twenty-eight. At thirty I surrendered, but it was a good act. And why not? I had been acting the role of Claire's Daughter all my life.

It took another two decades of therapy and self-healing to even grasp this. Claire's Daughter was expected to watch out and protect her mother, report how her mother was doing to her mother's friends and to her grandmother. Claire's Daughter was truly the neglected and abandoned Lenora Comstock—my mother's favorite victim heroine whom I rejected like the Black Plague. My mother did to me what she revered in girl character portraits, heroines: she victimized. To be Claire's Daughter was the hardest role I ever played. I must freely admit I could barely stretch that far—I was not born for the role. Yet as the consummate actress, I could play whatever I was expected to play while I was really watching other women and the girls to measure, compare, discern, and validate that there had to be something better out there to define female and woman than all the women in her family, my father's, and her friends.

The women of My Female Tales emerge as female archetypes we have yet to bring into consciousness. By this I mean they arise purely from female consciousness.

We need pure Female Archetypes, and I delineated these women to offer our first female archetypes. No more Hera, Electra, Venus, or Artemis. We must pull from our Own. And name them. And teach them. And become them.

Some were mothers of girls I knew in grammar school. Others, teachers. While others taught music in school. Two were guitar teachers outside the school. The women of my mother's family and my father's, friends of my mother's were Dark Force Female Traitors. And yet in contrast to them you will meet their uncommonly brave and beautiful daughters. Unforgettable, because someone had to tell and sketch their portraits for all female posterity. It is time their names, characters, and spirits were brought out into the world so that women and girls—today and for all time—will greet and gather them into their open arms. It is my Otherworld way of consecrating their characters, of all they endured that never saw the light of female consciousness.

I present them giving you the opportunity to honor the Great Sacred Girls in my state of Girlbeing, to hold them in your psyche as you live your female life. It is my prayer they will move you to remember and tell of the sacred girls and women who served as your female archetypes. They are part of female-being, which means creations of our new Female Culture. Welcome them.

I held them in my arms, cried with them, and rocked them to sleep. Held their space. Soothed us to sleep. Created magic rings to keep their abusers from breaking in. Taught guitar. Harmonized. Strummed alongside. Told their mothers how wonderful they were. Stayed a mile away from their older brothers. Observed, and when appropriate, loathed their fathers. I knew them in cardio-spirit arrest. In bedrooms for which there can be no rating. I calmed them, danced with them, observed our differences and commonalities. Brushed each other's hair, listened to transistor radios. Went through Archie and Veronica comic books like buzz saws. Sprayed our hair pink and gold, raided our mothers' makeup bags for green and blue shadow. Smoked pretend ciggies with baby-blue tips that puffed powder. I could mimic Bette Davis before the bathroom mirror, holding her cigarette like a stiletto knife, from what I remembered from an old movie (paraphrased) "Every time you touch me with your sticky little hands it makes me sick. Sick, do you hears?" Puff, puff, do it again, what a release. When no one was home to pester me, *what are you doing in there young lady?*

The Unforgettable: My Great Sacred Girls

I shall never forget their tears, clear beads of pink, brown, black, freckled sweat, tender Sacred Girl scalps. These tales are testaments to the Female Soul and my basic premise: Female Love is the only thing that keeps a girl going. It saved me and had to last me throughout the decades, long after the actual women and girls were out of my life.

Some were the Jane Eyres and Helen Burns whose lives of adult cruelty reflected my own. The way I see it, any female who has survived even one day in this hellhole we call life on earth deserves to be Female canonized and immortalized, recognized for the uncommon courage it takes to even sign on and show up.

The girls I knew deserve this much.

I had different feelings for each one. Some had not a thing in common. Others I admired from afar. While others were just passing in the night of female girl solitude. One saved me from suicide, though she never knew it. And one whom I chose not to write about was malignant in the bud. I kept my distance wisely. I was counseling in the sandbox. Knew a handful of empathetic, intuitive souls my first eight years; two were boys. Yet it was with the girls I was home. Home is how it felt, though I never knew the meaning of the word.

Many of the tales feature mothers and daughters, though they do not necessarily appear in the same vignette. I had a distinct advantage in being who I was. No one suspected my origins. How could they if I did not? I knew when a particular soul was to be courted. Urgency would propel, "go to her." None of us knows what it is like to live as a girl in a female-centered world—in other words, supported, surrounded, embraced by Female Culture. What I do know is what it was like to survive and suffer where female consciousness had all but deserted us.

This chapter is meant to catapult the Creation of Female Culture to the forefront. At some point my head was spinning. I knew and wanted to share so much. But I did not know where or how to begin.

Then a friend, very editorial-minded woman suggested I get centered to just pick one event. It worked like a charm. Events are the stuff of story, and story is medicine. Even if you suffered, when you share it with others, the healing begins. It is mutual and symbiotic. That is human. For females it is fodder, with nutrients only they know about in their bones. I could never get into any story told by a man, nor about guys no matter how civilized—if the girls and women were not the central characters, I could not relate. And when the girls and women were patriarchal puppets, I was done. The smell of libraries does not evoke much female imagination. They reek of decayed patriarchy. New ones, all glass and steel, are a veritable female imagination sterility.

We all have a story. Few cherish theirs. We would much rather hear someone else's, because it gives us a safe emotional distance while ironically inspires, influences, enlightens us consciously and subconsciously. As I shared, my respect for real-life stories was appalling. I demanded escape to beauty and people acting civilized, so whether it was loosely based on a real person or fictional, just keep it easy on the eyes and as far away from my life as possible. Nothing wrong with escapism, yet I learned the biggest lessons of all.

Your female tales—fully integrated and shared—allow you to see yourself in an inner reflection, whereas until then, you did not exist to you—only parts of you. The shards of abuse take the good with the bad—that is, what people either do not realize or at the least, accept. Well, there was not much good anyhow of me forty years ago. Here is the first thing I learned: Until you can tell your story in a fully integrated perspective (adult objectivity), you will always live half a life, or 20 percent—superficially—and if you have children, they are the ones who will suffer. That's why I got into RDFT. And with girls from eight to sixteen, it was a no-brainer. *Get thee to a therapist.* If you want a future with them, there are no easy ways out, and that was never my jam.

To bring me back in a safe, cohesive, cogent way, I started with my story belongs to ... to give me permission to tell about the actual environment I had blocked, hating SoCal because there was no respect for history and it never rained. No autumn. And the next logical step began on its own. My Female Tales organized itself—person by person, event by event.

THE GIRLS

The Bliss of Chris—The Sacred State of Girlbeing—Female Attunement

Every girl is entitled to a sacred attunement with a girl like Chris. The children in our class responded to her golden energy as children will do. She had a major magic energy. I used to think it was because she had straight A's and was so pretty that we were all in awe of her; she seemed to have every gift showered upon her. Yet looking back, there were other girls who had straight A's, beauty, were great on the field, could play the autoharp, sing, and harmonize, but they were not her. Chris would have been a magnetic female force no matter how many or how little achievements she chalked up, although it was our musical attunement through her dazzling personality that took us to the threshold of Otherworld Femality.

Chris Was My Fate When I Was Eight

I recognized her as my fate when I was eight. We had been in that school since the first grade, and while we may have had classes together, it wasn't until the third grade that I really saw her up close and very personal. Although my grandmother had blue eyes, it was as if I had never seen blue eyes until I saw Chris's. They were fairy-tale blue. Crystalline, chalcedony, otherworldly blue. Her smile as wide as a jack-o'-lantern's and dimples that I tried in every which way to drill into my own cheeks. Those dimples rendered her a certain elfin status. She had a perfect nose, the kind you cannot get with plastic surgery, and a wide Flemish forehead, hair sometimes shorn into a flip or its long, whipping will as she rounded the bases, an auburn mane with rainbow highlights, her temples throbbing like a Derby winner's.

She was as at home cracking a grand slam as dancing the swing, letting me lead her and laughing wholeheartedly at everything I said. That made me so much more comfortable with my own brilliance and wit; it was like been heard for the very first time. Like champagne, the first few swigs.

I was jealous to the point of being panicked of losing her attentions, but Chris's way of being was that no one girl took precedence over another.

The boys were another thing. Her old autograph slam book reads "Best Friend," and in her simple perfect handwriting reads my name, which I influenced her to put in. But somehow, even though I did, the courting there was nothing uncomfortable and showed no resistance. In fact, she was dazzled by my flair to take the stage and perform with aplomb and an ease that she herself did not possess. That never mattered to me because why would you need to be on a stage if you were playing Chris? You were on Life's Stage; to be in that body and genius was the role of a lifetime.

I taught her guitar. We strummed autoharps side by side from third grade to graduation. We sang up and down the hills in perfect two-part harmony, her alto to my soprano of what Mrs. Vischer had drilled us on in choir. "I Pledge Myself Faithful." *Brahms's Academic Festival Overture* was the one song I kept us practicing. Its lyrics prophetic:

"I pledge myself faithful with heart and with hand, to thee my own fair country to thee my native land ..."

Who could have told me our own fair country and native land was Femality? How could I have known? Except for female instincts I never questioned, nor did she question me. No matter what you said, it was never criticized. No matter what you wanted to do, she was willing to try and was more than able.

I convinced her to go shopping for matching outfits—in different colors; not to be twins but to be female colleagues. We wore each other's black ballerina flats until my feet grew past size five. We dived into her mother's makeup bag; she put on powder blue eye shadow and apricot lipstick. I wore green for my brown eyes, but alas, Yardley would not come out with brown shadow for five years hence. From the drug store, we sprayed our hair in the only crude available colors then. Chris, the golden Rapunzel's, and mine. Well, there was nothing for brunettes, so I chose pink. My father had a fit when he answered the door. I remember looking down at pink rivulets in the shower as I cried it all away.

I was only a child, yet it seemed the world of cosmetics favored the blonde beauties of the Breck set. Chris had to have known she was more than pretty, yet she took it in her stride; perhaps that was what made her so magnetic. A total lack of self-consciousness, the kind of confidence that comes from a strong mother and mother's love, that golden patina. It's what we all wanted. The boys because they loved shiny objects, and the girls—because we wanted to feel what it felt like to be her.

I loved this Sacred Girlbeing as I have never loved another. Her essence was authentic female being. She had that perfect balance of female/masculine-female/feminine energies that perfectly balanced with my own. We were at that peak age in the first stages of female consciousness. And that, at age eight, kept me from suicide.

The natural Sacred State of Girlbeing is the crux of my work and theme of this book.
This sphere does not turn by chance, whether you are a theoretical physicist, cosmologist. There is always the fundamental reality of the Invisibles, and they in turn refuse to be measured, categorized, or archived; only intuited.
Author, Nancy Llewellyn

We tapped into the womb at the center of the universe. Into FemaleLove (MotherDaughtering), bee-bopping to the beat of soulful gospelly music vibrations; The Del-Vikings' Come Go with Me-, Dell Shannon's Runaway, Frankie Lymon's Goody-Goody and Little Bitty Pretty One. It was one long perfect uterine fest.

To be with her, to be Us; that is what saved me from throwing myself in front of the oncoming train that ran past See's Candy and Whitefront, like all those teenage death of the Death Culture's era.

I knew Christine Lee S. when we were eight, nine, ten, and eleven; I was Nancy Lee, her bon vivant, elegant cavalier; she was my lovely muse. What she never knew that behind all this golden light of female love was a darkness I experienced my own exile from self, from mother, from women. It was a darkness few survive, a hell not of our own making.

Instead of the winsome consort, I played the active, receptive, healing femme to a different girl, a rejected daughter during that era of our first female consciousness.

Sacred Female Reunion: 2012

It took fifty years to find her again. Girls grow up. Women give away their sacred inner daughter names and then some. Yet fifty years practically to the day we reunited in San Francisco. She drove an hour to see me. I hadn't spoken on the phone with her, had flown across the country to visit with my daughter—home in Cali again when all these arrangements were communicated via email and text—no phone calls.

We arrived at the Chalet restaurant early. There was something synchronistic about her suggestion of this particular restaurant, overlooking the Pacific Ocean where we had known each other and I always associate with her and her mom when I drive from Emerald Bay into and past Laguna Beach. The smell of sea salt, sage, and eucalyptus will always waft Chris and her mom, Jeanne to my senses.

The Lucien Labaudt murals on the wall stood high and wide as reminder of the old California I had been missing, only realizing it when I temporarily moved to Ohio. It was a California never to come again; the population did not feel like a population. It was just LA, the Valley, the Beach, Beverly Hills, and downtown LA. Still, these murals featured a working-class California of the 1930s, not an era or images I recognized. It was the colors that spoke: Rust, ochre, blue jean blues that reminded me I was home. Waiting for her had me on pins and needles and at the same time, a relief.

It got later and later and I remembered how, like me, Chris would not be late. My cell rang. She said she was caught in traffic and on the way. *I had not heard that voice since we last spoke in June 1962, exactly half a century before.* I hung up and felt a calmness run through my veins, arteries, muscles—what we are supposed to feel when "mother has arrived." It was a feeling I had never known as a child or adult and I marked it well. It rocked me; it blew me away. It literally was a visceral thing, like someone had shot me full of Xanax and chicken soup. That was what she had offered me. it was the mother-daughter love all sacred girls carry—Chris's rare, in that it just fit. We were a sacred match at just the right ages of sacred girl reunions.

After lunch, we strolled along the foggy coast, reminiscing and adding bits and pieces to our memories neither of us would ever have known otherwise. Just like we were fifty years before, with wisdom sprinkled over and honeyed laughter spooned in.

Every girl is entitled to their own Chris & Nancy experience.

Female attunement is the seat of our Femality. It is the first time we experience what being female is and where creation originates.
If we do not hang on to it, we remain forever exiled from Sacred Female BodyPsyches.
Every girl is entitled to that.

We must name it.
Honor it.
Bring it into the light.

And culture it...

The Swan Called Madolyn

Some souls are aptly named for the archetype they carry, and no one was better christened than the swan called Madolyn. White platinum hair in a Dutch-boy cut, you could not miss her even across the blacktop, and when she sprung into full view, dark eyebrows, hazel green eyes full of clarity, turned-up nose, and spangling of light freckles arrested you on the spot.

Madolyn was noticed by all, because she was one of those straight-A students who had the icing on the cake—a child protégé pianist, one of those amazing souls who chose the perfect family to hone her art, parents who would encourage and educate to a high shine, their purpose for being.

She was by nature an introvert, had no hidden agendas, and wouldn't have known one had it fallen on her head from a hundred-story building. She had the same emotional IQ as my own. We never had much time to get to know each other, because girls were divided up by their moms who stuck with whatever race and religious group they blindly bleated to.

She did come to my house once, but when we dropped her off, I found it impossible to cross that threshold. A large A-frame house high atop the hills, with slanting cathedral light, her father an *actual real violinist in the LA Philharmonic,* and her mother played and taught piano—my self-esteem and all my father's "So she'll do without" abandoned me on the other side of Privileged, worst of all when it came to musicality and musicians.

Madolyn was on the side I identified with—the French looking navy blue and white Campfire Girls and Bluebirds. To my chagrin and ongoing frustration, I was relegated to the murky brown sack-looking shift and crude brown belt of Troop 2225—better known as the Brownies, headed up by mothers some of whom competed through their daughters. The more I tried to be friendly, the meaner some were.

Some were better than others. Mrs. Wolfson and Mrs. May never saw me as competition, but I so preferred Jeanne Breedlove and Eunice B. They were so much more real. There was something far more real about these midwestern women-turned-nurses, than the mothers like Mrs. G., who gave me a dirty look when I got all excited when her hair overnight went from a bowel brown to a champagne-colored beehive. I kept asking what she had done. It was so pretty, but her ire kept rising. In those days, one did not point out a woman had "done something" (dyed) to her hair, especially a know-nothing little girl.

If I wanted to have any time at all with this rare Odette, she would have to meet me inside my deeply secluded cove of classical music while I assumed the role of the black and white egret. To nestle-perch beside her and ask her to come over after school. We were sitting in class at recess, when holding my breath, I asked if she would like to come over after school. Since her after school agenda revolved around Madolyn's piano lessons, her mother said Thursday was fine. Part of me was ecstatic—the other part, was sick at heart.

These feelings played out in a book that found me when I was eighteen years old. Decades later, when I was deep in therapy and identifying what really went on in those sacred state of girl years. I realized the role and ritual I was enacted at eight, was articulated in the 1928 novel *The Well of Loneliness* by Radclyffe Hall.

The excitement and shame I felt was the same as Stephen Gordon's, the aristocratic young female heroine, when she awaits to visit her goddess, Angela. The wait is unbearable, yet worth it. The scene I came across in my first quarter in UCLA, took place on the grounds of Morton, her family estate.

In my psyche, Madolyn echoed Angela—or was it the reverse? Hall describes her with the same platinum hair bobbed in a medieval pageboy— just like Madolyn, that I intuited imbued the same Otherworldly look. I even thought she named her Angela for angel. The swan called Peter swims by as they come together. The desire to merge our energies I had enacted with cousin Ellen, I repeated at eight. Inviting Madolyn to play over after school, knew well the low-esteemed awkward eighteen-year-old Stephen does upon her arrival. My female archetypal imagination was firing on all nine pistons.

It was a new yet completely torturing place, for had I felt welcome in my own home, had my mother felt home in the house we squatted in, there would have been no shame or anxiety for my expectation of "my" Angela's visit, but it didn't go like that. In the end, when we got there my mother had left a note in in the old milk box holder (she called it 'the secret place') reminding me to *stay in the backyard*. She would not leave a key. She believed it was more dangerous for us to be left alone inside the house, so she left Rold Gold pretzels to munch on until she returned. And no water or juice. Stuck on an unkempt lawn. I hated, dog poop assaulting my nose, Madolyn never noticed, with only me to keep us entertained.

Dropping Madolyn off

I never went into that cedar-scented, holy cathedral house of real-live professional musicians.

Again, it was in those days as today, always about *the other*, and I have a gut feeling many of these moms did not give a fig about it but were following what their husbands expected. Religious institutions ruled. It crippled everyone and severed girls from each other, tried to separate all kids and succeeded and failed. You can bus, you may impose isolation, but know this; never forget the female souls they clicked with and never let go.

Madolyn lived in my mind's eye in a glass castle at the top of Coliseum, which in all reality was an A-framed house, I would learn later, her father had built. Mr. Swan was a lead violinist in the Los Angeles Philharmonic and worked two jobs so his budding family could live at the top of the hill in such a lovely and elegant home. It was my ideal—three-girl family inhabiting that modest, amazing, dazzling home, the youngest Madolyn as a gifted pianist and sacred girl.

Through Madolyn's Front Door and My Female Otherworldly Eyes

At the base of the cathedral lighting in the living room, pouring down on a golden archangel harp. I know they had a baby grand with a metronome and her mother was a piano teacher but there was just no sense of a casual running in and out of a house as nice as this one.

It was different at Chris's household, so open, wild, and wooly that there was nothing intimidating about the air, let alone the humble threshold. It was like all the tract houses not high on the hills, a three-bedroom tract home, modest to say the least, and lived in to the max thanks to Mrs. Jeanne Breedlove. Madolyn's, in contrast was a contained silent space.

Girls like Madolyn carried a rare navy royal blue parochial patina, which I read as: "I am wanted, treasured, and valued. My whole family makes certain I have the best because I am deserving of nothing less." I was too young to know that parochial schoolgirls were in as deadly an ism trap as my own. But I was desperate for proof, visible proof and trappings that being wealthy and privileged had its own image of existence. Plaid, white blouse, a Scottish lassie, high-class elegance. She had the look and feel of a wealthy parochial girl without literally dressing that way. And she was as real as real can be.

Brahms's Waltz in A-Flat: My night of daughter shame

I was no fool. Madolyn sat down at the ivories one hushed evening when we were seven years old, and all the parents in attendance knew this was going to be a fine treat. Mrs. Vischer, bursting with pride and excitement, introduced Madolyn, who would now play, for our listening pleasure, Brahms's Waltz in A-flat Major. I saw, heard, and intuited before I could prepare and brace myself, a world of privileged lullaby kids, and with bowed head, squeezed back the tears my body was quaking with. This melody, played to the hush of attentive adults and kids, was heart-twistingly unbearable. Something that had always been denied hit me: "So this is what my mother never wanted me to find out."

The Telling Lullaby Moment

A solemn warning to Stupid Adults who are in charge of children, be they parents, teachers, relatives, coaches, or someone else: Sacred children see, watch, observe, and never forget anything when they leave the isolation of home and family and attend school. Whatever my mother feared I would notice—all she and my father withheld—I observed in grammar school, other girls' households, and selfless teachers—all of whom she dismissed (pretended to not care one wit about). For all the bullying, and slings and arrows that occur in school, my point is if you think your child does not see what they are starved for, you are dead wrong. And contrary to what you think—like sacred elephants, they never forget.

Anecdote

Reuniting with old friends brings unexpected gifts of surprise Authenticity. Madolyn remembered how we used to go to the studios, *Desilu* near Ballona Creek. How we found the empty set of *Guestward, Ho!* with a discarded script. What I had not remembered was that I climbed the high fence to throw my body over, just to get into the lot. Me? The adult me only remembered a less than adventurous girl. I climbed over a fence? Ignoring Keep Out signs? It was remarkable, yet there lingered a trace of Character that was—I would stop at nothing between Hollywood sets and floating like Alice down their rabbit holes. Pseudo main streets, yes. That is where the security guard discovered us and we had to leave—but I had done it. At ten, with my brother and Madolyn. Oh, joy. What a great return of an authenticity trait I could never have remembered, save my sacred reunion with the Swan called Madolyn.

Helena and the Day Her Mother Called My Mother....

"Nancy! Go over to Helena's! She's huddled in her room, refuses to talk. Mrs. May is beside herself. She thinks you might be able to help. Maybe Helena will talk to you."

An old drill. Got a problem with your daughter? Call for Nancy. Maybe she can get to the bottom of it. I was the Mrs. Piggle-Wiggle of our class. Yet the problems rendering my peers were hardly the ones in Betty MacDonald's children's books. Mrs. Piggle-Wiggle, an old lady with a hump of magic on her back, long hair pulled up in a silver bun, in a house that smelled of gingerbread and even had an upside-down staircase built by her long lost husband. The cures I was called for were hardly The Answer-Backer and the Never Want to take a Bath-er Cure, though I do disagree with many of her cures. My world of suffering children was not meant for a child to heal, yet mothers recognized a gift in me they called mature. Although that much was true—I was perceived as so mature for my age, with a common sense wisdom their daughters desperately needed and had long ago left behind. Kids healing kids. Children raising each other as best they could. All because of SAs (Stupid Adults).

Crossing over the lawns and swinging around the corner, I could have told her mother a thing or two about the Dark Force that entrapped that house of toxic silence. Having witnessed what it felt like to sit at that dining room table trying to pretend everything was normal when it felt like you had fallen into Connell's *The Most Dangerous Game*, Helena and I sat together looking past her father and brother. Surveying high above was Mister Moosehead. The stink of boiled shrimp and grits wrinkling his nose. Another trophy for Helena's big white hunter father. It was impossible not to upchuck with whole damned scene. We ate in patriarchal silence, and I feared taking a shower that night even though Mrs. May gave me my own neatly folded fresh towel and washcloth. An unusual nicety I was unused to. I never took that shower because I knew other girls with older brothers in adjoining bedrooms stood no chance of privacy. Older brothers had friends who shot over as soon as they got wind their little sister had a friend spending the night. All of this is what I reflected upon in a quick flash as I considered Helena's sudden silence. I had known her since we were Brownies off and on for five years. We never really clicked, and I suspect it was because Helena's quiet, introverted nature chose different avenues in which to escape. Helena was not a performer, musician, or dancer, but I suspect she was of poet bent, a lovely girl with an arresting quality I believe her mother saw.

Helena was in that strange bind with a mother who didn't reject her yet did not find the courage to face the deadly bargain she made when she took those vows and bred with a monster in human disguise.

This was not a rare situation. In my world I cannot think of one girl who was not being abused; it was just a matter of degree, length of time, and where and how her imagination took her to survive. The key factor that separated girls like Helena was the absence of full-on daughter rejection. Any mother who was alarmed by her daughter's disturbing behavior and act by calling for the one girl she believed could help was not a rejecting mother. I did go. What I remember was the inertia in Helena's bedroom. I knew it well. It was not dark; it was even sunny, with plaid curtains of brown and yellow. She lay prone as a Buddha on her bed, nose in a book the way children act when they pretend if they do not see you, you can't see them. I pulled out my most subtle, gentle appeals. However, what I saw and felt was my friend in a deeply dissociative state. Nothing could break the spell. Nothing would draw her out. This was an old scene I had been playing out in girls' bedrooms since I cut my teeth. Her father was a brute, her brother, a brute in the making, and the only other soul who knew it besides her mother watched us at dinner high above the dining room wall. I pulled out every stop, called upon my most gentle, reserved, careful healing energies. It was strangely ironic since Helena was the kind of girl I stood in certain awe of. Tall, athletic prowess, solid frame, and brainy—very brainy. And because we were children, it was so easy to shut each other out. I made no effort to befriend Helena because when one is clinging to a life raft, one must save oneself first. I know the feeling of going under, and it is not something I would wish on anyone except an abuser. I did not feel I had failed that day. I did tell my mother to please tell Mrs. May that I did not know what was wrong and like my namesake

Nancy Drew, did not tell my mother what I really suspected. *Besides, it was the Sacred Girls' Coda not to tell what I had clearly deduced.* How would my mother begin to understand what she cared not a fig for? Tell her, Helena's bedroom had the same air of girl spirit death as in so many others. That it was the same inertia the black hole that was in my grandfather's garage when Al slammed the door shut? Same dark air in the Old Livery Stable at Knott's with an 1870s child size hearse with a diamond-shaped black coffin and gold-mitered edges awaiting the next child's body taken to its final resting place when the park closed?

Mourning Is Broken

It was around this time a new girl who had come to our school in the fifth grade, Maryanne, a girl who was adopted and whose parents had survived the Holocaust came into our lives and was very much like the clown she had dressed up as that last Halloween. So good natured, I recall the waxen nose melting from the bonfire. When I visited her home—a tiny apartment house—true, thick, eternal MotherDaughter Love sweetened the air with her baking. Mrs. DS did not call her Maryanne, she called her My-Anne, with an emphasis on the my. She served us homemade croissants with real bittersweet chocolate inside. They were Dutch. Concentrate camp survivors. Yet somehow they found and kept and gave a love for their daughter that I found to be all too rare. Maryanne was their life. Both her mother and father were utterly filled with joy and devoted to her. It was a happy family that laughed a lot. And then in October 1963, Maryanne died of a sudden brain hemorrhage. The whole class came to the funeral. As I entered the chapel, I made a beeline to Chris's side. In my usual dissociate state, I stumbled to find her up front and sat down next to her, instinctively homing in to the only MotherLove I'd ever known.

After the services I found myself sitting in PTSD silence in Helena's living room with all the girls of our Girl Scout troop, as Mrs. May took on the role of standing by us girls in this horrific nightmare. She and the other moms thought it best we all have a place to gather upon return. No one knew what to say, especially the moms. It was strictly let the girls figure it out together. A pall hung around that living room. The sudden shock and the unbearable funeral service. You could hear Maryanne's parents crying behind a veiled curtain. I had never been to a funeral. It did not go with the lively spirit of Maryanne, truly another Great Sacred Girl. And so sudden.

As I sat with all the girls in Helena's living room, no one said a word. Moms did not automatically think of counseling in those days, considered bona fide privileged adults. Children did not need therapy, especially in my mother's choice. What might I and my brother divulge to a therapist that might hold her and our father accountable? There was so much morbidity under Helena's as much as under the chapel roof in that awful House of Peace. The only difference was that here, on the sofa, there was no mourning. No one mourned my dear Helena's personal hell, and I wonder today if her mother ever found the courage to protect the daughter she so truly loved.

Cookie Sue Morse Was a Horse

Cookie Sue was a horse. She dreamed, ate, slept, whinnied, neighed, galloped, cantered, trotted, and loped. Lest you think she was lyrical, she was not. She was, as any Great Sacred Girl could be, the salt of the earth but with wounds that salt was thrown upon, and there is no doubt in my mind that when I ran into her mother in my late twenties and was told Cookie had moved out of state and changed her name. Hmm. Sounded like she was one of our scar clan, girls with abuse to overcome.

Cookie looked as if she stepped off the South Dakota prairie. Her real name was Carla, but to be honest, neither name fit. She had a solid, quiet, horsey way about her, where you might have called her Jesse, Chance, Chase, or Blue. And like many of the girls who were horse crazy, to walk into her bedroom was to walk into Plastic Horse City. There they were, all the models of paints, pintos, buckskins, and bays, but the one all the girls wanted to play with was the palomino because of its rare platinum mane and tail.

I remember visiting Cookie after she had moved to LA with her grandmother. It was a small duplex, and in her bedroom was every miniature bridle and saddle manufactured in the world. If she did not have her own horse by then, she still rode because we went to an exclusive stable where a very rich girl kept her horse. It was a country club stable in Windsor Hills, and wouldn't you just know it? Who was kicking up dust that day in his Tony Lamas was teen heartthrob Johnny Crawford from *The Rifleman*. A frantic female buzzing filled the air: "You will not believe it, you won't believe it, Johnny Crawford is here!"

He was just as he was on TV; shy, unassuming, knew he was a public figure, and was probably thrilled to be away from the set with real horses and real people. But I seem to remember him in jeans and chaps with a pockmarked complexion. He did not put off the air of many a smarmy, smartass child star; but even at twelve, I knew enough to respect a celebrity's space and did not approach.

This Horse World thing that this nucleus of girls from Windsor Hills shared was different from LA girls, because you had to be very rich and have well-off parents and your own horse(s) boarded at ritzy country clubs. If you were a more out-in-the-boonies girl in the San Fernando Valley with parents on self-supporting ranches, was also cool, but did not feel the same. The Brentwood girls of the world were hyper-aware of the privilege they wielded. Cookie Sue's friend dwelt in a million dollar house in the Windsor Hills. Lucie, a tiny girl with brunette bob, an older sister, both had horses. Yet I was not envious. After all, if it wasn't treading the boards, the movie sets were as close as the crow flied at Twentieth Century Fox, Desilu, or Paramount. It was not my jam.

It was the horse manic cadre of girls I felt both in awe and distance from. Since I could not even get my own mother to talk about her passion for horses, how could I expect Cookie Sue to? She was in it for the pure wild spirit, that mystical girl-horse-female-equine bond that is the Female Mythstery, and it was fast being crushed out of her in that house at the end of Silverfern.

My mother used to laugh about how I hated going near horses; I was terrified of their sheer magnitude and that I would shiver and say, "Yuck, green teeth," because I had been around with Cookie to see them chomping alfalfa. But my life was on such a shaky spiderweb thread that the last thing I needed was a thousand pounds of unpredictable horse power-bucking and rearing under me. I was *never not* protecting my body and psyche from threats unpredictable, because a higher power cautioned me *you don't want to end up with a broken neck and severed spine,* and even though I knew it could happen in other ways, I was fully aware putting that boot into an iron English stirrup—or worse still, that klutzy leather Western one—swinging over as the world slid to the left, was worse than any stage fright that anyone had ever described to me. (Not ever having stage fright I always needed people to describe what it felt like.) So while I was smart enough to stay away from horses and stables, I still clung to horse lore as the only avenue that might get my mother to bond with me. The Rearing-up Horsewoman I would never meet in her self-orchestrated publicity shots. Just like the character in du Maurier's *Rebecca,* digging her spurs into her horse, laughing over the blood they drew. Like Rebecca, my mother was not a horse-loving soul; she was She Who Rides as Dominatrix woman.

I spent a certain amount of time with Cookie, not a lot but enough to remember that awful night when she had my back, secretly warning me that her older brother and boys next door were going to try to see through the bathroom window when I took a shower. Cookie's older brother was among the budding *brute-snoops* of the neighborhood, the kind of older brothers who sole-soul existence centered on terrorizing girls, voyeurism, and conspiracy. It could be overt, covert, or both. I didn't shower that night, and even going to the bathroom to use the toilet was torture, throwing a towel over the rod and praying it would stay put. You could correlate the showers I didn't take depending on the households I stayed in. All Girl Households were the Safe Ones. Older Brother Households were hell. And No one knew it better than Helena and Cookie Sue. Obsessive voyeurs, they were *boyeurs*—and all girls knew it. Just like the whole of our sick sphere's society (i.e., Boys-will-be-boys shit and 'he only punches you because he likes you).

I have tried to find Cookie over five decades. When women get married it's difficult to find them again, yet with the internet I still held back. Because when a woman decides she does not want to be found, no one understands that better than I. We change our names and move away for good reason. Hiding is the illusion of safety at all costs.

A girl with flaxen blonde hair tinged with nutbrown in old-fashioned braids parted down the middle or a plain ponytail, with a slight hook nose, green eyes, and freckles. She was the epitome of Bar None Ranch. Right out of a Willa Cather novel. I do not remember Cookie's poetry and refused to trespass on her privacy. I acted on stage playing those scenes written from the Male Mindset—from Shakespeare to Tennessee Williams. Their Male Speake as well as the Dark Force Females who spit out their *merde* (Hellman, Clare Booth Luce), and all the rest who demonize, punish, and victimize girls and women in their so-called classic theatre and novels.

Love Letter to Cookie Sue

My dearest friend,

I was *there*. I am a witness to whatever truths you carry. I, too, changed my name when I hit twenty. I didn't just change the last name through marriage, I changed my first name because I could not move into adulthood when I was loathe to refer to myself as a woman and stalled that off until I was thirty. After I married and could not bear to be called Nancy another moment, I changed my name and tweaked it. I could never quite let go of the letters that lived within, so I chose my grandmother's Motherblood line. Welsh. And where they fled from, Mother Russia. To escape my low-class family, I required an aristocratic bent. From the princesses of The House of Romanov, I picked Tanya for Tatianna from ages twenty to forty-six. That allowed me to keep the a, n, and the y, enough to hold close to my heart my original N-a-n-c-y, yet took me out of this world and into a pantaloon-parasol pretend cosmic sphere, how I envisioned *elegance* and *civility*.

And when I told your mother I had changed my first name, she countered you had too. At the time I did not put two and two together. It would take me another fifteen years, another nervous breakdown, and twenty more years in therapy to know why we each had done it.

Why any person does, really. We change our first names to divorce ourselves from the toxic family identity thrust upon us like flimsy, ill-fitting cutouts they hang on paper dolls. Except our parents stick it on with Krazy Glue, pun intended.

Cookie, I was forty-six when I threw away my antidepressants and went back to the Nancy who went to your Halloween parties. Though the meds would be needed again, what I did not need to hide from was the Great Sacred Girl I always was, just had to meet and cherish her. Wherever you are, I never will forget you and wish we could have spoken our female truths back then, one Great Sacred Girl to another.

With all my equine awe, Nancy.

Eloise and the Nancy Drew Debacle

There wasn't anything Eloise B. did not have. She had the only real playhouse in the neighborhood, and there were girls in far grander homes. The playhouse, with windows and curtains, was big enough for a table and chairs and tea set. I did not know what to do in it as there were no costumes. It was in a boring backyard, but Madolyn remembers endless happy hours there.

I just was not the "pretend to pour tea" type. It had to real: bergamot, London Fog and Earl Grey with a jug of real milk. And where were the tea sandwiches? Cucumber at the very least. Still, I adored Mrs. B., and when she knew I was visiting, made my favorite macaroni salad with pickles and brought home from the Armenian bakery, picked up my absolute favorite, *lahmajoun*, an Armenian pizza.

Eloise's parents took her everywhere. Once, we went to Del Mar Beach Hotel where her father, not a young man, hit the indoor swimming pool and swam with us. I was astounded. It was a beautiful hotel, but I shall never forget what her mother drew out of a special suitcase: a hard, swift punch to my solar plexus. There on the twin bed, Mrs. B. laid out a pale yellow chiffon party dress, more museum than party.

It was like Helen Fenton on steroids, party dresses from a Hollywood movie.. With a stiff silken Edwardian bow in the back and full length, laced sleeves. Not only did it have a pinafore good enough for Marie Antoinette, it came with white lace pantaloons. No one ever saw pantaloons in real life, only in the movies— on Scarlet O'Hara, her little girl, Bonnie Blue, and Melanie.

How her mom found this rare treasure still mystifies me. She worked at Buffum's, so perhaps that made it available to her. I kept looking in the newspaper ads for pantaloons to appear. Eventually they took off but were nothing compared to Eloise's, satin bows, and all. I begged to no avail. My mother, like a cockatoo, just repeated the usual: "Ask Grandma." When I saw the newspaper's cheap ones were just a poor, thin echo of what had come out of Eloise's suitcase, and worst of all—I complained about wearing all of it. Whenever there was something I wanted, and was too young for even babysitting jobs, it was Grandma Mary who would pay. No matter what I wanted, my mother's reply was: "Where there's a will, there's a way." Followed by, "Hey, I had nothing as a kid. Just kick the can. Jacks and marbles. Why aren't marbles good enough for you?"

Hmmm. Marbles versus a frock like Vivienne Leigh's in *That Hamilton Woman*? My mother was an alien. We would never understand each other, nor care to.

Eloise was an only child. I got along swimmingly with her. She was one more nonjudgmental, non-hidden agenda girl I felt at total ease around. We laughed much over everything, let alone *Katy Keene* comics. We went to Santa Barbara on an overnight trip with her parents and visited Bill Wogan, creator of this comic book, in his own studio. Katy had ebony hair so black it had dark blue highlights. She was beautiful, forerunner of Wonder Woman and Xena, but she was not a superhero. Just glamourous and full of adventures that were also glamourous. After leaving his studio in total amazement, we were taken to lunch.

I will never forget siting in an exclusive, WASP country club in Santa Barbara and having fruit cocktails served to us in tall silver goblets. We also went downtown to Clifton's, and Mrs. Buckwalter knew well the Treasure Chest. Eloise always came away with some trinket. But Bill Woggon's was the treasured gift: seeing the actual artist in his garage studio with all the Katy Keenes on the walls, on his drawing boards, and even the upcoming ones. It was unbelievable. What is funny is that after all this time, Elaine has no recollection of the entire trip.

It begs the question: What? You don't remember being presented to the queen and visiting Sandringham?

The Nancy Drew Debacle- 'Do Not Tread on My Sacred Ground'

In grammar school, Eloise and I were knee-deep in Nancy Drews. One day after school, as we stepped down the salmon-sparkled steps, she boasted, "Carolyn Keene is really a man!"

The world stopped.

I looked at her like she was out of her girl-mind. Eloise was in one of her Mary O'Toole moods (from Mrs. Piggle-Wiggle's the *Answer-Backer Cure*), braids twitching with smugness framing a smart-ass jutting chin.

Dutifully, with all the female fealty within me, I apprised her: "That's a lie. I don't believe you."

"It's true. Carolyn Keene is really a *man. My father said so.*"

Her father was a reporter for the *Herald Examiner*, and he could have known publishers with behind the scenes details, but I knew a woman's voice when I read it. Nothing on this planet or any galaxy would ever convince me that Nancy Drew was written by any consciousness but a female's.

"*It's not true.*"

"Yes it is! My father wouldn't lie!"

"You can believe what you want. *Nancy Drew is a woman's voice.*"

Wheeling around on my saddle shoes, I left her standing, sputtering, red-faced fuming.

What Eloise *could not have known was that she was treading on my sacred ground, my religion, my spirit home.* We never argued again, and that was how it went with her. She held no grudges. In fact, she didn't even recall them.

I liked Eloise and stayed in touch when she moved away when we graduated.

Years later I read about Edward Strathmeyer and how he contracted with Mildred Wirt to ghostwrite as Carolyn Keene the first Nancy Drews from 1928 to 1959. There was a brief interlude when Wirt went on strike and a man filled in with *The Secret Letter*. But I knew female consciousness on the written page. I did not have the concept nor any word for it, but I intuited Nancy, Bess and George stood for the Triple Goddess and Femality. No male possessed the BodyPsyche to pull it off. No way.

Eloise laughs about all of this today. She is what I'd call a good sport. She was showered with dresses, toys, and had the first Barbie. Wanted for nothing yet I always felt a tension in the house. I remember her father was a fan of Ruth Etting, and since I had watched Doris Day in the movie, he was duly shocked when I sang along with all her recordings. It was always that way. Parents and grandparents were always asking me how I knew anything from past eras. I just smiled—it was who I am.

Femocratic note: *The Mystery of the Tolling Bell* is a Female Consciousness book if ever there was one. The womb-tomb metaphors along with Nancy and George's partnering to solve the mythstery is worthy of several reads.

The original pen name of Carolyn Keene belonged to Mildred Wirt Benson. From the very first, *The Secret of the Old Clock*, she was the one who created and gave voices of the Nancy Drew books, and in my mind she is *the* Nancy Drew author. She eventually identified herself as (one) Carolyn Keene in 1980 and was given a special Edgar Award for her contributions to the mystery genre.

Lila and the Comandante Table

The C.'s were the most unique family with whom I have ever broken bread. When you gathered to have a meal at the end of the day it was not dinner, it was supper, and it was not just supper—it was supper with the von Trapps. The C. dinner table commanded that one behave in the most civilized fashion: speak when spoken to, the cringy tings of silver on China. You half-expected Mr. C. to whip out his whistle and blow us all to silence if we giggled out of turn, while Mrs. C. shot in and out of a swinging door with each course to the tune of *The Russian Dances from the Nutcracker Suite*. Classical music for background was du riguer.

At these suppers, Mrs. C. ostensibly played the role of dutiful housekeeper a sort of Fraulein Rottenmeir revamped as a mild-mannered 1960s housewife. Yet she was really tough as nails, so we weren't fooled. She was that great combo of Dedicated Mom and First Commander.

When I look back on it—the civility, the continuity, the sheer Edwardian propriety with classical music playing in the background—it should have made me long for more dinners at the Commandante's table, but the truth was it would really be revisiting the Mays all over again, dining in yet a more civilized version of Patriarchy of Things Past. Father as Ruler, Commander in Chief. To be fair, Lila's father was not like Helen's. Having served in the military, he retained the butch haircut and corporal stance, but to my recollection did not carry brute energy. Had this been so, the upstairs bedroom girl's wing would not have rung with rollicking high-pitched shrieks of laughter, a family of three Great Sacred Girls' energy (except when they were being good little Liesls and Martas at the table).

In short, it did not feel like a household gripped by The Dark Force.

I credit this back to Mrs. C, who served the role of Strong Mother well, not unlike the mother in *National Velvet*. Mrs. Brown takes Velvet up to the attic and shows her the medal she won swimming the English Channel as a young woman. She genuinely understood her daughter's passion to ride her horse to victory in the Steeple Chase and sees to it her daughter will slip by disguised as a boy jockey, helping trim her brunette locks short under her riding helmet. Mrs. Brown possessed that rare quality I sought in real life women: the natural, powerful female, supporting and inspiring her daughters selflessly. And in real life, Lila's mother appeared to come the closest. Capable. Functioning. Fully present.

Like many women (recalling she may have been in the military) who married a military man, Mrs. C had a beautiful, transparent, masculine side, and her three lively, yet introverted daughters were unique and fascinating in their own ways. The middle sister, Ariadne, had the bibbidi-bobbidi-boo wave of Fate's magic wand; she actually got to study acting with the famous veteran character actress Lurene Tuttle. Ariadne was on TV regularly.

To my thirteen-year-old mind it was as hard to hear as it was harder to accept that something like this actually existed. I don't know which was harder, the fact that a studio existed that taught children how to act for film and television or that Lila's sister got to work on TV and movie sets. I would have practically sold my soul to have changed places, but then again, my soul was never for sale. And perhaps intuited to all that befalls a child left unattended in that Darkest Force of TV, Stage and Film.

Though I was there only once or twice, I recall a bustling upstairs and the tilt of dormer windows and ceilings that led to her sisters' bedrooms, but it is all jumbled now. I just see it as kind of like an all-girls bedtime free-for-all, like when Audrey Hepburn as Eliza Doolittle in *My Fair Lady* is singing *I could have Danced All Night* while getting dressed for bed by the lady servants. Heaven sent! No voyeuristic older brothers to have to contend with.

I was attracted to Lila's INFJ (a result from the Myers-Briggs Type Indicator (MBTI) test) brain. We met in English class where we were assigned to create a magazine. We dubbed it *Olypopla*—pig Latin for lollypop. Lila got the magazine concept whereas I was not at all into it but went along because we balanced each other with the words and images. My favorite was an ad for Booth's House of Lords gin she clipped from her father's zines, "Protest against the Rising Tide of Conformity." It was, after all, the early sixties.

With Lila, I could speak in metaphor and actually be understood and try to entice it out of her. She got to go to a camp along with Cookie Sue and Lucie. Somewhere in the mythological northeast of America. Until I was twelve, I believed that sort of fancy-camp only happened in *The Parent Trap* with Hayley Mills as the lucky duck.

So isolated was I from 'the well off girls' I simply could not imagine in real life girls being transported by an airplane paid for by their parents with all the camp gear, all the preparations, all the taking seriously their daughter's desires and to a *theatrical* camp that was so unique there was nothing else like it in the world. It had a name that I have never forgotten. Like a phantasmic violet-ultra-cobalt-blue forest sounded like *Ona Darkah (do not know its spelling)*, somewhere in Massachusetts, it was not just horses and riding in English gear so bourgeois for California girls, but it was designed around theatre. You could be an equestrian *and* an actress-in-the-making at Camp Ona Darkah. I always learned about these things in the aftermath, when summer was on the horizon and the girls were going back again. Whether I chose to show my feelings around my mother, they stung—a brutal shock of mother-daughter-rejection, like being backhanded with brass knuckles.

To My Dear Friend…

If I could say anything to my dear friend, it would be that I hope this memoir captures all I loved and envied about your unique and vivacious family, and I hope you are still making those beautiful clay pots and cups. *I still have mine, and coffee tastes best in it because it has your chi, your spirit embedded within.*

Athena & The Night We Kept Chernabog at Bay

Background Music: The Mystics – Hushabye, 1959; Dion and The Belmonts, "A Teenager in Love," 1959, "Tell Laura I Love Her, 1959 Ray Peterson, written by Jeff Barry and Ben Raleigh.

While some people should never be permitted to have the honor and privilege of raising children, others need execution before they have the honor and privilege to exist in the very sphere as children and animals. Knute and his battle-axe wife cohort were two such felons who believed they absconded from the capital offence of childhood sexual abuse. But I was there, the mouthpiece for Child Soul Murder, which is what went on under that profane, shabby, heinous roof. And I am here to tell it as I saw, heard, felt, and recorded it.

Athena. When I think of the name and all that it engenders, it is next to impossible to communicate the sheer magnitude of knowing her as one eight-year-old girl with another and how things coalesced, culminated, and transformed one brief-endless night in the searing, unforgiving heat only the San Fernando Valley can crank out.

'Twas an august, August night as it happened.

I do not remember their house in detail; it was the house they put a pool in. Likely her father had a hand in it as he did with all the brute force he applied to everything and everyone he touched. That was Athena's father. Knute the Brute. Blond going bald, thirty tops. Born with a toothpick in the crook of his cruel mouth. If he did not have a silver front tooth, he should have. Clomped around in steel-toed Doc Martens. Marlboros jammed under the rim of a biceped T-shirt. If T-shirts were offered with the evil Western Pest Extermination Mole Undertaker, he would have had a truck full. A mean cuss, dirty pooler. Never cracked a smile unless it was the sadist's smirk. A child's worst nightmare and a girl child's worst fate: her torture papers and death warrant signed by the Better Business Patriarchs and the women who colluded with them. Knute the Brute. Knute was Chernabog, sometimes referred to as Satan, the embodiment of Evil in Disney's *Fantasia* who resided on Bald Mountain. A demon of the Male Underworld, a Cobalt Beast pummeling his chest to his minions, bellowing in false bravado. Knute. Taloned soul. Forked spirit. Cloven psyche. *The real-life bogeyman who sexually abused children, recognized because they must live with him day in, day out, year upon year.* The one you must call Father, Dad, Daddy, the one who shovels down his ham and eggs, licking his chops *that way*, the one you must quake and quiver over in your shower with no locked door, freeze yourself in your own bed, straining to hear those shuffling paws down the eerily lit hallway. Your father—the man in the pencil-leaded game with tufts falling here and there under the plastic, tufts you have seen and abhor.

Knute should have been publicly drawn and quartered and left for the buzzards, if only they would have him, which they would not. His wife had a high-pitched voice, as if she had shrieked so much for so long it just stuck in that register. A sharp contrast to the heavyset creature in pin curls, eyebrows drawn on like a cartoon upside-down letter U. She quite resembled that horrific jealous queen creature in *Betty Boop's Snow White*, except instead of being emaciated, she was the Jack Sprat wife who could eat no lean. She was in some unspeakable way reminiscent of Kate Smith, without song or smile. Dark Force Females keep Dark Force Females their lifelong friends and their unwanted daughters suffer the consequences. My mother's old high school friend. I was told often enough by my mother, how Athena and I were strolled together in tailor tots because we were born two months apart. She in searing August, me in autumnal October. Our brothers came later, with mine a little older than hers. My mother loved to dig at me about the fact that when we were babies, and they took us to Delores's dining room, Athena would sit in her highchair with a breadstick in her mouth and just stare, while I was busy pulling at the tablecloth. *It drove us crazy; she told me. You were just impossible, not a good baby like Athena.* Good is one thing; dissociative quite another.

Athena and I were unwanted, despised, rejected daughters. Our mothers hated us in their own pathetic ways. In this they were alike. In their tension, like motors that never purred and idled. My mom was like a pot on the boil with the lid forever rattling; her mother was the fomenting red sauce spilling over the sides, shooting up to the ceiling, hissing all the way. Like the man she married and chose to stay with, her mom kept her poor bargain and abused the life she brought into this world. Frizzled hair from bad perms, sweating forever, I honestly do not know who I would cast to play her. An unknown. All I know is that her daughter was an innocent, beautiful child with her own shortcomings, treading the boiling waters of a hell not of her own making.

Athena had the typical early American little girl's pink chenille bedroom. Small shelves and smaller radio. That was the summer of the teenage funeral dirges: "Hushabye" and "A Teenage in Love" by Dion and the Belmonts wailing from station KRLA. Everywhere hung grief, death, and hopelessness. (The Teenage Death Wish tunes of that era should be explored in depth.) Just as I was wishing for Dion to stop wishing on the stars up above, Athena dropped to her knees to say something kids only do in the movies. Her prayers. Didn't I know this one? And so, when I heard her recite these words, I could not believe what I was hearing. Frozen in terror. *If I should die before I wake, I pray the lord my soul to take.*

Whaaat?

I literally could not believe what I was hearing. Why would anyone pray to have some pretend, punishing old man floating on a cloud pointing his finger-of-preference to another man—*to take your female soul?* Not on my watch. No one takes my soul, let alone the Imaginary Brute Male (the Giant again) that devised the cultural Child Hells we were trapped in.

Girls wore baby doll pajamas in those days, but Athena wore PJs. Athena got to use Breck creme rinse I always associated with haloed blondes' photos on the back of *Good Housekeeping* magazines. Pretty, fair, blonde girls with halos, and because my mother used Prell, I thought that was what brunette families used.

When her mother came to assist her in anything, there was always dissent, but now her mother had gone to work the night shift and Athena had turned confessional eyes upon me. She needed to tell someone what her father did to her. He used Coke bottles to rape her. I listened.

While another girl might have found it unbelievable, the part of me that had been raped by objects understood it was true. She flipped out, tears flying like they do in cartoons, sobbing the way I never thought someone as tall and strong as she could succumb to. Pounding her pillow, sobbing "I'm a pig; I look just like my father; my mother is right!" How could I deny this when just hours before in front if me, Knute yanked her backward, taunting her. "Ha, ha! She's a pig—you know you're a pig—listen to her squeal! Go on, pig!"

Athena shrieking in agony, trying in vain to get his paws off the topknot. If looks could have killed, my eyes annihilated him on the spot. He let go so she would fall to the floor. I knew had I not been there he would have kicked her with his steel-toed boots. I wanted to murder him by throwing acid in his eyes.

She grew hotter, shaking more, socking the face of pillow. "I'm ugly! Ugly! My mother's right! I look like my father. I hate myself! Hate, hate, hate!" Athena was one of those babies born with a cleft palette. The stiches from the scar showed, especially when she perspired as she did in front of me that hundred-degree hellish night. She was Stephen, my Stephen. Viking-like in her golden blondeness, taller and larger-boned than I. She could bully but knew she could not bully me.

Me: Athena, Athena! Listen to me. No. Your mother's wrong! Her: She's not! She knows! Look at me! Don't, don't.

She fell forward and cried so painfully I shut my eyes and took my cue. This was a certain onetime surrender, and I did what I did. Terrified her monster father would come back because her mother was out, what she did not count on was what I had up my sleeve—something in me knew he wouldn't dare come after her while I was there, but I was charged to do more than that.

I stopped trying to pat her back. She would not be touched or consoled. I got up and lay down on the other twin bed.

Me: *Athena. Come here.*

Stunned, I watched as she characteristically lumbered over like a polar bear. Gently I got her to lie on top of me. She was too tired, too spent to care.

Me: Look at me.

She blinked a blank stare. She had turned off her listening ears, but I did not care.

Me: You are beautiful. Handsome. So pretty.

Too exhausted to argue, she cried her heart out. When there was nothing left, I lifted her head and gently said, "Do you want to try something?" With no protest, I kept talking. I was getting my words from some faraway place. Pointing to my Queenie forehead, I whispered, "Kiss—*here.*" Just like Johnny kissed Queenie. Years later I would hear others calling that The Third Eye, for spiritual connection.

Still in a stupor, she complied, robot-like. No protests about her scar. No pushing me away. I used my Female Spirit Guides wand. The room spun like the white chalk circle the virgins draw when they need protection. Divinity protected us. We broke our sweats. I wanted her to see how beautiful she was. She did not know what was going on, but kissing my forehead took her to another state of being. Chaste. Sacred. Holy. I could feel her sobbing ebb as she slid her head to my shoulder. We were sweating and cooling together.

It is an amazing thing that can happen when the cosmic alchemy of two eight-year-old girls is harnessed. It was only one night of sparing her from Chernabog, but he did not darken her door. Over the next few years, I saw her off and on until we were about twelve; it was never comfortable—she was contentious, but I knew that her existence was on some level even more hellish than my own by its sheer brutality, mentally, physically, and spiritually. Athena was not possessed of the spiritual reserves I carried; but I know in my bones I could not have survived her particular hell. From seven-to-nine my life twisted in turns of Evil and Sublime.

Love letter to Athena… We were unwanted daughters, and our mothers were wickedly, unconscionably cruel to us and our siblings, each in their own sick-twisted way. I have thought of that sacred hellish August night. I want you to know I did the best I could to reflect back the truth of your beauty. No one else did or would, at least then. But it haunts me, what and all you were trapped in and abandoned to. Just know, my memory honors The Great Sacred Girl you were, under the worst of unthinkable circumstances. Any witness to violence is a victim of violence. I could not have withstood a father-monster as mentally-bodily-brutal as yours.

In loving remembrance,
Nancy

A note about Mothers and Daughters

Why I ended up suffering it out once again in the hellish Reseda heat was my mother's venal agenda. She would not have to tolerate me under her roof for at least one day and night. I hold her accountable for the women she chose to keep company with, for the Great Sacred Daughters violated, and for subjecting me to their criminal homes.

Girls of color stolen from me by Stupid & Ignorant Adults

There was something tacitly understood by all girls then who intuitively had learned—in certain households you may not be welcome. You could be white, gifted, and talented— but if you weren't part of their Bluebird mom's group, you were *the other*. I suffered in oddly reverse discrimination when black girls did not invite me over, though I tried with all my skills to suggest it.

Adair T. was a highly intellectual, introverted, arresting girl, in a word, my type: Otherworldly. She kept to herself and I admired that, but no hinting around as we walked her home could get her to break her family rules. Like a punch to my solar plexus, how could I blame her? Whites were forbidden. Can't trust 'em.

Lynne T

A few years later when I was also forming a friendship with a black girl who reminded me of Mr. Peabody and his Wayback Machine, on 'Rocky & His Friends.' Her voice even sounded like his; calm, unflappable beagle in a white lab coat, who gave wise counsel to his 'boy' Sherman. What a kick! We laughed ourselves silly with the wittiest puns. I adored Lynne. Her family lived on the rich streets named for the streets the houses were built upon. The Dons. It was said that was where Nat King Cole's family lived.

Lynne was from a highly successful and academic family. I was so excited for a day with this muse and wit, getting ready for my father to drive me over. I was told I was not going. What? I was sucker-punched. My parents had found out Lynne had brothers of my dating age and made it clear, 'we know what's best for you.' I cried and cried, when the real truth was they wanted what was best for them. The inevitable white flight fears of neighborhood gossip—like, did you hear that Llewellen girl hangs around with a black family? To this day I can hardly believe the ignorance and cruelty my parents harbored. The real tragedy? It was everywhere no matter what race or religion. All of us Great Sacred Girls lost out in so many ways of inner and outer integration. I still think of Lynn today, over sixty years later.

Bonny Ronny and the Boys

In my grammar school years, I spent my entire time in search of like-spirits. Any way I could seek out and find anyone where I might discover a kinship connection on any level.

With Chris, it was how she listened, her balanced presence, and something utterly Female Otherworld. Chris connected with My Female Girl Soul's Authenticity.

Then I met Ronny O. in third grade, and something about his crystal blues stopped me dead in my tracks. His good looks might have played a distinct disadvantage. I had learned from birth to avoid the "charm boys" and how they might weaponize their superficial good looks into manipulative agendas. Like how my handsome father (a precursor to Calvin Klein male models) took advantage of my innate child's trust and all the while plotted out the sexual abuse he would never be held accountable for. His sociopathic energies never left and served me lifelong. With me, it would always be, "Prove your worth step by step." Words are lies. Tone of voice speaks volumes. Behavior broadcasts the truth of your Character. Ronny—a cross between Tony Dow (Wally on *Leave It to* Beaver) and Brad Pitt—passed with flying colors.

Bonny Ronny and Backward Glances to Third Grade

I used to be on pins and needles until we finally got to the May Festival. Dancing do-si-dos, smacking our little lips with the moms' miniature Avon red lipstick samples (however inappropriate). And the costumes! Off we bowed and curtsied to "Wabash Cannonball" and "Tennessee Wig Walk." Then, in third grade, I was paired with Ronny to the ditty that remembered me from my homeland. Named "Home to the Isles," my body's psyche remembered it as home. Home in the Highlands, heather in the air. My plaid skirt a kilt, mandatory white knee socks, ballerina flats, and a paper tam that rippled in the soft breezes of Ladye Santa Ana's. Lassie Nancy and Bonny Ronny. This Ancient Otherworld Caledonian tune would lead me fifty years later to Scottish country dances in Ohio. Ronny was authentic as a friend. He helped me with things I would not, could not do; he sawed and sanded my tugboat and I painted it. We'd laugh, slathering tempera paints on those flapping newsprint papers on easels, far taller than us, in our fathers' old shirts.

The Mexican Fan Incident

My brother leapt out of the new white Ford Galaxie as we pulled into the driveway. Look! Look! His flushed face was the same as when he discovered our cat's newborn kittens. In his arms was one of those paper Mexican Rainbow folding fans, opened to a circle. Ronny did not have to leave a note because Davey knew. Wanted it to be a happy surprise for his big sister. That night at dinner found my father interrogating me about whom this Ronny lad was. We sat without mom at the pallid, sticky yellow Formica table that was steel-belted around the rim.

Dad: *Who is this lad?*

Me: He's so nice! I really like him.

Dad: (To my brother) Keep an eye on him … and your sister.

Casting my little brother as a spy-stalker I never knew might foretell, Honest John the Fox (in Disney's *Pinocchio*) manipulating his gullible sidekick, Gideon, to do his dirty work. I was ten when Disney rereleased this child-hating film; his threats made me feel like I was walking with shards of glass tumbling in my stomach, a kaleidoscope on steroids.

My brother, Dave, was always my champion, taking on bigger boys when they badmouthed me as a "prude" because I would not sleep around at twelve. I had his undying loyalty. Could blood sometimes be thicker than water? Could I live at school without worrying that Dave might get his own lying spies, lying about my every innocent move? The funny thing was, what my father could never have known was that my true heart's desire was Chris. Had he known, he would have laughed. Who takes girls and their little girlfriends seriously? No threat to his male ego. (Still, it would have freaked out my mother. I learned by her words, deeds, and butchfemme phobia to keep my feelings locked in a vault.)

Fast Forward: 2012, Fifty Years to the Date We Graduated

I reconnected with Ronny for a journey sentimental and sobering, through the old streets of our grammar school times all roads leading to our old school destination. Up the old salmon-sparkled steps that turned salmon-underbelly-gray in the rain. Right up to finding it chained and barred on weekends. The security guard gave us entry when we explained our sentimental journey. Soon we found ourselves back in the old "aud," me swinging my feet on the stage's apron, him at the still shiny black baby grand that Madolyn's fingertips sanctified with Brahms's *Waltz in A-Flat Major.* What with Ronny singing an old pop song, I got to see for the first time my friend's musicality. He wrote and produced songs and played piano effortlessly.

On stage I looked out longingly over those old precious seats of honeyed faux wood, the metal armrests long since repainted a powder blue, my favorite color. Was it small, or was it just the scale I always remembered? Had I ventured alone I may have explored the wings and walked on the spot where I led the China Boys from *The Nutcracker.* That night, when the audience kept laughing, but I did not know because it was happening behind me. I was as the leader. The reason? Celia's yellow silk PJ pants kept falling down.

Then, there was the night Chris and I played guitar side by side and what happened upon leaving—my mother's venal attack because I had "No personality," a paraphrase taken from the title of the Lloyd Price ditty. Apparently, a lady was complimenting me in the crowded throng, and I never heard her, so how could I thank her? Anything to weaponize my moments of joy, celebration of community, and audience appreciation, I learned early on that the spotlight proved more kryptonite than limelight. School allowed me to shine—until my mother got wind and threw me in my room to think about my rudeness and no personality.

And Then There Was David G.

David G. played the violin, and carrying its case gave him a middle-aged lawyer or accountant look. Like Madolyn, he was one of Mrs. Vischer's protégés. He was a profound introvert like me, the polar opposite of a jock, so we spent the World Series in one hundred-degree heat on the cracked, spackled gray benches under the only shade there was, the aud's overhang.

That day, a bully made it his agenda to humiliate me about wearing white after Labor Day. Sandy Koufax was hitting home runs on transistors all around us, and Alan F. was whacking them on the blacktop before us. As the bully smirked away, David leaned into me like Agatha Christie's detective, Hercule Poirot. Dave was *The Big Bang Theory's* Sheldon Cooper without the ego. That is part of why I looked up to him. He got science, the solar system, and his callow figure in gray cords that always threatened to slip off his non-hips. Dave was an empath.

I was crushed and slumped in shame. *How did I not know it was taboo to wear white now?*

Crossing the knee of his cords, he duly informed me that, "Dark colors absorb heat and make one hotter while white reflects the heat away."

So I was the Smart One after all!

All this shared from beneath his adenoidal glasses—gray on top, clear on the bottom, sports shirt buttoned to the nerd top. We might have been two Edwardian cohorts, convening about Pavlova, *Anna Karenina*, *Eugene Onegin* under chestnut trees, taking tea besides the Black Sea lapping at the shores.

Did I sport a Merry Widow chapeau, or Leghorn cartwheel, if in June? Did he wear spectacles and bump-toed spats like grandpa's daguerreotypes? Sipping a 'glass tea' Russian style from a samovar, or did we choose Poirot's blackcurrant sirops and tisanes? There was, after all, French somewhere in Grandpa's bloodline

Herbert F-Our class Battalion Chief

Herbert and Gail were twins. Each had a very mature air about them. Straight-A students, if memory serves me right. Fifth grade was adventurous, if you had an archetypal imagination starved to be fed. The teacher told us the LA fire department would be coming to school and our class had to vote who would be our "battalion chief." In some intrinsic way, we all knew it should be Herbert. He carried certain natural leader energies: trustworthy, steady as a rock, with an empathy he wore like his softly ironed shirts. There was no question about it. He won the honored title.

The battalion chief or representative from the LA fire department arrived to our school in his red engine. So charming. Kids kept asking, "What's your name?" as he would ping-pong back, "Puttin' Dame. Ask me again and I'll tell you the same." This went on and on to peals of laughter, a funny little game he must have done at every school.

I remember the monolithic red of the fire engine. I remember the novelty to our daily grind. What I most remember was Herbert being introduced as our battalion chief and crowned with an authentic red plastic hat and something pinned on his jacket. This stuck in my head when I dreamt in early therapy years, of Herbert standing in front of the map of the United States. He was the Churchill of our class.

His sister was also forty at fourteen. Maturity itself. I had just completed our morning performance of *The Music Man,* as the leading lady, Marian the Librarian. We ate lunch on the lawn by the aud, and she gave me a compliment, a Great Sacred Girl reflection I will forever treasure. "You looked like nothing in the world could move you from that stage," were her words. Talk about the actor's highest compliment and we were just chatting. No one before had ever complimented me, and I never acted for fame. I acted automatically for my spirit guides. But Gail's selfless adult perception remains in my heart today. Gail and Herb live in my distilled memories as a most underappreciated pair, each for his or her own gifts of what we all needed: Maturity, goodness; role models without ego. In short, the definition of real deal Peer Leadership.

Ah, Alan—The Sandy Koufax of BHS, Lefthanded Pitcher Extraordinaire

Alan F. was baseball itself; baseball Incarnate. Even his flattop sported a baseball diamond. The embodiment in America's late 1950 and early '60s. Known for an incomparable pitch (he was the only lefty besides me, so we sat together at the end of a row every semester). I rarely conversed with this clique of boys, but Alan, Danny, and their crew will always serve as background for those last torpid autumn days of the famous 1963 rivalry between the LA Dodgers and NY Giants, reaching a fevered pitch in Danny Kaye's spunky 'D-O-D-G-E-R-S' song.

Meantime, David, and I sat pensively, sipping our imaginary sirop de cassis, wondering what sports was all about.

THE WOMEN

Grandma Mary wore the pants in the family.

She neither saw through Female Eyes nor heard through Female Ears. In short, she bowed down to the male altar, body, and soul.

My grandmother came of age in a time I call *when the divine female surfaced once again in the blink of an eye.* Call it the turn of the last century, pure Edwardian. The Edwardian Age to the Roaring Twenties. Zeitgeist. It was an era where *female* was divinely fluid and this image took on a full female wholeness.

She used to say how Marlene Dietrich was the first woman to wear trousers. It was a bold move, and people of her generation still remembered the beautiful shock. Of course, she never referenced the film and that shock sequence where Dietrich struts her stuff in a tuxedo and topper in the film *Morocco,* directed by Joseph von Sternberg. It was 1930. Her film debut. She appears in an elegantly tailor-made white tie and tails, silk topper, boutonniere, and figure-forming waistcoat.

The scene takes place in a low boîte, where she embodies the evening's entertainment. There she swaggers, ciggy as much a part of her demeanor as her own being. Riveting. Obviously a woman, spectacularly a beauty of her own kind. She affects the mannerisms of men, pocketing one hand behind the tails, letting it fall forward, resting an entitled leg on a table, leans forward, balanced on her elbow. We get it.

Up to a table of diners, without asking first, she plucks a flower from a young lady's hair. "May I have this?"

"Of course," the shyly blushing stranger says.

While other adults look on, Dietrich inhales its fragrance, bends down, and beneath the satin tilt of her topper, we see her kiss this stranger full on the lips. It is quick. Almost too quick. Rather forced, though no one else reacts that way. It is meant to be male titillating. Everyone is appropriately shocked (as if Berliners in 1930 would be shocked by anything—let alone this ridiculous fast-and-it's-over kiss).

What women fail to grasp about this male fantasy infamous woman-on-woman scene:

Dietrich is exploiting the whole idea of FemaleLove. The woman at the table is never portrayed as having a will of her own. Dietrich manipulates her for pure amusement—hers, and by proxy, her audience's. No one shows concern that the young woman has been objectified. It is a turn on. Dietrich laughs at her triumph, swaggers away, taps her hat, a Bantam cock. Eases on down the dance floor to Gary Cooper and the rest of the boys.

I doubt my grandmother ever saw the film. She would not have understood this iconic moment had it been explained to her a trillion times. For Grandma, gender was served rigidly. Men were men (and oh so handsome!), and women were women (so in love with the handsome men!), and never the twain would meet. She was not female phobic as much as limited in her female imagination. Whenever she raved about an adorable baby, it was a boy.

In short, Grandma Mary bowed down to the Male Altar, body, and soul.

She was fifty years old when I was born and took care of me until she was fifty-six. I used to believe I was her pride and joy.

My upbringing in those years turned on her clockwork; body clock and everyday take-care-of-business clock. She was chief cook and bottle washer, and no one could touch her for her way with food. If she had a restaurant today it would be called Mary's Eat Yourself into a Happy Stupor Cafe and there would be a never-ending line out the door. Hers was good, solid, staples—European stock. Yet it was not so much *what* it was, it was *how* it was, and how it was, was Mary.

To watch her strain gravy was beyond vestal virgins tending devotional altars; it was a deeply religious act. Her dishes were presented simply. Bone

China was white with magenta trim. Butter dishes and glass side plates were Depression glass in peach and tourmaline green. Tea was Lipton. She and my grandfather did not preserve elegant old Russians ways, with samovars and tea glasses in brass holders. Although the joke about the expression of was, "Have a glass tea," I never heard her say it.

She cooked for three days straight for Thanksgiving. The dining room table groaned under the weight of Grandma's marvels: Turkey that melted in your mouth; gravy from the heavens; potatoes she had mashed forever with just the right texture—no lumps, God forbid. Real green beans. Sour cream herring and borsht, laverbread, Welsh cakes, all I loathed yet everyone else wolfed down, raving, "Mother, you should open a restaurant!" Chicken soup that floated noodles in rainbow circlets. And her sole décor: parsley sprigs with spiced crab apples that left magenta stains on the lime green sour cream Jell-O mold.

You could not separate Grandma Mary from her cooking. Her cooking and all the cookfires were her. The foods, the selection of it, arguing with the butcher, the dissection and deveining bloody liver and chicken entrails to the old meat grinder, so pioneer-like—all was her, her root self. Yet there were other sides to her I got glimpses of—and pursued like a starving artist salivating for her muse.

The Mary Llewelyn I never knew had been a millineress of her hat shop Chef-d'Oeuvre (French for masterpiece) by the Black Sea at the last century's turn. She created chapeaus for the upper middle class and aristocrats. My grandfather ran his gambling casino in Yevpatoria.

Imagination can plague you when you must romanticize other eras, other lifetimes, Otherworld. Another era, another lifetime. I used to picture her Zhivago-style somewhere off Ulitsa Pushkinskaya Street, while Pavlova at the Marinsky Theatre dazzled in *Swan Lake*.

I was always pumping her for information on her past life. Like squeezing a half-dried tube of caulk but worth it. Eventually learned she had once seen the tsar and tsarina with all five children at a railroad stop. The four girls, OTMA (Olga, Tatiana, Maria, and Anastasia): "In their Liberty frocks, long curls and 'beeg' bows. So fetching, so becoming. And the boy—the sick one, so cute, so sweet in his sailor suit and cap!" It was always the boy where her heart flew, let alone a sickly one.

She may have even caught sight of Maria Fedorova in a Lucille gown. Ropes and ropes of rare pearls. At least, that is how I painted her into this railroad reverie, just like her famed mauve boudoir in Livadia. Grandma had visited Livadia, boasting about the gigantic grapes as long as your fingers. It was like a neighbor to where she lived, this royal summer palace. I have seen photographs of the girls leaning over balustrades with spiky palm trees behind them as the Black Sea forms the backdrop. All of them holding their prized turn-of-the-century cameras.

It always sank my heart to learn that Great Britain's King Edward had the power to save his look-alike cousin, and his young family. What struck me as barbaric was the children's fate. The way they were murdered haunts me, and I wondered what Grandma felt, though I was smart enough not to raise that red flag.

Over the course of many, many years I pumped her enough to discover as a little girl she'd had a beloved baby goat. She laughed, telling me that this baby goat really did follow her to school, and the children used to call her "Mary had a little lamb." It was something I treasured, like a Faberge egg. I got her to tap into this girlhood memory, because we were talking about Grandpa's paintings that hung in the dining room.

Paintings in the Dining Room: Young Females as Victims

A pre-Raphaelite assortment of patriarchal fantasies of peasant girls. Lugging heavy clay jugs to and from the village font, portrayed as happy to be barefoot instead of wearing comfortable satin slippers, dirty, barefoot, and bare shouldered. I hated that painting because the world was blind to what these young women must have felt like. Sore muscles. Strained backs. And I knew the homes they returned to as well. It was such an offensive exploitation of the Great Sacred Girl in all her subjugation—enslaved in every way, but the same as my most abhorred one, the one that my own grandfather bought and hung behind him head of the table.

Sexual Harassment on Sweet Potato Mountain

Pure pre-Raphaelite. The painter's signature stamped in red in the corner. It is the archetypal Nell begging the landlord (Snidely Whiplash?) "Oh, please, dear landlord. I can't pay the rent, do not tarnish my virtue, sir!" The landlord in question (forcing himself upon this "sweet young thing," looking like Charlie Chaplin as his trademark Little Tramp). Pencil thin turn of the century villain's mustache, black hair parted down the middle, crazed waves as if he will fly away, taking her captive like Thumbelina. In old-time undertaker's cutaways, like Mister Mole Western Pest Undertaker pressing against her near naked body--the sheer inequity of their bodies--made me want to take a machete to it and hack it to shreds. This was a travesty to the Great Sacred Girl and Woman, and it boiled my blood.

On Sweet Potato Mountain: On a peak that looks like frothy whipped sweet potatoes and yams. She, the archetypal Male Fantasy just like the Edward Gorey lady, helpless on her back on the pointy rooftop, ankles tied, from BBC series Masterpiece *Mystery*. In this painting the same thing is happening, and begs in a sheer peignoir slipping off her shoulders for the male gaze. He paws her, forces his will on her. "I must have you. Surrender!"

At age four, I recognized my own victimization from my father and uncle. I recognized my own victimization from my father and uncle. Her fingers in a tremble I had felt many times, half-frozen in the orange tufts. A dead giveaway.

I read her Female Code. She was a trapped animal, painted isolated and alone for those male-gaze voyeurs enjoying the 'young girl kill.'

That Grandma was married to a man who went out and bought these images at auction and hung them over the dining table wall, sent a message loud and clear what women were for in this family and the world family.

Twenty-two years younger than he, the glaring irony was that she was the one who wore the metaphorical trousers. Head of the family, not only did she bring home the bacon, she cooked it. Balanced the books which she pronounced "b*oo*ks" and handled all the leases, purchases, and negotiations with the man she became coquettish over whenever his name was mentioned. On their twenty-fifth anniversary, he sent a silver tea service. Grandma sparkled around Mr. N. and the buildings she leased from him that gradually morphed into purchases. By the beginning of the second world war, Mary had built up modest wealth. Unlike Dietrich, who wore *actual* trousers. Yet just like Dietrich's character, it was to and for men she lived. Her husband's real desires and false beliefs about the Great Sacred Girl and Woman hung on the walls, a window into their souls.

Their Living Room at Sundown-My Duntreath Castle

I remember the smell of that house. It had a heavy old European musty, rotting green-velvet odor beyond mothballs. A sick house. Elder decay was my night nursery. It was as if all the curses, tragedies, crumpled dreams, and bruised fantasies found their way into that back bedroom where my grandparents slept.

Grandpa's linen suits, batiste shirts, Maurice Chevalier straw boaters, fedoras, Malacca cane, and voile handkerchiefs lived in the cedar consciousness of his Otherworld armoire. Imperial Cologne's domed bottle with crystal stopper rested on its Art Deco bureau throne. My grandmother's ablutions, what little she kept: Maja soap and Ponds Cold Cream waited patiently on the Art Nouveau inlaid vanity in the master bedroom where my parents slept.

Grandpa had high arches and kept shoe trees in his old-fashioned bump-toed lace-up shoes. He still wore brown leather slippers like the children's character Crispin Crispian, in Mister Dog written by Margaret Wise Brown. Reminiscent of that patron saint of cobblers, curriers, tanners, and leather workers, thin robes reminiscent of the Turkish baths he regularly patronized on Wilshire Boulevard. He kept to his Old World Gentleman's Ways, a most elderly septuagenarian for whom no music need play, no fires stoked nor kindled. Odd since it was said he had been a lumber provider before the revolution. He was old-peasant, non-pagan Russia itself. The Baba Yaga and Wolves in the Forest drove his every footfall. I used to think Khrushchev looked and sounded like him, but I was wrong. My mother always said he had Tartar roots, with tip-tilted eyes. Scratch a Russian—find a Tartar.

His eyes were Kurganesque. My cousin Ricky inherited that Mongolian look, so easy to miss in Caucasian features. As like the Tarim mummies in China, Grandpa was ginger haired, extremely pale skinned, and green-eyed and at least six feet. Skin so fair he had to hide it from the sun. Indo-Euro Tartar as he appears in the daguerreotype, he poses with handlebar mustaches and Edwardian linen suit. Someone has written on the back a love note in Russian about his handsome ginger beard. He is the Male Archetypal Zeitgeist Dandy and owner of his successful gambling casino by The Black Sea.

When I lived with him was in his final years, keeping to old ways reenacting his gambling casino days on Saturday nights with his east European English and Welsh cronies, who seemed to come right out of Grimm's and Aesop's, smiling, hacking from heavy smoking, with iron-lung voices over shots of whiskey, cheek pinching and eyes with closed doors behind them.

Those Eisenhower-era folk in fox furs and pancake makeup were identical to the TV shows in the early fifties. Mrs. Pritkin (we nicknamed her Pritakatoe) wore Ethel Mertz-like navy blue, white polka dot sheaths with black shellacked low hair buns; Harry S. in funny fedoras, and coke bottle glasses with gurgling accents were my only playmates, amused by whatever I said and did.

After a few minutes of "Tete à Tetes with Mary's little granddaughter," I was off like a good Edwardian child, summarily tucked into my Uncle R's army cot, on the floor below Grandma Mary's bedside. He had served during the WW2 and received the Purple Heart. In the BBC series *Foyle's War,* the war rooms of Britain look and feel oddly familiar, those maps with stickpins. My mother confirmed he was in Britain and for the liberation of concentration camps. My therapist speculated, perhaps the cot was still hot with energies I picked up on in my sleep from ages two to five. I do not doubt it.

79

Meanwhile, lollygagging in my stiff little cot while the cronies played poker, my imagination was still in the thirty-foot barrel-vaulted living room, around the green baize poker tables; red, white, and blue chips and ice clinking together; See's Candy disappearing fast, sucked down while Grandma was finally coaxed to stop waiting on everyone and sit down. When she finally did, she played them all under the table. She was known to keep her cool, with a mind wired for what card games require: intuition plus math. She was what temperament sorters call the Intuitive Thinker.

Her feelings never fully integrated, her temperament quick to panic. Rage rode shotgun over Full Blown Panic Attacks. The real things that called her to attention; her child predator son, the red flags of lethal child death traps like the open-flamed incinerator legal in those days in the neglected backyard. It was next to Grandpa's vegetable garden, its gigantic sentry sunflowers, where neighborhood animals would cotton to him as he rested contentedly in his director's chair, fanning himself with his straw boater. Any curious child or animal could have seriously become injured lost their life with that open door cover.

1997—My Mandatory Healing Pilgrimage: Visit to Their Graves

I visited her grave in the throes of the second stage of my healing. It was 1997 and near her birthday time, which fell ironically on Mother's Day. I brought a dozen pink roses, placing half in my grandfather's vase and the rest in hers. I sat there disoriented in the eerie encampment of The Death Culture. One more creepy mortuary forever clawing at girls and women's hems.

Squatting I stared at over-looping streams of ants dotting and dashing around the words on her gravestone I saw for the very first time:

Mary Llewellyn.
Beloved Wife, Mother, and Grandmother.
May 14, 1899–1984

I noted the darkly chiseled, elegant Edwardian roses. When I put my hand on it there was a low vibrational hum. I read her the riot act with all the love and fury she had to hear. The cars crawled by, the ants crawled round her headstone, and my head crawled into a nightmare she left me in when I was four. (See: If you could peer back, Uncle Al was really The Big Bad Wolf)

Grandpa's was stone cold, no vibrations. Back to his origins of Russia via Wales, he long ago left this toxic family.

She is not gone from my life. I doubt during this lifetime she ever will be, for she appears in dreams occasionally, with good solid common sense about my future successes. Not a Guide but a Witness.

Today's Perspective from Phoetics and EMDR (Eye Movement Desensitization and Reprocessing)

I had romanticized my grandmother's early days beyond all reason and with idealistic practicality and hardcore necessity. She was a survivor of something I thankfully never knew.

To have the Bolshevik Dark Force take over your *house with the ebony furniture*, its own library, to give birth under those circumstances, to slip away in the dead of night with only your husband, two little boys, and jewels sewn in the hem of your garments, to leave your mother and your mother country, to board a train with all the shades pulled down, to catch the next boat from Riga and wake up to a country where you had ancient roots but do not speak its language and stay as boarders rather than wealthy owners, at age twenty-one—that will never be in my trauma repertoire.

That she survived four years in quarantine in Southampton, England, sailed to Chicago in first class on the White Star Line paid for by her wealthy American in-laws, only to be mocked and rejected by that family; to leave for a better life to the southern tip of this new country—in a warmer climate like the one they had left, a rough, wild place to be sure, scrubbing floors of apartment buildings, putting her boys to work until she owned the buildings. Then on to that final destination—Los Angeles—making a financial success of her life; all walked in those Mandel pumps with bursting bunions and teeth I never knew were false.

What was false was *the life she chose not to lead.* I would never benefit from knowing the girlhood she experienced, the young woman she grew into. My grandmother, as would my mother, withheld her story. Most women do not value their story and never share it, what little they remembered or not.

I do not take it as a personal travesty. It is just one more loss for Femality: one more creative woman who refused to step up to her gifts and potential and her Fundamental Female Obligation. To integrate and gift her story to her daughter and their daughters and female culture. And so I filled in all the blanks of what I would never know. Had we been contemporaries, we would have been only passing friends and gone our separate ways, for Mary Llewellyn was not my kind of female and never would be.

She bowed down to all that was male, and like a gay man, worshipped at the Altar of Male Eros. She was not female phobic (as was my mother) and had a female confident in Uncle R's wife, her daughter-in-law. She had once a close girlfriend who fled Russia to China, but that was as far as her need for female bonding and attunement went. For Grandma's perspective, women existed to gather with and worship those brave, devoted, oh-so-handsome men.

Once I realized how traumatized she was, I accepted that her story and its details would have to be gleaned from books like [4]*Before the Revolution,* and what snippets I could extract from her by carefully juggling the objective: easier accessible memories while never pressing the Bolshevik-Cossack button.

---

[4] Before the Revolution, 1978, by Kyril Fitz Lyon (Author), Tatiana Browning (Author)

Mary's Mantra: "I Know My Obligations"

This was said by patting the back of her right hand into the palm of her left hand. Her obligations were defined by the male mindset of the Death Culture: dutiful wife, obligated to bear, feed, and clothe children, higher educate the males, all while making a *decent living*. Those were her obligations, including insurance, taxes, accounting, deeds, contracts, and the endless lists of Yellow Pages plumbers for her many apartment buildings. But she did not know, nor ever questioned, her true Female Obligations. She was not a womanly woman. She did not derive from Femality; her character was in diametric opposition.

She did not view life through female eyes, did not hear through female ears. In this tragic way, she was the male wolf's accomplice in grandmother clothing.

I was the only daughter of her daughter. Had she seen through female eyes, I would have been sacred, as would have all her children and grandchildren. But that was not her. She doted on my cousin Rick, born premature, and seeing through Patriarchal Victim-Hero eyes, provided her with an excuse and need to fill: align with a helpless, immature male and play the role as the rescuing mother figure. When we would watch television on the living room floor, she would run plates back and forth, precutting his food, making everything just so. During Mickey Mouse Club I'd catch my mother hollering from the back bedroom, "For God's sakes, Mother! He's a big strapping kid. He can cut his own meat, stop catering to him!" Ricky favored Grandpa in his inherited features, so she seized the opportunity to feed her toxic enabling.

She did not read. Only the Yellow Pages for plumbers and accountants. She did not write. Music was nonessential. I doubt she would know poetry if it flew at her like a flock of wild geese, but what she did do was provide me with the poetic image that was a portal to the females who were My Own to find, females of her generation. Yes, they too were not possessed of a character that would fulfill Real Deal Female obligations of telling their integrated stories, even though these women were poets, Women's Women, but they were respectfully awaiting my return.

She did not find women's stories interesting or of value. How could she when men were the center of her world? My brother always thought of her as a man. In her sixties, he asked me, "Doesn't she remind you of that picture of George Washington?" He was partly right. Silver haired in temple rows, similar profile, she might have been Washington's mother or sister. He caught her British roots and transparent masculine side.

My grandmother never told her story because in her mind, she never had one. She carried a giant memory-event eraser and rubbed away every last event. However, she unwittingly gave me a story to follow, a touchstone to muse by when I was left with nothing but my imagination to keep me company for four long years. It was as if My Ladyefolke made certain that this forty-pound leaded glass and bronze-framed image, as tall as me, would remain tilted against the wall at ground level to commune with. And commune I did.

At four, her formal portrait of 1917 would serve as my Personal Portal to Femality. Cosmically placed there by my spirit guides, the Ladyefolke. Whatever she did not give me in Protection, word, gesture, music, or dance, she gave to me a cosmic Motherblood link. Her Mythograph.

My Mother's Mythograph: Claire's Stare

Photographs do have a will and intention all their own. You must respect their choices: to be seen when and where or go AWOL. This particular one my brother and I knew as *The Big Horse* was missing when I unpacked the huge box laden with every era of family photos he sent across the country after her death. He still swears he packed it along with all the others, but no luck. I believe him. He would have placed this right on top. As far as her prior horse-life, there were the few I recognized from the old Griffith Park stables. Yet these were small, three by fives with 1940s pinking shear framing; her spirit was just different, posing in front of a shack with my aunts Sally and Jane in jodhpurs.

Where was The Biggie? I remember because I first found it when I was about seven, rummaging through a drawer of family photos when we still had a den, before it became my brother's room with beds and bolsters. *The Huge Horse*, rearing up with a young woman waving her hat, was gone. Had I not cultivated my respect for the energies and wonts of photographs—especially those when we are children (or the child within is so fully present), I would not have had the sacred gnosis to honor its absence. It was almost easy, because every childhood photograph is sacred and we must honor their wishes. If they decide to be found again, that is their agenda. If not, there is good reason.

Its sheer size would have made it easy to find, even with so many pictures. So much larger than the rest, she had enlarged it to eight by ten, developed in grays and milky whites. The eye is pulled to the lower right-hand corner; a celebrity fountain pen jumps out in midnight India ink: *To Mom and Dad, From that Rootin' Rootin' Gal from El Paso.* Tumbleweed frames it. Tumbleweed in the dust clouds kicked up by her horse. She said it was in the Mojave Desert, but to me it looked like the floor of Hades, for it was in Death Valley, in the northern Mojave Desert, *the hottest place on Earth during summer.* Hades, indeed. Her domicile. I always wondered who took such a worm's eye view, giving her that larger-than-life pose of *Heigh Ho Silver, Away!* One would have to have been chest-to-the-ground with the cameras those days. Was she alone? I never asked. And she never told me. Silence was her language, like her mother before her.

Mother's Mythograph

There she is. Glued to the saddle upon this giant of an equine pawing the heavens. The cliché of that wave of a ten-gallon hat. Boots, Levi's, dark hair fluffy from a pin curl brushing out. Red lipstick reads black as it does in old black and whites. Plucked 1940s brows. When I started admiring it in total daughter-awe, I brought it to her attention and shouted, "Mommy, is this you?"

She came out of her bedroom when she saw what it was on my lap and immediately went, "See? See? I have on all my makeup. *I never lost my femininity!*"

What? What did that have to do with this hugely archetypal image, like a statue sprung to life. I did not understand why she rushed over and why wearing makeup mattered, as if she were stark naked without it. I was seven, left with *what in the world is she seeing that I did not?* Figure this one out.

This bold-as-brass woman, age sixteen looking more like in her twenties, had nothing to do with the woman I knew as my mother. Who was this? The woman I knew, the one I called Mommy, could not drive, leave the house, take an elevator, be in crowds, or get out of the passenger seat. *This could not be the same person. It looked and did not look like her.*

Why did she not ride anymore? And like her mother before her, I got the same silent treatment. I would never know if she had her way. but even if it took me a lifetime I made it my business to figure out what had happened. I was hardly horse crazy but admired the girls who were. When I returned from visiting stables, my sole response was "green teeth" from the alfalfa they chewed. She always reminded me of that. It tickled her. The truth was, the sheer bulk, size combined with their unpredictability I backed away from. Human beings were scary enough and unpredictable. But girls and women who rode with the boss-mare look of this photo were pure Female Otherworld.

When I reached my forties I braved dressage because it was dancing with the horse. Once, as I watched my trainer put her horse through the paces, she came to a stop, hoisted her leg over the saddle horn, lit up a ciggy and exhaling, looked up and threw me a wink. In truth, it was more, "Aren't I great?" than flirting, but I nearly fell off the fence. It took all my strength not to. I will never forget that time-stopping moment.

Today, after decades of study, of self-study, of therapy beyond all reason and for it, I still do know what my mom's *makeup* hang-up was. She was dreadfully terrified that anyone should brand her as butch, because in her mind (as in many others in those eras), women who became grownup tomboys were perceived as masculine, attracted to women = lesbians. So, since she was attracted to women, her secret would be out. She boasted this was the horse no one would ride. So on one hand, she was boasting, broadcasting her competence and bravery by the sheer archetypal female masculine-magnitude of the photo, but on the other, she made certain that she was not to be taken as "One of *those you-know-who's.*"

I began to put her stories together, whenever the subject surfaced through my late childhood, early teens. There was a female cashier at a market that she perceived found her older sister Sally attractive. In that Claire-stare, she told me, really speaking to herself, "Hah. I know what she wanted!" Likely this was one of those branded as a butch lesbian.

Whether this was true or not, it was that ironic funny scene in *Golden Girls.* Blanche, the ultimate high femme, is told by Dorothy that her gay woman friend has fallen in love with Rose. The audience waits. Certain that Blanche's ignorance of what a lesbian is, she instead blows up like her ego is shot through. "She likes ... Rose! Rose? Now you tell me, Dorothy. Who would you pick? Me or Rose?"

In more than one way this was my mother. Jealous to the point of toxic envy of every woman on earth. Any woman I admired—teacher, mother, whomever—she shot down. What I get out of this was not *what* she wanted but *who* she wanted ... and perhaps, the what was known to my mom because that mirrored her own secret desires. Remember, you could be thrown in jail, ostracized, or alienated from your family in those times (that still occurs today). Her broken record was always, "Sally got everything." What is pathetic about women who compare themselves to other women and immerse themselves in the tub of Envy miss out on all the love and beauty within that is the gift of the Great Sacred Girl and Woman.

We worshiped at different altars...

Whereas I was drawn like a magnet to women shining from transparent female masculinity, she could only see the camouflage of her deepest attractions. This so-called butch image is equated with lesbian feelings. Why does it threaten women? Because it makes feelings *visible*. This does not imply that women with natural transparent masculinity are not attracted to men as well, or solely. Sexuality is fluid. And it has been noted by many women's women writers, "How do you tell a femme?" Those women are attracted to women. Can't pass as straight because under the Death Culture, what else could you be? *Normal* qualified as attraction firstly to males. For cowardly or insecure men, to accept that is not true is too threatening to their egos. However, in those days as in most, it branded you on the spot. And because the sacred strength of Nature's Female Masculinity is most threatening, they are punished by the Death Culture, they are punished by the Death Culture.

Decades before Stonewall, men and women did go to jail if discovered. Suffragettes. Force-fed through a tube in their nose. What my mother was likely ignorant of were the subcultural signs women's women used to be safely visible to each other. Wearing violets from the Victorian and Edwardian eras, the Suffragette Movement, in the 1920s and '30s, monocles and suits and ties. With the 1940s and '50's came the pinky rings and loafers. My mother's girlfriend gave her a set of teacups that I was crazy about. Pastel Victorian green, richly colored violets around the golden rim and saucer. As years went on, I begged my mom to tell me where those went.

Her reply, as to everything, was always: "I can never hold on to anything."

That much was true. Once I dived deeply into my own Female Studies a la Nancy, on my own volition, I knew damn well why she did not hold to them or anything else. It is somewhat relative to having a Borderline Personality, but that is another story.

In the lower right-hand corner of this eight by ten scrolls her Claire-font: "To Mom & Dad, From that *Rootin' Rootin' Gal from El Paso." The woman who wrote that did not jive with* the woman I lived with as Mommy. Her greasepaint was Anita of Denmark's *Day Dew—"What all the Gabor sisters wore."* Circlets of her eyebrow pencil on her bed as she arched hers like Maleficent and the Stepmother in *Cinderella*—I just could not integrate or marry the two energies. Not with her. Why? Because neither her feminine nor masculine was natural. She got her beliefs from the Unnatural Death Culture, never questioning any gaslit "beliefs." So glad that I know what I know now, able to teach any girl or woman confused as I was, or gaslit by the Death Culture.

Diving Deeper: Beneath My Mother's Mythograph

Rebecca, by Daphne du Maurier, 1938

Our natural Female Masculine-Feminine energies did not live in my mother.

In DFFs (Dark Force Females), this is their missing piece of Femality. Do not be fooled by women who break glass ceilings solely to become trapped once in those same top floors with a window office. It is one more Ism.

Rule of Thumb: If She Does Not Put Children (and Animals, Dependents) First, She Is Likely a DFF.

As a female, my mother was intellectually, emotionally, and spiritually bereft. She bought into what many talented women writers bought into, and sure enough it all came out when she talked about Daphne du Maurier's *Rebecca*. I was always turning to her for book references (it was one more ploy to get her to even talk to me), and she boasted that as a girl, she always had her nose in a book, munching on graham crackers and butter under a tree. I guessed that meant she certainly had more up her literary sleeve, right? As it washed out, I hated the stories and characters she loved.

Female Victims. And animals too. Young death. Mean adults. Elnora Comstock in *Girl of the Limberlost*—motherless, neglected, and dirt poor only intensified my suicidal wishes. *Ramona,* her fave, where they did the pageant every year in Hemet, now the Ramona Hills. Beautiful blue-eyed Ramona, abused by a cliché Evil Stepmother Moreno (my mother's eyes squinted that Claire-stare whenever she said her name), who falls in love with Alessandro, an American Indian. Only to be left a widow with his baby when he is murdered. Girls and women crying for their dead lovers. So sick.

Oh, but that was not *Rebecca*. Quite the opposite.

Today I know my mother's and Daphne du Maurier's psyches. I listened as my mother took on the role of Mrs. Danvers right in front of my eyes. The weird thing was, I was a powerful onstage actress. However, her acting took place behind closed doors. Comedy. Tragedy. Murder mysteries. That was the kicker.

My mother could be zany, inching on her derrière, legs straight out a la Jack LaLane, but hell to pay if I did not laugh at her antics. My father did the same thing. It was a "Look at me, Ma!" thing because they never got attention as kids and never grew up. She would bend toward the vacuum and throw one bent leg backward, waiting for me to fake any laughter. I learned by six it is one thing to watch Carol Burnett or Lucille Ball acting zany on TV; quite another to have the characters they played as your mother in real life.

What she never realized was that when you don't remember to sign school papers, supply your daughter with back-to-school required tools, and have other moms get the Brownie uniforms because you couldn't leave the house—somehow dampened the funniness. Besides, why did a kid have to be the audience for the grownup? When I got the sillies, it was *for my kids' enjoyment and participation*, not for my ego-applause. But that is another writing.

Carol Burnett did spoof *Rebecca* and Mrs. Danvers, but it could not compare to my mother's, and hers was no spoof. I had my own private performance in the front row. She raised one eyebrow, telling me about how she loved this one particular scene of Hitchcock's. The unnamed young heroine (played by Joan Fontaine) is brought to the casement windows of the dead Rebecca's boudoir by the evil housekeeper, Mrs. Danvers. (In the book, Danny is described with a skull face, but Judith Anderson did not have that. In the '80s BBC version, Anna Massey was incomparable.) But my mother deserved an Academy Award for "Mrs. Danvers, Mothers Who Torment and Terrorize Daughters."

In her head she was living Hitchcock's scene, the filmy floor-length drapes are blowing, her voice fawning. *Danny takes her arm and holds it like a vise.* Then she makes a gesture like she's pushing Fontaine toward the open windows. My mom memorized this famous scene so well she jumps right into that infamous monologue:

Mom/Mrs. Danvers: "Look, down there. It's easy, isn't it? Why don't you just jump? It won't hurt ... why don't you try it?" And then, looking me dead in the eye, my mother murmurs to me like Anderson does to Fontaine: "Why—don't—you—just—jump?"

It has taken six decades of constant study of MotherDaughtering Love; Female Love; the Collapsed Mother in *The Ugly Duckling*; the Unhealed Daughter's Search for Her Mother; Understanding the Borderline Mother; and so much more to understand where Daphne got her characters and writing chops from. While it is totally beyond my soul's imagination to grasp a mother rejecting a daughter, it occurs more than the Death Culture would ever admit to. Mom is to blame for everything, but when it comes to the daughter's experiences, feelings, and viewpoint, there is always a reason that forgives the male or female writers. Especially for American audiences. But to have to face and accept that your own mother was downright evil takes many decades, if you can ever accept it at all, and emotionally I have had to. Truth—no matter how ugly—must be confronted. And accepted. So we may move on.

It has been well-documented that du Maurier abhorred Hitchcock's version, and since he was such a female-phobe, I cannot blame her. I would never have signed off to have him nor any male director or producer touch my masterpiece.

The point?

During this time I dreamed about my mother throwing a knife at me. In between us is a wedding cake that catches it. I am no more than two and my father is next to me. My therapist wondered if maybe the marriage stopped her from acting upon these feelings. *Nothing is worse than knowing your own mother wants you dead. Wishes you were never born.* I heard my grandmother wanted to abort her but didn't. Apparently, it was a toxic cycle. One that I broke when I had each sacred daughter.

Nature's Grandeur Default: Female Femininity and Masculinity

In the SoCal 1950s women were very laid back. Some wore make up, but the average housewife did not. I wanted to be in a more sophisticated era, the Edwardian into the Art Deco periods, but Southern California, didn't call for hats and gloves. The odd thing was, I was one of those girls who was called the 'epitome of femininity.'

I was comfy in dresses, felt like my true self in long gowns and downright miserable in jeans, shorts, or slacks. My mom ratted her hair like Elizabeth Taylor's bubble, wore the same Cleopatra eyeliner, and when she left the house on rare occasions, she dressed in Leed's stilettos dyed to match her Jackie Kennedy shifts.

Yet this went root deep. Her issues. It would take me more than half a lifetime to figure out what the hell it was, and it was linked to my calling. Her dreaded fear of "masculine-looking women" became the horns of my dilemma.

My Sacred Altar Was Her Bogeywoman

Was there something wrong with me? Not only was it a new foreign idea, there was also no one to talk to about it. Once, when I was waxing poetic about Mrs. Stuart, she stopped me like a veritable Mrs. Danvers and sighed. "Jeanne is a nice person. I have nothing against her. But don't you think she's a little too *masculine?"*

The funny part was, yes, that was part and parcel of why I found her so alluring, along with what made that wild woman come to life. It did not matter who I liked, if it was another woman, she tried to redact my perceptions, likes, admirations. This was the same young woman waving her hat on the floor of hell in the middle of the 1940s, a woman I would never meet.

On the other hand, when I was studying my grandma's Mythograph for the umpteenth time, I was lost in the outfit she designed and handmade. A dark jacket nipped at the waist, with a huge white collar splayed widely and black buttons the size of quarters like huge exclamation points, all the way down the front and on each cuff. After she corrected me that these were not high button shoes but "high laced, darling, *high laced,*" she pointed out that she was not fat. "What? *You see there? I am pregnant with Al. I was never fat.*"

So, Grandma's hang-up was that most women under the Death Culture suffered from body image. Masculine energies in females did not faze her. She never even paid attention so zeroed in on the male. She was the one who told me about the first woman to wear slacks, Marlene Dietrich. Quite an emboldened thing in the early 1930s. That dazzling tuxedo and top hat she rocked had the world of women and men all aflutter. The irony was that like Betty Grable, she was known for the most beautiful legs in the world. Grandma wore palazzo pants to the beach, but that was it, refusing to wear pantsuits in the 1960s though we begged her. "Come on, Gram. You have such great gams. Raise your hems a little."

This was met with, "I know my limits. No more talk."

Mothers and Daughters may worship at very different altars, and that was never truer than my grandmother, her mother, and myself.

In the piles of photos my brother packed, there was one I had never seen of her barefoot and bareback in a long shot galloping pell-mell, hell-bent-for-leather by the LA basins.

How could this person be my mother? The same woman who could not drive the freeways. Not take an elevator? Not even leave the house until I hit my teens. Agoraphobia ran in the family. In a way, that disorder gave her the perfect excuse to feign headaches in order to get out of seeing the events of my early life. I was often in the spotlight, due to teachers showcasing my musicality. But even graduations and open houses were rarely attended. I had to start my crusades for anything I wanted that was normal for a parent to take joy in weeks, even months ahead of time. My father considered his family of origin to be his family. I don't know what he considered us.

Still, as much as she took no interest in what I liked, I took unending interest in her early years. At the beach, at my age it was like looking back at me. *Look! Look! That looks just like me.*

"Do not be ridiculous, Nancy. Look at my hair. It is nothing like yours. You got your father's hair. *You look nothing like me!* Be thankful you did not get mine."

There were the LA High pics, her smiling in saddle shoes with Dita, the one she always talked about, with beautiful blonde braids on top of her head. On the other side was Lucy in heels. Very pretty, she remained my mom's friend and followed her around like Marcie to Peppermint Patty.

In packing up her photos, my brother swore he packed our mother's Mythograph. It was gone with the wind. My brother and I could not make sense of it, but this I know. Photographs have their own agendas. And the energy in this one was a doozie. In those days, teenage girls looked so much older. She was no more than sixteen yet appeared in her early twenties. A few short years later she married and had me and my brother.

94

When I was two and Davey was six months, we all went to live at Grandma's house. Grandpa lived there too but it was always "Grandma's house." We were taken in because my father couldn't make a decent living. I would not learn the real truth until I was twenty-eight with a two-year-old daughter and had a nervous breakdown. I was convinced I was dying. Dr. S. looked at me and suggested short-term therapy. He referred me to a psychiatrist around the corner from the ones my mom used to visit. I could literally look out his window and see the buildings where I was abused by my pediatricians, and behind those buildings, her old haunts with Drs. S. and F. I took his suggestion, because he said short term, and I found a nervous breakdown unbearable. Two sacred little Great Sacred Girls depending on me deserved nothing less.

Nervous Breakdown Number 2: 1978

Dr. F's office was right around the corner from my mother's old psychiatrists in Beverly Hills. I sank into a well-worn leather chair too soft to crackle, and he asked me a simple question.

Him: Why are you here?
Me: I don't know. I had a very happy childhood.
Bursting like a long dormant volcano, I nearly choked to death on entombed toxic tears.
Him: How do you know that?
Me: My mother told me.

As I said this, the mental image painted by her, a veritable Walt Disney production complete with Cinderella's birdies chirping in bonnets, looping blue ribbons across the screen: "Nancy's Happy Childhood."

After a few sessions, he asked me why, if my grandparents were well off, did they not help with living expenses and rent until my father got on his feet? Four years is a long time to live there.

He was right; something did not jive. Since Grandma Mary was still alive and alert, and he asked me to ask her. So I took her to her favorite hangout on Restaurant Row. We were dining in Lawry's, where Aunt Sally would also take her, and asked why, as she was poking prongs at her filet of sole almandine.

Lawry's Indoor Atrium Room: Gram's favorite on Restaurant Row, 1977

Stilted, dead air, with all the earmarks of the Sinatra era.

Me: Gram, why did we live at your house?

Gram: You mean Mother's breakdown?

She didn't miss a beat, more interested in her almondine. Everyone knew but me.

Me: What do you mean?

I waited and watched to discern if anything was going on under those deeply hooded, almost gypsy eyes.

Gram: Ah. Who knew? Postpartum? Not even doctors. What is there to talk? Forget. Forget.

So my mother had lied to me all my life.

When I got into RDFT (Real Deal Female Therapy) I took advantage of my Aunt Jane's memory and recorded her answers. After all, they all got married and had babies within the same era. She had married Uncle R. I asked her what really happened, and when she tried to describe the conditions, Gram found us, and words would not come. Her face told it all. I did not pursue the details; no one wants to hear about a childhood of neglect, abandonment, and abuse. There would be time for that when I was ready.

Dr. F. was right. Now it was starting to make sense. All those psychiatric trips to Beverly Hills, several days a week. I loved it because I got to tap dance for people before my father yanked me away. Once we were at the diner on the corner, and someone said to my father, "Hey, you should put her in the movies." Growling back, he's grumble "Yeah, yeah, just throw quarters."

Beverly Hills meant Schwab's, getting to eat the Hi-Low plate, getting spoonfuls of coffee in my milk, and best of all—visiting Blanche and Ginger. Yet like all kids, I did not question my routines by Stupid Adults (SAs). We were doing this from three until about nine. After school, we'd park in front of the building and kill time, having a burger and Daddy buying cigars, red hots, Rollo's for me and baseball cards with bubble gum for Dave.

I did know a few things, though memory skips around. Mom proudly bragged the maternity nurses called Dave 'butch' because he was "all boy"—born breach, perfect face, almost ten pounds. It was only after I started RDFT that I started to put two and two together. She would always wince, scrunch her face over, and grumble, "Those damned forceps." Had I not resurrected all the details of what befell me those four years I survived at Gram's house, I'd be left without any dots to connect my entitled truths—and not my mother's evil fiction. Connecting them took a decade, and connect I did.

How I Figured out What Triggered Her back in 1952

After I delivered my second daughter, I found a theory going around that girls who are sexually abused often do not dilate past two; a self-protection reflex. *The body remembers what the mind forgets.* Why did I always need Pitocin to induce labor? I hated the unnatural contractions, coming way too fast. It felt like the steel pieces they whipped back and forth backstage to make it sound like thunder. My uterus was at the mercy of this damned drug.

I was abused by the same sadist brother as my mother had been as a girl. Her eldest brother Al used to abuse me with tools, and hang me upside down over makeshift-torture "operating" tables in Grandma's apartment basements. He must have done the same to her which she confessed to me in my thirties. So when those awful forceps entered her to bring my baby brother out, it had to have triggered the abuse hibernating in her body.

I remembered how she used to shiver and curse "those damned forceps." Forceps indeed.

MotherDaughter Wounding: Daphne, Rebecca, Mrs. Danvers, and My Mother

There are girls like me who would not, could not hurt a fly. There are Dark Force Females like Daphne and my mother who see through the eyes of Death Culture Evil. They may find that other girls and women attract them, but it is not for the sacred. Daphne had a gallows imagination, as did my mother. How I ended up with a Dark Force Mother is the subject of this book and all I have gleaned from a lifelong study, through brilliant authors like Dr. Christine Anne Lawson's *The Borderline Mother* and my own parallels to fictional characters and biographical facts of writers like du Maurier and many others.

Why should this scene of Mrs. Danvers carry such power in my mother's psyche that she had to share it with me? *Rebecca* is one amazing mystery, but I read it before and after I watched the film. My mother took the easy way out and watched Hitchcock's version, which Daphne rightfully hated. Bottom line, I accept today my mother's death wish for me. Too many dreams are crystal clear that she wanted to murder me, but the malignant Death Culture spirits hosted by women like these I am well acquainted with.

It was Mrs. Danvers recalling how at sixteen (the same age my mother is in her Mythograph) Rebecca mounted "a brute of an animal" (reminiscent of Mr. Rochester's steed, Mesrour) that the groom claimed was too hot to ride. Yet she stuck to him just like my mother stuck to hers, dark hair flying behind her, and Danny's evil glee of Rebecca digging her spurs in his sides, drawing blood. "He was trembling all over when she got off him." The sheer brute mentality of sadism really hit me between the eyes as I first read those words. "That will teach him, won't it, Danny?" Rebecca bragged.

I froze and turned the book face down. Too close for any comforting denial, I heard my mother's own memoir as she boasted that no one else would ride him, and her words—eerily familiar: "I showed him who's boss." I kept reading in shock.

My Mother's Mantra: 'Never trust a woman. The only woman you can trust is your own mother.'

No daughter wants to confront a sadistic streak in her own mother. The very person who is supposed to serve as your home, safe place, calming harbor. Yet I had been in therapy so long I was finally able to face, accept, and go forward with: Yes. My mother was *Rebecca*. My mother was Danny, *Mrs. Danvers*. And it came upon me, that yes, I was the young, terrorized, isolated, unmothered daughter who married Max de Winter, a transparent father figure, as far as du Maurier was concerned, in her real life. In the film 2007 *Daphne*, she speaks about how she pegs characters on to people she has known. In both *Rebecca* and *My Cousin Rachel*, she creates Dark Force Females that revealed the dark truths about her own MotherDaughterhood. And since I am not a writer of fiction, it fell to me after three decades of therapy, research, and Phoetics that I indeed had to admit my mother was, in word and deed, a Dark Force Female.

Photos Heralding Unspeakable Female Truths

It was my mother's custom to write on the back of every photo she took (she was a bit of a photo bug) the names and date of its taking. There was the one on that pinto, where she gallops pell-mell, bareback, barefoot in the basins of Griffith Park area. On the back of the pinto photo, she scrawls *Claire on Paint, 1946.*

Synchronicity has its own cosmic calendar. Why did it never occur to me to look on the back of my mother's Mythograph as I had all the others? Was it too big? Too intuitively scary? One fine day I suddenly flipped it over. There in faded brown ink, bled my mother's authentic truth: *'Claire on Satan'*

Jeanne Breedlove S. The Mother I Wanted at Eight

I remember the day Chris finally revealed her mother's maiden name (I had begged her). When she finally told me, I refused to accept that anyone could have a name like that, let alone the woman who literally radiated female love. It was just too ironic, too perfect, yet it was true. Here then is my toast to the woman who in word, deed, and female spirit did indeed "breed love."

Jeanne Breedlove S. I will forever see her in her muumuus and T-shirts, serving up spaghetti at the kitchen table, throwing back her head in that gutsy sailor's bellow over something that got her good. The new pool was in, and the four of us girls had been swimming all day.

"Hah, you shoulda' seen it, Dean!" Her hands arced like dolphins in the waves. "One bare butt, another bare butt … and then a black and white striped butt!" She just about split a gut, pounding the table.

The black and white striped butt was mine. I could never swim in the nude. My Barbie swimsuit in 1959 was my only protection, yet in some unknown way I stood in awe of how Chris and her sisters could be so natural in the clear-blue waters. No shame there.

We were eating her spaghetti, as tears squeezed out the corners of her eyes and Salems burned in ash piles on the table. Her whole being shook with unabashed laughter. I wanted to burrow my head in her generous chest, drop anchor, and never return to my funeral parlor house.

The world was *her*. It turned on her axis. A green eyed Simone Signoret beauty, American to the core and yet as real and old as the Venus of Willendorf, the wild, raucous Baubo goddess, Butch and Femme in one amazing flesh and blood female; Celtic to the core, echoing the character Bloody Mary from *South Pacific*, her favorite musical, with her favorite knock-knock jokes.

Jeanne: Knock-knock.
Me: Who's there?

Jeanne: Sam.

Me: Sam who?

Jeanne: (Hand draped over the steering wheel, she bellowed in her best baritone) *Sam- Enchanted Evening!*

That was the Jeanne I knew as we curved down and around the Pacific Coast Highway in their station wagon in the early California June fog. It felt like she sang for me alone. I stared from the front seat at her in absolute awe as she sang song after song from her day and even before …

"We'll build a bungalow
Big enough for two,
Big enough for two, my honey,
Big enough for two.
And when we're married,
Happy we'll be,
Underneath the bamboo,
Underneath the bamboo tree!"

Right then and there I wanted to have "'Tea for Two" with her "Under the Bamboo Tree" and live alone in mother-child bliss forever. I could hardly believe such a being existed. A mom who was also a nurse. Gave shots to her own kids who weren't afraid at all. A mom who took her kids to piano lessons and would one future time, divorced and alone, put all three daughters through college. A mom who left at my front door pink, blue, and green meringue Easter eggs in a basket (like Queenie's eggs in the hexagons). Poufy sugar clouds billowing in your mouth and slid down your throat like pastel velvet.

That mom was my heart's desire.

Teachers

A brief overview

What an odd turn of events when we all arrived at Lady Santa Ana's hot breaths searing up our thighs as back-to-school time hit. The High Holidays and September's desert heat swirled, whirled down Her mountain passes, turning my soft curls and waves into straight hair, much to my temporary thrill. It was for me a Sacred Time because I believed this year, every year She would show up. I sought in vain for her scarlet maple leaf cuffs, burned copper offerings, yellow flaming updos against her cobalt skies.

Los Angeles's way of promising a change of season was how the leaves seemed to choke from the smog, shrivel up and drop dead in sneezy piles from sycamores with that awful dust we nearly choked to death on ourselves. Yet Her sacred autumnal promise could be morphed into the figure of a woman as I was to discover. It was a weird and wild eventful first week when I first arrived in a nightmarish situation I never could have anticipated. Like all the kids, I wondered who I would get for the next grade. Up to that point we took each teacher in stride.

Mrs. Hewlett was second grade: felt press-ons, apples, oranges, and Christmas trees in her far-off bungalow near the benches. She was like a petite Mrs. Tiggy-Winkle. I liked her. She was not scary. Once a week, Mrs. Vischer arrived with maracas and her basket of noise-making musical instruments. Second grade at least got me to third. And third brought the most popular and coveted teacher in the school: Miss Woodward.

Carolyn Woodward. Her name looped in the air, italicized, gold-tinted in Olde English font, reminiscent of Jennifer Jones in *The Song of Bernadette*, the original Lady Madonna in her sway, hush puppy-ed down a breezeway. Her every day "uniform" was an ankle-length, knobby, mauve, dirndl skirt, white cotton, short-sleeved, batiste blouse, navy blue sweater (not ribbed just simple), and soft, not buttoned to reveal her untouchable crucifix dangling from a fairy chain. She sported an ankle bracelet above her tanned hush puppies worn with stockings and her hair rather à la

Hepburn—Katherine, not Audrey—in a turn-of-the-century topknot right out of a Gibson Girl painting. She never pulled it straight and tight; rather, it was poufy, coppery with silver and gold wiry strands lending her that pre-Raphaelite aura.

One morning she called me up, explaining or asking something. I fell into another world, riveted by the golden cross dangling from her dainty clavicle through a gossamer batiste peephole, her reddish golden aura like a Byzantine saint.

As she pointed at something in her simple nun-like costume, I pictured a baker's dozen hung from hooks in an oaken armoire, lavender bunches hung upside down from ribbons like Hildegarde of Bingham in her abyss. The olde British folk lyrics, 'Hey Nonny, nonny,' kept swirling round my head,' watching her sway down the breezeway, mimeographed papers taking flight from the crook of her elbow.

"Nancy, would you please try to find the papers for class? Some blew away outside."

Of course I would. Rousing myself out of my Renaissance reverie, I promenaded, pranced, and even grand-jetèd out into the morning mists, pouncing on each purple inked (mimeographed) paper for my mistress.

Such was third grade.

From Carolyn Woodward I segued into the next angel Lady Synchronicity sent my way- Gloria Mize.

Mrs. Mize the Wise--Grade Four

Miss Mize was classically gorgeous. Her image was very Bryn Mawr. All of twenty-five, tops. She lived in the off limits of the mythical Village Green. Some of the kids claimed to know which door was the witch's, the one you had to run past to get to the signal because the crossing guard, Loretta, with the flaming red hair, would not hear your screams if a long, boney hand suddenly snatched you inside, never to be heard from again.

The Village Green was built to house the 1936 Olympic athletes. Twenty years hence, they were opened to the general public as apartments, unusual in appearance for a Los Angeles suburb. The architecture took on a distinct mythological fairy-tale aura; a village of classic uniformity and no on in their right mind dared cross that border, much less walk inside on the green grass if one valued one's life, limb, and mortal soul. We never knew in what apartment lived our Mrs. M. and marveled at her courage.

Mrs. M. was amazing (or amizing?). I was the only lefty out of one hundred in our class except for Allan F. In my head I was the odd girl out, but when Mrs. M. in all her glory showed up—sporting a beehive French twist, smart dove gray suit fit for a Ford model, complete with the pumps, legs, and smile to match, an actress Joanna Barnes type—we all flipped. And to my absolute amazement, *Mrs. M. was a lefty.* This was the year and the grade I was to learn and master longhand. And because she identified with left-handedness, she offered me her special attention.

I practiced like crazy and stumbled upon some handwriting alchemy: how nice my letters looked after I had erased a few times the newsprint to a nubby tooth that grabbed the pencil lead and transformed it to something far more beautiful. It turned out handwriting was my forte. To split up letters in harsh, linear, perpendicular lines, even if there was the occasional circles and ovals, was ... unnatural. To have a way to communicate in a free-flowing, loopy, curvy slant made sense. Never did she have to teach me how to hold the pencil. To twist-warp my left wrist like many lefties did was crazy.

How my penwomanship looked meant the world to me. And Mrs. M. understood. Recorded in the inner office notes teachers did not share in our report cards are her thoughts: "Cares so much about her handwriting. Really a lovely child." Fourth Grade ended on a beautiful note.

Fifth Grade gave us Mrs. Henry, an elderly lady the kids made fun of. Once she accidently dropped her gold compact, spilling face powder on the floor, and I was appalled to hear laughter. The cruelty of my cohorts never ceased to shock. Mrs. Henry was a good lady. She got up every morning at her age, when her hands shook and her voice broke. She was a precursor to my favorite screen actress, Edna Oliver. (See: Edna May Oliver)

Same equine-shaped face, with a prim and proper outer layer. White hair, Avon red lipstick that showed the creases of a long life. I never got to know her, but I didn't have to. I just appreciated that she showed up at all and seemed to still care when had I been teaching such fools would have given up long ago.

The hot summer winds died down for the time being. March would bring the only rain we'd see.

This was when I found myself in the worst shock of school I had ever experienced. Our class had been together since first grade, long enough to know each other and small enough to fill two classrooms. We knew each other's ways and quirks in a world that seemed forever poised to pull the rug out from under us. At least there was comfort to sit across from familiar faces, voices, sneezes, coughs, and whispers.

What we didn't know was our class had grown so large that they had to split us up into three classrooms. That third teacher, a last-ditch effort, became my booby prize. Mrs. Shapell taught the younger grades we had long since left. She was a bleating sheep, with tight white curls as in the days of the 1930;s or even the 1830's. Her voice was mind-numbing.

To add insult to injury, all the straight-A girls got Mrs. Butler, the most popular teacher in the school. In her fifties, she dressed well, had a Midwestern style with sophistication. Right out of Disney. She was the quick, sharp teacher with the wink in her eye in everything she did. Known for being strict, fun, challenging and worth the challenge.

In stark contrast and tragic irony, Mrs. Shapell was right out of Disney too except she was Miss Inch in *The Parent Trap,* the epitome of incompetence, failing to rescue the cake while the punch bowl goes sloshing off the table. Sitting in her static classroom was a guaranteed ticket to La La Land, and this flagrant rejection hit me like a backhanded slap across the face. Worst of all was what I could not tell anyone: Chris was not going to be by my side. To be separated was unbearable. I was not a complainer, never a troublemaker, but this brought something out in me that was unacceptable. I was defiant. No one and nothing could keep me away from Chris.

Love, war, and grammar school make for some mighty strange bedfellows. Kathy K. was rather new to the school and I could not bear her. A permanent scowl and a lack of humanity just made me nonplussed around her. I couldn't get her, and when I saw how phony she was, didn't want to. But Irony gifted that the very reason I couldn't tolerate her would be my saving grace. Kathy was the original American Princess, and all she had to do to wave her magic wand and turn Mrs. Shapell into something better than glass slippers. All she had to do was cry to her mother.

A regular Maestra.

No one in that school had ever protested the class they were assigned. Kids might cry to their parents, but that was at home. But Kathy was born with major spoilt artillery: her mother. No one made Mrs. K.'s darling daughter cry, and even though the teachers and office administrators were baffled when the two of us ran to the nurse's office crying our eyes out and refusing to return to class, they did not know what to do. I will never know what Mrs. K. did, but Kathy whispered that her mother confided—they had tried a little experiment with us kids keeping us together for all these years and then poof! Watched to see how we would handle such a radical change. And guess what? The other teachers knew Mrs. Shapell was not for our grade level, and the school had made a big mistake.

The ladies in the office promised if we went back to the classroom and were patient; *a brand new teacher* would arrive in two weeks. That event would change my life. That new teacher would be my first Real Deal MotherDaughtering event at ten years of age.

Barbara, whom we called Mrs. A., had such an impact on me—as a teacher, a grown-up woman but not so old she could be my mother (she was twenty-two to our ten), and Female archetypal versions. "Barb'ry Allen," the Scottish lassie she sang about from the infamous ballad, that in and of itself plays into my Character and Calling, and she was there for me as I for her, courtesy of Ladye Fate. She was Teacher, role model, and for me—Grand Muse.

Barbara A

Here are the inspirational views I was privileged to in those pivotal years when Great Sacred Girls need more than ever: a disciplined, self-effacing, out of the box, creative, and unflappable young woman as a mentor, role model. and muse.

1. *"It was synchronicity's gift"* covers how she came to be our teacher in a most unconventional yet fated way, and you will notice several other teachers in cameos as the predecessors to her, our last teacher in fifth and sixth grades, before culminations. This sets the psychological stage for her entrance, important if only for her uniqueness and our good fortune.
2. *"To be in Mrs. A.'s class"* tells what it was like to experience this richly engaged young woman (teaching her first class, so I recall learning later), and how she mixed up what we were learning about (e.g., the white folk moving west, the Cumberland Gap, annihilating "heathen" Indians), yet we got to wear costumes made by generous, talented moms, and what else? Carving and sanding guns for Flintlock rifles. What great American heroic story isn't complete without guns and the bad guys whose land you trespassed, invaded, stole, and blamed for killing your own? All fallacies aside, I wanted to express from my point of view and absence of being appreciated at home, how that fed me in her class. You will see how much one teacher can do that lasts and stays a lifetime.
3. *Was An Enchantress*
4. *"And her name was Barb'ry Allen"* can only be appreciated by reading. How one woman can contribute to one's fiery imagination, the proof we all are potential muses for each other, no matter what age (children included). Teachers can be our most powerful models unwittingly, perhaps because they, too, had inspirational teachers,

coaches, and tutors. However, this song, its original truth and the twisted meaning over the centuries hit me between the eyes and I hope it does for you.

5. Chance Meeting 1967
6. Mrs. A. Reflections 2015

Barbara A. was the non-teacher, the anti-teacher as teachers went. Never the Los Angeles Unified School District flunky, she taught from her intuitive essence and her popularity and improved grade point averages bore her out.

I forever see her in my mind's eye, freckled in the most subtle tones, auburn hair that shined in rainbows where the sun hit. So soft was the cuticle you could see where bobby pins had left their indentations from the set the night before. She wore it alternately in flips and pageboy fluffs and spring saw her in belted, seersucker, sleeveless shifts in powder blue or yellow with a matching cardigan fastened across her delicate shoulders with icy blue pearlized sweater clips.

She was all of twenty-four with a certain Miss Brodie quality when it came to reining in unruly students. Barbara took no prisoners. You got with the program fast. No chitchatting; eyes forward, but it was hardly a challenge, she was so damned mesmerizing. She made the Cumberland Gap more interesting than it really was. We built a covered wagon, and she asked me if I would write a play that would revolve around a family going west. I wrote it and added a singalong with myself playing the guitar. I even named a character Nancy and cast Madolyn in the role, whispering in the cloakroom with Bobby L. as lines handwritten morphed into lavender mimeographed pages to put on our play.

She planned for us to have, as part of our authentic gear, gunpowder horns. Procured them—rough-edged and dried out from a local slaughterhouse— with our mothers sternly cautioned to *boil all weekend* and *throw away the pot*. Shellacked and baked in the kiln, we drilled holes in the circles and threaded leather strings to tie around the boy's belts.

Barbara A. was my fifth grade teacher, and she was more than my fifth grade teacher. She was, in every way, my muse.

She was one more goddess remnant, echo, and the first woman to offer me the gift of her own time with nothing expected in return. I was far too young to understand this selfless gift, because I lived in the throes of constant guilt with a ticking clock of justification. To be able to fully hug anything that was freely given was a complete unknown, and I wouldn't have understood even if it had been explained to me. But I held fast to some deep-seated hope that there were women in the world who did give selflessly despite the ongoing anti-female propaganda war my mother waged.

Mrs. A. was the first woman to touch my fingers, safe, intentional, and with no hidden agenda, placing them on the frets of her sacred Goya. *A mother's touch or lack thereof is a girl's key to her Authenticity.* I was ten, and while it was the first momentous time, it lingered just below consciousness. To have this gift freely given—her full presence so overwhelming—it helped ground me in the act itself of strumming "up down-up damp" and "thumb behind the neck" (I can still see it), kept me fully in the moment. Free guitar lessons on her magical Goya after school in a sacred space no Evil could penetrate. Trusting comfort, a primal swaddling, rapt in that mother-daughter eye-to-eye connection. While my conscious mind drew in draughts from these First Moments of Female Primacy, they put me in mind of the Animal World—that indeed, there were mothers who did reject their own babies. So stunting to the Great Female Brain, Kathie Carson covers in *In Her Image, The Unhealed Daughter's Search for her Mother,* a chapter "Touch Starved, Touch Phobic." So primal deep, she shares that this one subject was always the most difficult workshop for women to participate in, bar none.

I remember her hands, sprinkled with a redhead's freckles, her knuckles and knees brightening when bent, her Barbara Wholeness—sustained me. Her presence of Order, sticking to the rules, the marvelous magical chords produced in kind. Had it not been for her, I should not have met Harriet and Molly, a life-altering experience. Again, while it was ostensibly about advanced guitar and singing American Folk songs of the Death Culture (which catapulted me down a rabbit hole of child and female depression), it was another annunciation of my true calling, FemaleLove. Two adult women living a boldly chosen life for those days. Frankly, I was more dazzled by Molly and Harriet's mutual competence, and just the sheer cosmic energies my body picked up from that humble house a few feet from the boulevard, under the powerlines. My fairy tale, eclipsed. (See Are You Going to Harriets?)

To Be in Mrs. A.'s class

To be in Mrs. A.'s class was like living in a sonnet, a tale, a place where Otherworlds overlapped and blended. The American West, where it was rooted in Anglo Celtic lore. I didn't know it then, but the vibrations of the songs she sang and us singing together—the covered wagon we built, the flintlock rifles, aprons, and hollowed-out horns for gunpowder, the visits prior to Knott's—all seemed to soften the psychic soil, to go deeper by tunnels laden with stalactites and stalagmites through the mining shafts of the Miners 49ers, into the real ones with amethyst and the fool's gold turned to opalescence, fires of tanzanite in young, open minds, and Great Sacred Girls, though they were unaware of it.

Mrs. A. was an enchantress—it showed in the energies of those who picked up on it. She added touches of mythos and playacting, sprinkled with song, dance, costumes, sawing, and sanding, painting transcended us to Female Child Otherworld.

We were pretend pioneers, a naïve yet necessary enactment to make the Cumberland Gap not a dull study on worn, smelly pages. Under her thrall, it became Adventureland. No truth of the real pioneer history (His Story): the unspeakable cruelties, hardships, prejudices, the white supremacy importing and enslaving Chinese "coolies" to build the railroads, not to mention anyone who was not lily white—but if you had to be a kid in the fifties and sixties, it was a better than those duller than dishwater school films. To whitewash it, victimizing the ones they victimized was soul sickening, but at least she added a fifth dimension: Pretend. Time Travel. Music and the vibration that allowed for the time travel itself.

We were a family in that bungalow—not a very close-knit family but a pretend family, and we sang the songs by Peter Seeger and old American folk songs that she mimeographed in purple. Too bad they were saturated in Death Culture toxicity. With girls and women, no matter what their color, we are always the targets of blame. I had to put what I felt intrinsically aside, at her request that I write a play with Bobby for the semester's finale of our Pioneer Studies. We played a pioneer family and danced as we learned for the May Festival "The Tennessee Wig Walk."

After school, Chris and I kept dancing this with a sense I had no word for. It was Joy. Pure, unadulterated (by any Stupid Adult) child joy. When you dance and you feel that syncopation in your body and feet, it was pure joy.

> "I'm a bow-legged chicken, I'm a knock-kneed hen.
> Never been so happy since I don't know when.
> I walk with a wiggle and a giggle and a squawk
> Doin' the Tennessee Wig Walk!"

Happiness spilled over from that bungalow and the blacktop, and Chris and I squeezed it until it from sunup to sundown.

Mrs. A. Archetypes

You could have dressed her in a prim schoolmarm's two-paneled skirt, with high-collared chambray shirt, and arranged her hair in braids that twined in a knot at the nape of her neck, or in a 1920s Miss Jean Brodie outfit complete with instep-strapped spindle heels, straight kick-pleat skirt, simple sweaters she wore, and a flapper pageboy bob, which was her hairstyle off and on. She also had the physiognomy of Caddie Woodlawn (the title character in a book by Carol Ryrie Brink) herself; there was a freckle-faced, wild, redhaired tomgirl quality about her that I didn't know how to discuss, because Caddie didn't cross the patriarchal barrier into *Pippi Longstocking* territory, female fortitude, and fealty.

I had a fealty with her. We all did.

Yet when she sang "Barb'ry Allen," my heart twisted because no one had ever connected the female dots for me. In the Death Culture, this was indeed a blaming, shaming, vicious, vitriolic attack on the sovereign beauty of a young woman who stayed feral in the original version and stood fast against the Dark Force ploy to play the victim card.

"And Her Name Was Barb'ry Allen"

"Barb'ry Allen" is one of the oldest songs of Anglican Scottish Celtic folklore. Its roots honor the wild female sovereign soul spirit. I don't believe the lyrics that a trickster switched the message throughout. The song has its *roots* in the wild feral female sovereign spirit. If you look it up and trace it back, the original message was that she stood fast against male entitlement. She is approached because she is beautiful on the outside from within by the Dark Force male named Sweet William because he wants to suck and syphon the Female Light from her.

She does not want him, and she informs him thusly. But the Dark Force wants the light of her female soul, and he is rooted in the wild sovereign soil of the female spirit. It is about the Dark Force and its plays to entitlement, and it preys upon this sovereign Female Love brilliance luminosity that it in BA innate beauty beatific.

In the town where I was born in the place where I was dwelling, there lived a fair maid, and her name was Barb'ry. Over the centuries, this once-heroine became demonized. From a persona as powerful Queen Boudicca, reduced to an obedient servant of the Patriarchy, killing herself to be buried next to Sweet William—a bully who had pronounced she belonged to him, like a doll in a shop window.

And over the eons, instead of its original female tale, the lore of the leer of male entitlement being flat-out refused, and She who prevails has infantilized female spirit because it rewrites the story and trespasses into an anti-female propaganda.

I was ten years old when Mrs. A. sang this song, and she became the full embodiment of the spirit of her namesake.

It took fifty-five years to figure out the agony of the beauty that kept twisting and morphing similar to the changing pictures ... only in my changing pictures—the strong, powerful female on the outside was erased. Instead, she was rewritten as the selfish, man-hating femme fatale, a tease who would be punished by gaslight and believed the distorted mirrors held up by the Dark Force. Instead of fighting back, she surrendered and became an accomplice in her own death.

How patriarchy twisted, demonized her honorable character. I have written more times about Barbara A. than I could count. Not because she was who she was (though that is a part of it), but what an emotional Female Shift she caused in my young girl's life.

The timing was perfect. The subject was perfectly fit. Her graciousness was right on time. Her physiognomy matching a key song sealed the testament of the Sacred State of Female Being under the Death Culture. What has made it so confusing and overladen with meaning contributes to telling my story's chapter of Barbara A. and me. She selflessly offered the gift of her precious time to single me out for my talents.

She chose me. No one ever chose me. Although ballet and tap teachers did try to encourage my parents to do the right thing for their daughter's future, to keep me on track as a professional ballerina or dancer of any sort, especially tap. With Barbara, it was what it was supposed to be. *What I needed more than anything was the gift of a grown woman's appreciation of my natural gifts (musicality) and the desire to cultivate it. In simple terms: I desperately needed healthy MotherDaughter scenarios that were real and initiated by her. I was worth her precious time. I was her choice. And she did not have "pets."*

In learning guitar, she knew she could only take me so far and then off to Harriet's, but mostly with her taking the action to start the growth, the watering, pruning, cultivation—there would never have been any transplantation, no Harriet and Molly. They, in turn, were a milestone in my female life. It was all connected. And it started with Barbara's love of teaching children. I was that lucky duckling.

How do I unravel how it all happened? Mrs. A. brought her Goya, slung its lanyard over her slender shoulder, and sang American folk songs to us, teaching us, her fifth-grade class, Never fond of any of these songs—grown male mindset about guns, rifles, wagons, freedom, mountains that belonged to them, and miners 49ers. I was still part of it all. She noticed my accompaniment on the autoharp with Chris and Madolyn, naturally extremely talented musicians. Madolyn was a piano protégé. Chris would go on to entertain in her own folk band. To be singled out over these two, my best friends no less, was truly unbelievable. Yet it became believable because I had to get permission from my mom and not tell any other students.

I took her offer in my stride. She spoke as always, as was her style, in earnest. So I asked my mother for permission to stay one hour after school on Thursdays to take guitar. Always relieved to have me out of the house, she only insisted that I not take the shortcut because a girl was attacked there. it was a path secreted by high bushes, ideal for predators to strike. However, she never considered the other route I took walking along in the late-afternoon darkness. I would not have my own guitar until kids got on the bandwagon and started at Harriet's, but I was used to being last, with Grandma chipping in for the cheapest instrument I could find. Even Goyas were considered moderately pricey in those days.

Her sweet-smelling Goya's honeyed scent emanated her female energies. It even looked like her. Same complexion. And that red dotted necklace around its open circle looked like her. The shape of a guitar is the shape of a woman. I was blessed to press my fingers on the same frets and strings and move the same capo that her sacred fingers were fast friends with. Those yellow-knuckled fingers, moving mine correctly over the frets (I see your thumb; arch that wrist), that same white-yellow when she crossed her knees under nylons and slender legs, a redhead's complexion. At long last I entered Female Otherworld with an enchantress.

Barb'ry Allen was the song that made her morph before my female eyes into that fair maiden. Harriet sang it too—but Barbara became Barb'ry Allen.

Barbara A. was the antithesis of a teacher's pet type.

Settled upon a high wooden stool, [5]Loreena McKennitt-like, her Goya now a lute, strawberry blonde tresses springing and cascading down her forest-green bodice. A Scottish lass, hardworking barmaid whose simple crucifix dangled over the frayed lace at her bosom. The scent of wild achillea filled the air. I was in her thrall. She strummed....

> "In Scarlet Town, where I was bound,
> There was a fair maid dwelling,
> Whom I had chosen to be my own,
> And her name 'twas Barb'ry Allen."

Yet the lyrics she crooned over our heads shocked me. About a bully who had the gall to "choose her to be my own," demonizing the strong, brave-hearted lady of Scottish lore. They lyrics reflect his name as Sweet William, when the truth was he was poisonous as hemlock. Portrayed himself as dying of love for the sovereign Great Sacred Female who refused him.

> "So slowly, slowly she got up,
> And so slowly she came neigh him.
> And all she said when she came there,
> Young man, I think you are a dying.
>
> He turn'd his face unto her then:
> 'If you be Barbara Allen,
> My dear,' said he, 'Come pity me,
> As on my deathbed I am lying."

Come pity me, said the Victim Cards my father had stockpiled. Hah. Had I been in her place, I would have done the same thing. Her response, though inferred as heartless, would have been my response, for he arrogated his "entitlement" he had "chosen her." He did not ask her for her hand. She did not want him. A woman under patriarchy's iron fist has no say in the

---

[5] Loreena McKennitt, Canadian singer-songwriter

matter—just as in my day was mistreated as my father's plaything and child mistress.

> "'If on your deathbed you be lying,
>   What is that to Barbara Allen?
> I cannot keep you from your death;
>   So farewell,' said Barbara Allen."

Again, it echoed my father's playing the Put-upon Rejected Victim of a cold-hearted woman, a real Hard-Hearted Hannah—"Put the Blame on Mame" (from the movie *Gilda*).

I wanted to shout: "No! No! Don't go near him. He's only pretending, like the Wolf in *Little Red Riding Hood*. He will grab your hand and pull you onto him. He is faking death. Even if dying, he would find a way to shame you one last time!"

However, "farewell" was more than I would have wished him and his trickery. But deeper betrayal was that my muse, my goddess, my one fair lady should sing such a lyrics was a terrible shock. I trusted and adored her. I believed her to be smart, savvy, all-seeing. Again, I was faced with, "Do you know what you are singing?" Lyrics through the ages chastise girls and women. From "Barb'ry Allen" to "Put the Blame on Mame" to "Hard-Hearted Hannah" (what my father called me at six). Sadly, I was alone in grief and shock with the hideous truths women had suffered eternally, refusing to awaken, and by taking arms, oppose them—the Death Culture.

> "'And mother, father, go dig my grave.
>   Make it both long and narrow.
> Sweet William died on yesterday,
>   And I will die tomorrow.'
> Barbara Allen was buried in the old churchyard;
>   Sweet William was buried beside her.
> Out of Sweet William's heart there grew a rose,
>   Out of Barbara Allen's, a briar.
> They grew and grew in the old churchyard
>   Till they could grow no higher.

At the end they formed a true lover's knot,
And the rose grew 'round the briar."

The Irony of red rose and the briar twisted my gut. To hear her singing those lyrics meant to me that she not only did not admonish such a travesty, to gaslight a young woman (older girl) to accept and not revile and fight against the lies of one vicious male and the chorus of townsfolk who bought into his crap—that she was responsible for a man's death by rejecting his advances.

The strawberry blonde maiden whose hands moved my fingers so gently and firmly on the frets at our lessons after school betrayed me, albeit unknowingly. Her beauty still dazzled but was diminished. Not tarnished. Just diminished. I was not the only kid who lived in her thrall. But this song—its mournful sound, the similarity in names and physiognomy, threw me for a loop. Continually betrayed by my mother, grandmothers, and all the aunts on both sides of the family, I was now learning another girl-reality: that a woman could be kind, giving, selfless, and beautiful from within yet could betray unwittingly Great Sacred Girls—the Female Truth under the Death Culture.

5. A Chance Meeting Spring of '67

Hippies, drugs, and hypocrisy abounded. I was sixteen, working at Field's in Century City. One day, I suddenly became aware of a vibration. I looked up, and across the floor, there she was. I had that distinct feeling that she had already seen me, that weirdness of the unspoken. If she did, why didn't she acknowledge it?

She looked nothing like the Mrs. A. I had known five years prior. It was a busy, crowded, fast-paced Saturday, and she was nonchalantly threading though the aisle near the registers. So much had happened since then. Mary Anne's sudden death in seventh grade. Kennedy's assassination. MLK. Bobby Kennedy. Maryanne. So much violence. The Watts riots. The biggest thing to hit the planet: The Beatles. And now this hippie thing that took on so many images, influenced by them. Edwardian. Western. East Indian. Nehru jackets.

Gone were the days of Jackie Kennedy's pillbox hats and signature triple-stranded pearls. As I crept behind milling customers and made my way cautiously, breathlessly toward her, thoughts ran through my head like a movie reel in a foreign film all about the girls I'd graduated with; the ones who went to Hammy (Hamilton High) lived in her neighborhood, and I discovered they used to babysit for the little boy she had after we graduated. The closer I got to that side of the store, the more I became aware of never returning to visit the school. That would mean seeing her again. Why did I never go back anywhere? Should I feel guilty? Did she hold resentment? How could I tell her that even though I'd had her for class, nothing was ever the same. We were all changing, but I had counted on her staying the same. My parents actually came to open house after weeks of my campaigning and met her.

Of course they skipped graduation. As all the parents and kids were scattering back to the parking lot, I tiptoed like a homing pigeon to the auditorium. There stood Mrs. Vischer's black lacquered baby grand. And the stage where I performed in the Brownies, and that night I played guitar with Chris. That night my mother threw me in my bedroom to teach me a lesson for not turning around when a woman was complimenting me on my playing. I never even heard her, so squeezed were throngs of parents and kids in the child-sized aisles.

After, I did the solo at Mrs. Vischer's request to be the sandpiper's voice: "Ooo, lee, lee, aaa." Her go-to soprano had me take on the role of this refrain in what we kids never knew was an old sacred Hawaiian lullaby. As I crept closer, she dived deeper into the clothes. Or did she? Sucking in my breath, imagination running riot, all the pain, confusion, isolation, and left-out feelings came rushing back in fast-frames.

> Oh, Mrs. A. … do you recall my awful earache in the schoolyard when the blustery winds kicked up—not hot but cold? I covered my ears and you offered me one of your scarves. That was why you always wore one; you got the same earaches too. And the girls were so jealous when they caught me wearing one. They never knew there was

nothing to be jealous over. They had mothers who took care of them, or so I believed.

Certainly, they got excited enough to watch the clock when it approached and ran out like bats out of hell, whereas I felt sick at heart every day. I never wanted to go home. And now sixth grade was shutting the gates on me forever. Still, something was not the same. All the girls knew something I did not. She was pregnant. No, no, it could not be true. I ran up the bungalow stairs, knocked on the door, and when you came out, I asked you point blank: "Is that really a maternity top?" And you nodded with that Mrs. A. grin. "Why, yes." I stood there dumbfounded. Suddenly I was Peter to her Wendy-bird.

Me: But you can't have a baby! We're your children!

How that amused her. I sulked and skulked away from the bungalow in shock and dejection. Small wonder I never went back. Little did I know neither would she for more than one semester. It was too close to turn around. Too late to turn back, I decided someone had to be the bigger one. If there was one thing that surpassed my linear age it was rising to an occasion. I had no tolerance for pretense. No one, but no one, would ever dare to pretend to not recognize me, especially when I hadn't changed that much.

As she drifted to the right, I wondered what had happened to the Fair Maiden I had known, on the blacktop, whistle to her lips in that stiletto up-tilt. Left up. Shift weight. Right up. Women's feet were killing them in those days. Trench coat, very Burberry's, long scarf billowing as Barb'ry Allen, in a coach four-in-hand.

All this was ricocheting around my psyche as she came into full view, and suddenly the gulf of five years became five-and-twenty. I would recognize her a football field away. Gone were the pumps, kick-pleated skirts, seersucker shifts and belts, bangs, and pageboy flip.

I was looking at some creature who had stepped out of a pre-Raphaelite prairie, not quite Wyeth's *Christina*. More Judy Collins meets Loreena

McKennitt. Hair actually wound down her shoulders as I had pictured her when she sang that song, golden tresses in a frizzled, orange burnished halo, full-length Western skirt, turquoise concha belts, and dangling earrings. Pure hippie chic. This new creature was, perhaps by then, a divorcée. Going through her late twenties in that phase of life, with a six-year-old son. Single mom or not, she remade herself, and good for her.

Confusing to me to have to approach her as if I was some groupie, or young suitor approaching his past love. How the mother wounds propel us lifelong. Authors Daphne du Maurier, Radclyffe Hall, Adrienne Rich, Dorothy Allison, Vita Sackville, Violet Trefusis, Virginia Woolf, Lillian Hellman. The list was legion. I was only sixteen and had no idea what was making me so ill with fear and hope. The Rejected Daughter and the Collapsed Mother had yet to be written about.

Me: Mrs. A.? Do you remember me?

She: Yes, murmured the Sphinx.

Perhaps I was to her an uncomfortable reminder of the self she had left behind. An unwanted visitor from her earlier eras. Perhaps, like me, once she left one life phase, a school, a phase she never wanted to reflect upon, she never returned. This was the new Barbara. Beautiful with echoes of Barb'ry Allen in her long skirts and full-blow hair. I never got over that unexpected encounter until I turned forty, started RDFT, named it as Phoetics took me on the trail of Female Love.

When I was thirty, this identical scenario played out with the female OBGYN who delivered my second daughter and saw me through the whole pregnancy. Every woman who has gone through this knows what an intimate, mothering-daughtering sense of vulnerability and trust goes on during this sacred time of her life. One would hope for the doctor, too, but I was to hit another wall more ready than when I was sixteen.

A year after she delivered my daughter, I caught sight of her in the distance as she passed around, politicking as I see it now, with the high rollers of the Orange County Performing Arts Center. Another hoity-toity fundraiser.

I was on the Opera Ball committee, and this event had something to do with it. I weaved closer and closer but this time did not approach her. How could she miss me? She didn't; I knew she recognized me. But today I see that I was not one of the ladies who ran the opera committee and certainly not a wealthy doyenne. She could not gain anything in her practice by my acquaintance. The same shock but not a sucker punch. I was older and wiser.

6. My Sixty-Five to Her Seventy-Two - 2015

Facebook. Never a fan, but it helped me to help myself in a fifty-six-year search to find Mrs. A. Women marry. Remarry. Change their last names. Now Ladye Fortune was by my side when I came upon her daughter. She was receptive, and after a few texts, I gave her my number and it ended in her giving me Barbara's. I went to my car on a lunch hour shaking like a leaf on one hand, calm and fateful-grateful on the other when she answered: "Hello, Nancy." She knew I would be calling and I supposed my caller ID showed up. Her voice had changed even sounded like an aunt of mine, a smoky, chesty voice.

Me: Hello! Do you remember me?
Barbara: Of course.
Me: How are you?

The conversation went immediately to guitar, our lessons, and how laughed together about her old refrain when you surpassed her teaching level, "You need to go to Harriet's."

Me: What do you remember about me?
She: You were very pretty.
Me: Anything else?
She: Very sweet.
Me: Was your birthday really November the thirtieth? (I had wrestled forever that she may have told us the thirty-first to keep from answering.)

She: Yes.

It went on from there, and we tried to get together, but I worked during the week, and she had busy weekends. But after several cancellations, I saw or felt some secret part of her did not want to, and I honor every soul's choices. They owe me no explanation. Treat them as I want to be treated.

She hadn't remembered my Unforgettable Chris. And I learned she had left the school after teaching kindergarten when we left and then went on for her PhD in psychology and worked at the VA. It all was great validation. In my first notes about her, I realized she had to be an INFJ, and that was why her teaching style was magic. An INFJ, like me.

But on that phone call was the same Sphinx-like quality to her voice, like she had a cap on how much and little she would say and for that conversation I am satisfied. Grateful for her gift of selfless voluntary teaching. Even Mrs. Mize showed me special attention because she was a lefty too, in the very grade when longhand-script is taught. The years I needed a mother's love, validation, and appreciation of my authentic self was provided by all those women in that school. Gifts from my Female Otherworld ancestresses. Gifted to keep me going. Death wishes quelled off and on, but they gave me what a girl needs most—a sense of worth. I was worth their time. Now that is real MotherDaughter FemaleLove alchemy.

To my dearest Barbara,

Should you ever read this, thank you. For Barb'ry Allen. For choosing me to write the class play. For giving your time to teach me on your magical Goya on all those transcendent Thursday afternoons. And for taking my call, fifty-six years later.

Love forever,

Nancy

Mrs. Woodward, Swaying Like a Nun

Some teachers carry an aura only children can see. For Carolyn Woodward, it was a golden haze like saintly pre-Gregorian leitmotif, radiating as if the sun was shining from within or as if backlit from a cathedral window. Yet she possessed a steady, sturdy steely resolve like Hildegard of Bingham.

In other words, children loved that they respected her and respected how they loved her.

To get into her class was considered hitting the jackpot of your third grade year, even if it meant only one semester. I was one of the lucky ducks, and the memory of her as well as her very existence went a long way to keep me going through the most grueling and disturbing times of my young life. My very sanity depended on the visible proof-the existence of female consciousness. As long as I caught sight of it whether on a real-life, in-the-flesh woman or her archetypal equivalent in storybook form; like the good nun Miss Clavel in *Madeline* or Miss Pross in the film of *Tale of Two Cities*. Something in me was temporarily quelled. A great sacred female was present.

I remember distinctly, in the middle of my father's nightly molestations, forcing myself to focus on what she had asked us all to bring for our assignment about the Yagna Indians and their wickiups and how they turned corn into a fine powder, grinding it in a mortar and pestle. And while this bored me to no end, the tedium of their daily labors, the utter lack of wit, whimsy, and sophistication in music and dance, it served to anchor me by its sheer mundaneness. And since my mother dismissed it outright ("Where in the world am I supposed to find *cornmeal,* of all things?") I kept running over the monotony of the day's lesson and the mental note to find some friend who might share hers found by some responsible mother.

In those days, female teachers were always dubbed Mrs. Even when they were single. It reeks of patriarchy, but who knows? Miss Woodward was listed on the roster as Mrs., yet little girls intuited the Virgin archetype—and dubbed, nay, christened her *Miss Woody Word.*

123

I refused to join their infantile chants, but their antics were an instinctive response to long-lost female idolatry, to the missing female culture we each still carried within; the Kore, the Woman Who Belongs to Herself. This trait so radiated from her that when she swayed down the quay, the open breezeway of unfurling spider ferns, a fresh pile of purple mimeographed papers nestled in her arms, it was like seeing the Great Daughter of the Great Mother. Nubby, rust-colored dirndl skirts brushed tops of tan Hush Puppies and on one ankle, the popular anklet. A blue-stone sweater guard clipped to her navy cardigans.

As I stood at her side waiting my turn at her desk, taking in the delicacy of her filmy white batiste blouse as if the finest fingers of a long-lost Belgian nunnery had embroidered it just for her in the gathering of infinitesimal folds and pleats, gave way to the full slip that peeked through here and there … and that crucifix of gold, resting in repose upon her clavicle.

Her hair was pure Kate Hepburn from *The African Queen*, a hastily piled up pompadour of auburn that refused to be lacquered, sprayed, dyed, or netted. The finest down on her cheek and jawline, without a stitch of makeup save some old-fashioned Papier Poudre blotting papers. Caroline Woodward was to girls—an anomaly, a mystic who could never have born any real children but more like grownup Shirley Temple on Sunday night's *Fairy Tale Theatre,* who played a charming Mother Goose. For in all her essence, that was who and what she was. Strict yet fun, creative yet by-the-rules storyteller and teacher, keeper of small children's souls until they passed into the next grade.

Looking back, Miss Carolyn Wood was a *girl's teacher.*

Mrs. Vischer could spot a gifted child a mile away. You did not have to be Madolyn for her to ask you to lead the choir in "Here We Come A-Wassailing" to sing a soprano solo for events. All you had to do was throw back a fierce look that said, "Yes!" and you were on her respectable stage for the duration. Maude's nod met my glance many-a-time.

She would not take no for an answer. She might let you buy time but expected performance, polished matching her eagerness. She expected what my parents forbade: Allegiance, joy, passion, dedication to the musical gifts that ran rampant in my female being.

To wit, Maude demanded that I shine.

Maude's Nod

The Wild Woman, wildly Teutonic, ran like spring sap in Mrs. Vischer's pulsating temples, arterial nostrils flaring each time she taught us new harmony and lifted her baton in organza sleeves turned up at the cuffs. *Fait attencion.*We were learning how to pay homage to the maven, a conductress for all time, and an echo of old Europe itself.

Maude Vischer (dubbed Maude Vicious by the boys) did not walk. She did not shuffle. Nor did she waltz around. She would not have known how to mince. In her sensible pumps with legs tapered like the baby grand upon she accompanied us, Maud Vischer *strode. With her scooped basket filled with all kinds of noise making ditties.*

Was she Dickensian? Rabelaisian? Shakespearean? Yes and no. She was— after all was said and sung—of hugely archetypal proportions. In another day and age, she might have smelted iron in leather aprons and arm protectors. Or bore many daughters and commandeered a chariot against the Romans. She might have leaned Edwardian-diva style against a proper upright on the gaslit stage, sucking in her gut to warble out "God Save the Queen" followed by a resounding chorus of "Knees up, Mother Brown."

But from 1957–62 she was music teacher extraordinaire for children who couldn't have cared less about Bach, Beethoven, and Brahms were only too happy to get a break from the three R's to shake, rattle, and roll her brassy maracas, shivery sandpaper sliders, and dainty finger cymbals. I do not remember her in class her visits were about once a month.

My reveries hover in the "aud," learning melodies and lyrics of places I understood better than my own hometown. When we sang "On the Bridge of Avignon" I got a funny feeling, a strange ache as we grew older, and "Alan-A-Dale Went A-Hunting" kept time with her pointer finger metronome. I fell into a Sherwood Forest trance that was not Sherwood Forest at all, for that is where Maud and the music took me.

Home. To Otherworld. Wild. Female. Resounding. Trumpeting. Those batting organza sleeves. Her Magic Wand baton, that clicking metronome.

Maude's Nod was pure MotherDaughter alchemy showered upon me, though I doubt she never knew it. Thank you, for demanding my musicality shine. And for the archetypal energies I needed to see in motion, as proof their did exist strong, sovereign adult women dedicated impassioned to bring the magic of music to children who might never had it otherwise.

Are You Going to Harriet's?

That was the constant refrain sung by every young girl lucky enough to darken and lighten the doorstep of Harriet William's Guitar Studio, which was, in all reality, just a modest home where La Cienega, Venice, and Washington all cleaved together. Beneath the power lines' hiss and crackle, just inches off the beaten path where cars hacked out smutty emissions, in the humblest of abodes resided Harriet Williams and her partner, Molly.

Harriet taught the advanced kids in the darkened living room while Molly—amid creaking bunk beds, dusty saddles, and Indian horse blankets in the detached garage—patiently tended to the beginners. In overalls, squaw boots, and one long silver plait dangling mightily down her broad back, Molly was the archetypal masculine female. If you turned around, you were shocked the voice behind you came from a woman. I was at once shocked, then enthralled. I could picture her whittling a corncob pipe on a cane rocking chair, kitten on her lap, her private blue eyes concealing ... well, I never knew what, but I sure longed to.

It was the 1950s, and women, let alone black women, let alone black women who chose to love *other* women, let alone a black woman who chose to love another (ahem!) *white* woman ... was downright dangerous. Whether or not Harriet gave a rat's ass I will never know, but she lived contentedly, openly, rooted to the land as well as to the purple mimeographed papers that bespoke of lands that she passed out to us each week. She and Molly possessed a beautiful mountain cabin that was more chalet with a charming white wooden staircase than rustic A-frame. They generously gave of it each time a new class of girls graduated in June 1962, we were driven up to Idyllwild for a weekend of laughter, popcorn, and singing, singing, strumming, and singing.

My fondest memory of Harriet is of her bending over me to say goodnight after we had sung ourselves into an all-night, tingly, tuning-fork frenzy. She kissed me on my forehead and said sweet dreams. She reminded me of singer and actress Ketty Lester, with those same Max Factor jungle-red lips; crisp, close-cut hair with a little salt and pepper; and she moved, walked, glided like a Nubian statue come to life in calf length leotards, thongs with poinsettia nail polish. Part of the Beat Generation and somehow, not. A beatnik with elegance. Somehow, I was always aware that right outside her door were nightspots and bars, where West Coast jazz was constellating. In some inarticulate, inexplicable way I intuited that Harriet was and yet was not part of that Jack Kerouac-Chet Baker scene. What she did when we girls went home and until we saw her again remained a mystery.

They ran a childcare center during the day, but after our lessons, when night fell, when the last Brownie mom closed the last door on the last station wagon, when once again, I was forced to go home ... well, I did not think about what Harriet and Molly did. I was too young. Too shell-shocked and too much a child to think they actually existed after the last check was slipped into the mailbox, the last girl swung herself down the garden path, flipping her guitar case back and forth in whip-snake fashion, all the better to trip up her balance. All that counted to me was that there was a clear and appropriate line: we were children, they were adults, and never the twain would meet.

It was as if I had died and gone to some heaven I never knew existed, a place with only women and girls. I was so safe with these women, so offbeat-eccentric-exotic compared to the white-bread, straight-as-an-arrow, duller-than-dishwater patriarchal world I was forced to exist in that I both honed and homed *to* them. Had any Fairy Goddess Mother asked me to make a wish or Jiminy Cricket to wish upon a star, mine would have been to have had two moms just like them: making their own authentic lives, strong, needing no man's approval, soft when it counted, self-sufficient, in love with each other, and dedicated to teaching children the beauty of music.

I doubt any of my cohorts ever saw what I saw but I was not like them, and I was not there for learning the chord families, memorizing Pete Seeger tunes or how to keep holding my wrist up so that my thumb wouldn't hang over the fret. Besides, I had already mastered it the day Mrs. A. smiled at me and slowly shook her auburn bob. "I'm sorry, Nancy. You have surpassed me. I cannot teach you anymore. *You need to go to Harriet's.*"

And so, as La Fortuna would have it, I found my way to Harriet and Molly's. My mother never found her way and stayed in her dark bedroom. And since I was so advanced and a quick study, it afforded me oodles of time to study Harriet when she wasn't studying me.

She did not know—nor could she and Molly have ever known—that they indeed were my life's work.

6

MY SCARY TALES

If You Were to Peer Back to 1954

If you were to peer back to 1954 and part the twin veils of Child Hate and Child Phobia, you would find a four-year-old girl with soft, brunette curls screaming at the top of her lungs on top of a tool table, her Mary Janes fighting for her life, throttled by a looming goon in overalls brandishing a rusty saw over her half-naked body.

"Shut up! Shut up! I'll kill you; I'll kill you!" He growls just like the Big Bad Wolf, and he means it.

Freeze frame.

Pan back to a deserted Southern California driveway; low, boxed Eugenia bushes line its borders. The house is a strictly Spanish LA Confidential-style. Concealed in its center, a patio littered with long-dead banyan leaves, stems shriveled, so coarse, so protruded and blackened you could charcoal sketch with them; a bird fountain, bird shit petrified on the bull-nosed lip. No one remembers when it last flowed; it has been stagnant forever.

A dog barks uncontrollably in the distance. A red and white Beware of Dog sign dangles off-kilter from the next-door neighbor's chain-link fence, piles of decaying, calcifying animal excrement butt up to it. In the middle of the driveway, no more than ten feet from the garage, a square blue-green child's plastic pool stops sloshing, with every shriek its sea horses shrink from its floor.

The air in the garage is the same air that hangs in the Old Livery Stable in Knott's Ghost Town on Boot Hill. Staid, static, sarcophagic air; black air, off-the-air air, a black void, a black hole, the same kind of black void where a child's screams for mercy never reach the ears of the living ... let alone a savvy woman who might happen by.

No savvy woman will happen by. Woman has been abandoned. The girl will survive. She will write, speak, sing, dance, draw, act, and teach women who they really are and what is wrong with the world and how to fix it and how to fix themselves for the benefit of children in their family and the world's Great Sacred Girls & Boys.

This girl does not abandon Woman because Woman will not abandon her. For she is the one who sees through Female Eyes.

Uncle Al, The Big Bad Wolf

I was always dancing. With oodles of time on my hands, I would practice what I saw in old movies and do my versions of Shirley Temple's routines, Darla Hood's (Darla from *Little Rascals*) songs, tapping and selling it to my heart's content. I had my own spot, the second mini arch from the front door. All in all there were four as seen in my parents' wedding photos and portraits of my mother and her sister in Hollywood glamour shots in gowns and shorts.

I thought every kid had pictures like these, but my mother and aunt were different. Grandma was a milliner and a whiz at dressmaking. They were caught up in the Betty Grable, Ava Gardner era and it was their dress-up time, their family publicity shots. I would learn that whenever my mom told my father to take me to the front yard to take pictures in a new Easter dress or swimsuit—these pictures were my mother's superficial proof that she was a good mom.

As long as her daughter appeared well fed, well shod, and the mandatory cheese smile, no one could ever accuse her of the abuse behind closed doors. The photos she never counted on were my reflective, pensive, candid shots where I am captured, confused, and depressed as to what was really going on in this upside-down, inside-out world in the cloistered home of Grandma and as it was reflected in the outside world.

I had no idea I was being spied on. Got in trouble for hanging on the wrought iron gate and using the sprinkler rod as a walking cane for my top hat and tails rendition of "It's a Broadway Mel-o-dy!"

"Who's been hanging on the gate again? Damned kids," growled the Big Bad Wolf.

Little Red Riding Hood

He was the spy who one day assaulted me like *Little Red Riding Hood*. This cartoon back in 1932 had all the elements of my life from two to five. That is when we lived at Grandma's house—mother, father, baby brother because, as my mother lied, "Dad could not make a good living." The statement was true but not the entire nitty-gritty reason. She had a complete nervous breakdown after my brother's birth. It was a breech and that is why he came out with a perfect head and the nurses all called him butch. She used to shudder, "Those awful forceps." No surprise she flipped out. It was what he did to her when she was my age. Cold steel shoved inside your birth canal. I fell victim to the same abuse that day he grabbed me by the scruff of my Helen Fenton dress and threw me on the tool table in Grandpa's garage. It was that Little Red Riding Hood captured in the cartoon, after the wolf attempts to beguile her in a ballet costume, camping, dragging it out when Red appropriately huddles away. She knows a Big Bad Wolf when she sees one.

"If You Were to Peer Back" perfectly captures that day in which Evil was unleashed. Yes, he screamed at me to stop screaming or he would saw me in half. Yes, he abused me with his tools. And yes, I left my body, took the hand of The White Rock Fairy and we hid in Grandpa's gigantic sunflowers. This majorly repressed event only burst alive that day in Pat's office when under hypnosis I relived his paws around my neck, throttling lest I make a peep. The garage doors slammed. I remember the urine-stained stench of the old mattresses, of male sweat mixed with mechanic's oil. It was the world of mechanical clues that I would figure out decades later.

It is hard to remember the order of the attacks, because he took me for a ride in his pea-green 1935 flatbed truck to carpet one of Grandma's apartment houses, and that was where I was kidnapped down into the basement where he did his evil works. When it was all over, I recall sobbing into his dirty flannel shirt and that perverse, soul-sickening sense when a predator "comforts" the prey like nothing happened. Gaslighting to the max, I never thought I was going crazy. I just wanted out.

Instead, I had to wait while he thumped with his knee the carpet knee knicker for what seemed like an eternity. What I had not remembered, until that day in Pat's, was I left my body all that time and stared at an empty light socket.

As I stared at the light socket in Pat's office, my mouth divulged "Uncle Al pretends to be Goofy, but he's really the Big Bad Wolf."

I asked Pat, "What just happened?"

She replied, "I think little Nancy just came out."

While these episodes of horrific child abuse fade back and forth into each other, the day I cried not to take a ride with Uncle Al, all hell broke loose, and I put together the puzzles of that scenario and what it all meant.

It Was All a Game!

It all started when my mother suggested that I take a ride with him. Always pill popping in bed, flipping through Photoplays, I wonder if she wanted me to suffer her same hell. She was a sadist. She had not repressed her abuse. She even told me about it during our last phone call before I hung up for the last time. Like all child sufferers of the Abuse Trap Cycle, I knew what that ride meant. Like the other time he took me with him to Felix Chevrolet to play poker with the men in the back. Wads of bills exchanged hands, and I was passed from each to sit on their dirty overalls. Next, abandoned to the back of the store, where boys were peeing against the wall. Felix the Cat high above and godlike on a huge billboard smirked down on me. "Hah, Nancy. Just another victor of Child Abuses, of the Death Culture Death Culture."

For decades I had a nightmare of being stuck at the junction of San Vicente and Fairfax, just a mile away from Grandma's house, with the Big Bad Wolf catching me to reach the handle too high for me. It was a replay of what actually had happened. A PTSD moment my psyche knew I was ready to consciously remember.

"You will never see Grandma again," he growled. He saw that I recognized we were close to her neighborhood and considered jumping out.

I may have even been in diapers. But his hairy paw on the stick shift and heavy black work boots confirmed who I was with, and I kept quiet and prayed I'd see her again. She was the closest thing to a mother figure I had then. My mother abdicated her role from the time I was born and flipped out after Davey's birth two years later. Grandma came and rescued us all—I have this from my auntie Janie. Interviewed her in my forties to find out what really had happened, versus my mother's toxic fiction. Auntie made a face. She could not bring herself to describe the scene Grandma found us in. Apparently, a social worker would have reported us to the authorities for sheer neglect.

So how did "It was all just a game" happen? When my mother said I should take a ride with Al, I freaked out. No way was I going to be trapped with the Big Bad Wolf again. I was so hysterical, my grandmother asked what was going on. She found me in the driveway, refusing to get into his truck. What clues/red flags came back to me in a rush? Grandma beating him on a chest she could barely reach, yelling, "Again? Again?" (She pronounced it a-gain.)

Being found out, he put on his Goofy act. "Ma, ma, she's just a kid. Dunna know what she's talkin' about!" His hands thrown above his head at six foot two, made him more giant-like.

After this altercation she turned on her Mandel pumps and went back to her inner sanctum and denial chamber, the kitchen. I had hoped she would do the right thing and take me away with her. But instead, I was left abandoned to the evil the whole family knew about. A four-year-old child handed over to a six-foot-two Moriarty.

He must have really panicked, because I found us sitting on the driveway slope, me focused on my precious baby brother doing summersaults in his diapers on the lawn.

Then, the moment he looked at me, locking eyes: *Don't you trust your Uncle Al?*

My answer showed through my female eyes: *Not as far as I can throw you.*

His eyes were the worst. It only came back after Pat read *The Prince of Tides*. I did not like the book but did confess: "Al is Callanwolde," an evil character in the book. It was one sentence that was in neon to me: "His unbalanced eyes." That was my gaze. His muddy hazel eyes, intense, like Rasputin's. It was becoming obvious I did not buy into this *game* thing, so he used my baby brother in his desperate scheme.

A last-ditch effort, he came up with Let's show Davey! Before I knew it we were in the garage with my brother on the tool table with Al brandishing his saw over Davey's sacred flesh. He screamed. Then Uncle Al took the saw away, laughing along with Dallas, his gardening helper, to play along. See? It's only a game! My brother was too young to get what was going on, but I was no fool. Fool me once, uh huh. Fool me twice—don't even try.

Such was The Saw Game. Big Bad Wolf foiled again. But that never stopped him from terrorizing me across the Thanksgiving table. When there was a party at his house, I protested, told my mother I would not go. Why? I don't like Uncle Al. Why? He's scary. Don't be silly. Uncle Al is as good as gold, an oft-used phrase by Grandma. In the end I was forced to attend but was old enough to avoid him, but it was horrific. I hated the pall that hung over that house and wonder whether whomever lived there later was visited by the ghosts of all the souls he murdered. All the violence. For that is the definition of Child Abuse—Soul Murder.

Grandma's Funeral: 1984 in the Gray Limousine

At my grandmother's funeral in '84 I had just had a new baby. Still, I had to show my respects and attend, along with my husband, and as much as I dreaded it, I went. The room for loved ones was choking me with a deadly sick rose scent, as if it was pumped in by the undertakers themselves. What I had blanked out was that when it came time for pallbearers, my husband was one of them. I found myself in a light gray limousine that would go up the hill to graveside, but not before l jumped in and slammed the door. Al had the bloody nerve to play the woe is me victim card, sighing just like my father, "Ah Nancy, Nancy," putting his paw on my bare knee. I froze. I do not know how I got up the hill, but it proved a major triggering episode—my entire past with him was well repressed. Shocked at his nerve, but there was something old about it and identical to my father's MO. It did not come up to consciousness, my body sure as hell recoiled, remembering for me how evil he was. Riding in a dove grey limo to my grandmother's graveside, was too much to bear.

In 1992 I sent letters priority mail to my mother, father, and uncle with copies to their siblings. It told it all—what my father did to me, and Al's Big Bad Wolf days and ways. Each letter was ninety pages on both sides, handwritten. I never heard back and did not have to, did not want to. I asked Pat if she thought my mother would read it. No doubt, she nodded. Absolutely.

So that is the story of my version of Little Red Riding Hood. I was Red. Grandma was not the sick one in bed; instead; it was my mother. She did not send me into the woods to bring goodies to Grandma but instead to get in the vehicle with the Big Bad Wolf, her brother. The grandmother was fit, ambulatory, and the mother of the Big Bad Wolf. What's more, she knew he was Dangerous and Evil. She, too, abandoned me to his lair. And that was not all—I would come to be cast in many other scary tales with my father.

But this was going on simultaneously. How did I survive? As my second RDFT told me, "You had resources. Imagination and Spiritual."

Perhaps I always knew these tales might benefit girls in the future. And publish them to change the world back to Female Centricity, through our Authentic Female Selves banding together and sharing. There is no other way to preserve this sphere.

Uncle Al & My Father

My Father-The archetypes of Evil that kept on coming...

I take umbrage with Tolstoy's famous line, "Happy families are all alike; every unhappy family is unhappy in its own way." Number one, there is no such thing as "happy families" under the Death Culture, and as far as unhappy families? Unhappy in their own way applies to both. Tolstoy was not a woman, unqualified to characterize a woman as in Anna Karenina—a woman's victimization if ever there was one. Same applies to Emile Zola's *Nana,* a poor abandoned girl who becomes a prostitute to stay alive. Zola, the male chauvinist, got away with the portrayal of this victimized female as a man-eater and therefore "corrupt within." He writes "her true character is concealed by her outer beauty" and erupts for all the world to see, thereby punishing and threatening women at large and readers.

He has her contract smallpox. "What lay on the pillow was a charnel house, a heap of pus and blood, a shovelful of putrid flesh. The pustules had invaded the whole face, so that one pock touched the next."

I was a teenager when I read this. Intrigued because it was one of my father's nicknames for me when he wanted to express his incestuous desires. Nana. (Nana Lee, my in-trouble name.) As I beheld this ending, I wanted to burn the book and Zola with it. Not to mention *Lolita* and Nabokov on the same funeral pyre with all female demonizing male writers, and some females (to be covered in book two, *The Dark Force's Death Culture: A Look beneath and above the Surface of Anti-Female Smut Called Literature*).

By the time I was thirteen, I begged my mother to divorce my father. Every day I prayed for it. She dragged her heels, only until I was seventeen, and started proceedings. Why would a child beg for divorce unless there was such criminal happenings she could not bear, contemplating suicide since age six? These events seen through Female Eyes. My father was more Death Culture Archetype than I can cover here, can even name, but the standouts I share here, telling my story to the best of my true sense of sacred Femality.

My Father's Earliest Archetype: *The Grasshopper and the Ants,* Disney's 1934 version

The song the grasshopper warbles, fiddling literally and figuratively his time away, goes: "Oh the world owes me a living, deedle, deedle, diddle dee!" That was my father in a nutshell—or rather, the green disguise of Mr. Grasshopper. What goes on in this morality tale was the tug of my grandmother's and father's theme. He refused to make a decent living, screwing around from coffee shop to drug store counters everywhere, from LA proper, East LA, Hollywood, North Hollywood, Montebello, Monrovia, and whatever was part of his territory. This sales job enabled him to goof off, coffee-klatching with every waitress who could tolerate his moves.

The scene where the Grasshopper is fiddling and warbling this tune entrances the Ant Queen's workers as they drop their work and dance around when her carriage pulls up. Mortified, she sends her workers back to do their important jobs while warning Mr. Grasshopper that he'll be sorry when winter comes.

"You have to put away supplies" for the long winter.

"Ha, ha," he chortles, and picks up his fiddle as her carriage rolls away.

Winter hits. Shivering, he sees the happy dancing in her warm inner tree palace and knocks on the door.

She shows him mercy, and he is fed. He changes his tune to, "Oh, I owe the world a living ..."

In truth, my father never learned his lesson, though he grifted off my grandmother until Mom divorced him. This was disturbing, and the earliest animation brought his true character in focus on the old Zenith set. I was ashamed of him from the start, but it got worse as I attended school with kids whose fathers kept jobs, and even a few of the mothers. His character was rotten to the core, and I would have to deal with this reality my entire childhood and teens. What made the whole thing too close to home was the way the Grasshopper spat out tobacco goo, looking and sounding exactly like my father. It was uncanny. To walk beside him, that is what he did all day long. Spitting his mucous on every street in Beverly

Hills while we waited for Mom to come out of the psychiatrist's office. Like Mr. Grasshopper, the whole world was his spittoon. As an intuitive, extremely sensitive child, one can only imagine how this commonality hit me between the eyes.

That was the first archetype, along with the Bald Man on the red tray with pencil lead you could move around to make different man faces. Why this struck me as uncomfortable; my father was gaining weight and starting to resemble males like this one as well as Bluto in Popeye.

Archetypes 2, 3, and 4: Mr. Caterpillar in Disney's *Alice in Wonderland*; "In the Hall of the Mountain King" and *Anitra's Dance* from *Peer Gynt* by Henrik Ibsen; and Chernabog in Disney's *Fantasia*.

In his young adulthood, he resembled Robert Wagner. Before I came along, black and whites reveal a lean Calvin Klein model, shift T-shirts, slightly caved-in chest, slick hair—the cover of Harry Connick Jr.'s album *Blue Light, Red Light* is practically a dead ringer. Uncanny. I did a double take, Dad in the 1940s. As he aged and put on weight from my grandmother's amazing homestyle dishes, he changed into Orson Welles: froglike, pale-green eyes, sinister, always nursing his pipes and offensive cigars.

He was arrogant and insensitive, like the Mr. Caterpillar on his divan in *Alice in Wonderland*, puffing out smoky words from his hookah. "And who are you?" to my tiny Alice looking up, unable to make sense of his gobbledygook speak. This went on with every guy I had to deal with. Like Raymond (*Everybody Loves Raymond*) punting back to Debra's repeating the question, asking, "What do you mean (repeat her words)" I was nonplussed. Why am I always looking at some guy who is Mr. Caterpillar, Mr. Grasshopper, Chernabog, and so many more?

I can distinctly go back to when I was three, alone in my parents' master bed. He is peeking under the sheets. Above me is a Jack Nicolson, high-eyebrow, maniacal look. He thinks he is playing a game, but I don't like it. *But all little girls like it.* Well, not this cookie.

I remember the day he tried jealousy. I was five. "Well, maybe I'll just have to find another girl who does." I immediately thought of my cousin Rosalie, and it shocked and chilled me to have felt threatened by your father's boyfriend-girlfriend jealousy ploys clobbering my psyche. Something, many things, was very wrong.

By the time I was nine, I put the kibosh on whatever he was trying to get me to do. That was the Hunter's bookstore Beverly Hills incident. I was getting curious about how babies are created and asked the saleslady where a book like that might be. It was very ahead of its time, watercolor illustration, side views of the baby in the womb. Quite a beautiful presentation, but it also showed how the baby got there.

When he caught me reading that book, he yelled at the lady and dragged me out into the searing sunlight on Beverly and Canon. Soon we were at that corner across from the coffee shop, him leaning against the cement ledges. He was laughing. "You can't get pregnant!" He knew about periods and ovulation, but I didn't have to. I knew it in my Uterine Wisdom. The whole thing was sick, bizarre, and twisted. I said no. He laughed again. This time I thought, *Go find someone else.* I was done. *Come near me again, and I'll tell Mom.* That was my get out of jail ticket.

How I Always Felt when my Father crawled into bed with me.

143

Her psychiatrist had advised Dave and I were too old to be sharing a room. What he did not anticipate was that it opened the gate for the fox to gobble the baby chicken.

There is a distinct memory where my mother in her nightgown lit from the hallway, saying, "What's going on in here?"

Aww, he said, the kid had another nightmare. The irony was that he was the nightmare. I used to dream of black snakes under my bed. Now I know why. When I watched Dr. Christine Blasey Ford speaking of the gang rape she endured, she emphasized that "It was the laughter" that traumatized her forever. I identified: been there, know that, and she had my total admiration. Brava.

Anitra's Dance and Giselle's Grave

My father was a classical music freak.

He would pound the dashboard to Beethoven's *Symphony No. 9* as we passed by the nearby radio station broadcasting it. Dried tobacco rinds jumping in peril. A tailgater on steroids, he would bellow, "Crackpot!" and slam the brakes. I can't guess how many times I was catapulted against the glove compartment.

Being strong musically, I loved many of the tunes, but not as much as Lehar's operettas. Once he brought me the album of *Giselle*, the cover very dreamy with the Willies and the words Adolph Adam scrawled across in faded red. When I learned *Giselle* was coming to The Greek Theater with Alicia Alonso, I begged and begged for him to take me.

My mother didn't get it. "Sid, you love this music. Why don't you go?"

We went. I already knew the score and hummed along. I was not prepared for the moment when Giselle returns to her grave, as her betrayed lover cradles her toward her grave. She steps ballet style onto what became a live grave, taking her back to death. Her death. There was no second chance. If you hear the music as he gently lifts her onto the mound, it is too much to bear.

While I never knew how devastating it would hit, it was me with braids peasant style on top of my head because my mom reminded me, "You know your father loves the peasant girl look." I did not but went along with it because I knew I could be Giselle one day if only someone would get me ballet lessons. But it was more than that. A girl trapped in the father-daughter incest psychodrama is always between life and death. It is a surreal bad dream life. In some symbolic way I was watching my life, always returning to the incest's grave only to resurface for school, topside activities but knowing my home was an ongoing death. Just like the demon Chernabog became symbolic of my father and fathers of girls I knew.

Chernabog.[6] Beating his cobalt blue chest, horned and taloned, the embodiment of Evil that should never have passed the critic's muster for child material. I felt at once Anitra to his Mountain King and listened to it frozen on my brother's bolstered bed. The whole damned score was terrifying, a classical music score for evil. Somewhere deep inside I felt I had to dance for my supper. Anitra's dance is mystifying. But she does escape the Mountain King's clutches, only to face the demon on that mount. Evil, as male prerogative, as domination over all innocent and sacred life, inescapable, irrevocable, and ubiquitous.

He used to do that Vincent Price voice to terrorize me. Once, as a teenager trying to do my homework, he kept making noises to make me look up. He was in my mother's brunette fall, her black bra and girdle, laughing with tears in his eyes, like a little boy trying to get his mother's attention. I was soul-sick. Such was my school life, trying to figure out algebra, history, and science, with no adults to help me. My mother's response: Where there's a will there's a way.

Getting back to happy versus unhappy families, the very statement demonstrates a total ignorance of life on this planet. It is a naïve mindset perspective, devoid of all Female Truth. What I want women to know, respect, and practice is that under the Death Culture, there is no such thing as a happy family. That life in this sphere is inside-out, upside-down, and ass-backwards, and we are the

---

[6] Chernabog. Walt Disney's most evil creation, being half Mayan bat god called Camazotz, and half Minotaur. He was also referred to as Satan or The Devil by both Deems Taylor and Walt Disney himself.

ones—the only ones—to turn it back on its female axis. All child abuse screws with your reality and hinders your brain. You can reclaim and detoxify your lack of full authenticity via Phoetics. That is what works for me. Childhood photographs resound with our original Authenticity.

Sid was always faking in his transparent, obvious, evil disguise. His Predator's MO: "Nana Lee, don't you recognize me? I'm your gentle Grandma!"

I sure do, you bastard.

And my mother slept in the next bedroom, never to rescue me.

My father was the patriarchal archetype that kept on morphing. He was the Big Bad Wolf, the Grasshopper in Disney's *The Grasshopper and the Ants*, the Caterpillar puffing away on his hookah in Disney's *Alice in Wonderland*, the Lion in Saint-Saëns's *Carnival of the Animals,* the Mountain King in *Peer Gynt.*

My father resonated endless archetypes, but the most painful one to write about was J. Worthington Foulfellow, aka Honest John, The Fox in Disney's *Pinocchio.*

My Father: J Worthington Foul Fellow-Honest John.

I only remembered this when a memory became conscious when I slashed with a pen an image inside the book of this evil character with his sidekick, Gideon. I was in a rage when I recognized him, and it was all could do to release my ire when I was ten. It proved to lead to worse trauma, where my brother was accused and took the blame for me.

My mother said, "Nancy is not destructive," and I was terrified to admit I had done it because she would ask why, and I could not lie. What was I supposed to answer? That is Daddy and Davey and I hate him! Gideon the cat was my little brother, as Dad's sidekick and lacky. Our father would make him spy on me and report back who I played with, which lads I liked.

They beat him. Get the belt. Dave shared with me as adults that it was with a hanger. He took it in his PTSD stride. Beatings were "normal." Weren't they? They beat the boy and punished the girl with verbal abuse, sexual abuse, and neglect to the Nth degree.

Walt Disney's Version, Pinocchio: Animated, 1948—Every Pedophile's and Child Trafficker's dream

The whole animation is terrorism to children, in particular male children. Everyone is a child predator=trafficker. Jiminy Cricket provides psychic relief as Conscience guiding Pinocchio through Good versus Evil, Right from Wrong. Let your conscience be your guide, but this wooden puppet is naïve, impulsive, and takes any lure. (It should be noted that in the original Italian fable, Pinocchio beats the cricket to death.) No matter how you tell it, it is a dark, evil, anti-child propaganda tale, but then again, so is everything called a fairy tale or fable. That is why these stories were told to kids—control over us for the rest of our unauthentic lives.

Disney knew his audience. Some American mindsets bow down to the Sentimental and Innocence Altars. Instead of having Jiminy mercilessly pummeled to death, Disney had the "bad boys" punished. The whole story is about child trafficking, how it pretends to be innocent, the disguise of the fox J. Worthington Foulfellow. He is the first link in child trafficking Pinocchio will meet on his journey of "innocence" and wanting to be "a real live boy." When we see what Disney portends should happen to real-life boys who are tricked into going to Treasure Island, we have only to think of the internet and how children are innocently lured (never say groomed) who have every right to trust, and with no guidance and adult supervision, fall prey to the Honest Johns of this world. I know. That was my father. I will never know how many girls he abused, but I do know he abused me in my bed, in his mother's, in his and my mother's, and in motels.

If you go to YouTube and scroll through the comments about this 1948 animation, today's adults write they have never gotten over some of the most terrifying scenes that turn boys into half donkeys, only to become beasts of burden and die on Treasure Island. The entire film is saturated in child-hatred, and the only two females are the Blue Fairy, and Cleo the Goldfish, cramped and trapped in Geppetto's tiny glass bowl.

For me, as a child the only saving grace was the hope that someone in this colorized world of predatory males and child-terrorists, there was one iota of common sense and seeing through my kind of eyes. Jiminy dressed like a gentleman reminded me of Churchill because not only did he warn Pinocchio of the epitome of Evil as the smarmy salesperson presenting himself as "Honest John," but all the time I knew he was really the Fox, J. Worthington Foulfellow (JWF), trickster and child trafficker.

The image I murdered (See page 132): The fox, putting on his act of 'Honest John,' was drawn and painted with such predatory evil it shook me to the core. Next to him, his sidekick, Gideon, the scraggly cat, reminded me of my little brother, who looked up to this soul-murderer and at the same time fought with him. My brother was not stupid. But he chose to remain duped. And I did not take the blame for what was to befall him, and in my tunneled psyche, redacted what prevailed for thirty-odd years.

During the first five years of my existence in this sick and twisted male-run sphere, I heard and saw *Pinocchio's* theme every which way I turned. On the radio, the lyrics to "Swing on a Star" not only terrorized children but demonized animals on land and sea. Donkeys in particular were always portrayed as stupid. How I hated that game to pin the tail on one and refused to participate. Pin the tail on the evil adults who came up with it would have been more apropos.

That song played on the Hit Parade nonstop during the early fifties. I hated Crosby's voice, his face, his dark energy, and those lyrics that posited if you don't want to go to school, you may grow up to be a mule? "A mule is an animal with long funny ears, kicks up at anything he hears, his back is brawny but his brain is weak. He's just plain stupid with a stubborn streak."

Mules and donkeys are among the smartest, wisest, and most loving beings on the face of this planet. Between those lyrics, sung by the voice of alleged child abuser by his real-life son—juxtaposed with the donkey-boys in the cartoon, I had no peace. Don't get me wrong. The incest with my father was always looming, along with the threat of him crawling into my bed at night, but the day I tore into that image of J Worthington Foul Fellow and Gideon, I was no longer four but ten, learning how babies are made. My father was forever trying to cajole me into letting him do to me what I would not allow. No matter how he tried to talk me into it, with the usual predator accusations of abnormally: "Oh, but all little girls like it!" I stood facing him, feeling a Churchillian feeling. Put my foot down. And he was a giant compared to my size but I saw him as stupid, reckless, and disrespectful of all life, mostly the Great Sacred Girl and Female.

To have seen *Johnny The Giant Killer* at four and then at ten, Disney's *Pinocchio*, knowing I lived with J. Worthington Foulfellow, one cannot imagine how I survived a life of unbearable child terror. Not because these were minimized by SAs as "just a cartoon" and "silly songs," they were propaganda in the War against Children, to quote psychiatrist Alice Miller. Her pleadings years ago did not reach or impact the world because she was too much of an academician. In order to teach, you have to know your story. When you know your story, give it your voice. And I have come to see that when you add humor to any villain, it is a disguise to soften the evil within.

Children, abused and inescapable in their own private Treasure Islands behind closed doors of houses, churches, temples, schools, doctor's offices, and other places are thrilled to see the Giant shrink down to the size of the bugs he torments, paraded along in a caged wagon at the end of the film. For that is what these grownups are to children: giants. Either a good one, a loving one, or evil with many disguises. Not only was my father J. Worthington Foulfellow, but an earlier version of his selfish, cowardly character, the Grasshopper, sang, "Oh the world owes me a living." Unlike the Grasshopper, he never learned his lesson and never did an honest day's work. My grandmother was the Ant Queen, warning him what would happen if he did not put away for the winter, instead of him literally fiddling away. But that is another fable for the table of our Feast of Female Truths.

As sacred children, we did not have that promise of hope that we could shrink our giant terrorists. Life was either captive inside the belly of the great male whale, or back with a selfish old man who created us as his puppet, to sleep beside him, only to escape and be waylaid by the evil child traffickers, Stromboli, Lampwick, and J. Worthington Foulfellow.

My father was a salesman who never met his quotas. Fired left and right, coffee-klatching with every waitress from LA, North Hollywood, and Gardena. Words like quota, territory, nomenclature, and whining "they let me go" were bantered about constantly. When he wanted extra pity, his shoulders slumped, and his evil face looked just like the fox's. Playing the trickster Honest John in a tattered waistcoat, fingerless gloves, and a walking stick with an obvious faux diamond, he was the epitome of a down-on-his-luck actor. But Pinocchio does not see through the obvious disguise, as I did my father's.

He used to put his head on my three-year-old lap and weep, "Nana, oh Nana, I've lost her. She's left me." My mother's breakdown was his selfish resentment rather than a supportive partner. And thus, he used-abused me as a substitute wife for comfort and physical "love."

Every Witness to Violence Is a Victim of Violence

I could add more to that because it is a mare's nest. That is what happens in family units of Incest Inc. All the kids suffer. The following trauma was repressed to survive since the day my mother found the *Pinocchio* book with that image of my father and brother slashed to pieces with my pen. Only she saw two cartooned figures. She never saw behind the Honest John façade when it came to anyone but herself.

"You know your father loves you in that dress; pull the shoulders down, it's so alluring," and "Let's pin your hair back on one side and let it fall over your eyes like Veronica Lake." She pimped me out. Isn't that what little daughters are for?

The song lyrics of,"Thank Heaven for Little Girls," by Lerner and Loewe, soul-sickened me. "Those little eyes, so helpless and appealing" sung by another dirty old man onscreen, in *Gigi*—the novel by Colette about a young girl being readied to make a good courtesan (sex slave) in 1890s Paris. Really? Twelve when I saw the movie, I was so sick, how I held down the vomit I'll never know. What was this shit that adults proffered? What place was this world where we, the Great Sacred Girls, were pimped out, as if it were some honor to be in an arranged pimped marriage . It was set to music and costumes, so that made it all right, right? And don't get me started on George B. Shaw's *Pygmalion*, otherwise known as the musical *My Fair Lady, (the pimping out a great sacred girl to be enslaved to a dull rich man.)*

So she found the book and went ballistic. Borderlines do not have yellow lights. No ability to reflect. Impulsive. And see only in black/white or either/or. "Who did this?" howled the wicked witch. I honestly hadn't remembered doing it until she confronted me with the book. My way of lashing out, never thinking my mother would find it or give a damn.

It was an exquisitely wrought book, more like a bible, with white organza cover and onionskin pages before every eight by ten of the characters. The one I recall is the Blue Fairy, and I stared and stared at her for hours, wishing for blue hair, but the good slashing I gave my father I had repressed. Wouldn't anyone know it was him and Dave? What I never understood was how no one else could see the evil under the disguise. The closer the archetype came to her, the less she recognized it.

I denied it, almost losing my bladder. Knees knocking. Now hot on the trail, she would get to the bottom of this heinous act.

When my brother acted innocent, she yelled, "Don't lie to me! Your sister does not lie. And she does not destroy things. You're the destroyer!"

They beat him. My father and mother with a belt or hanger, holding him down. I curled into a fetal position, because it was so much contrary to my Character. I was the one who stood up for everyone. At school, anywhere. My brother remembers I screamed at the kids for calling Kathleen, the first Japanese student, "flat face." I went to the principal. That was me. This was the witness to violence that I was, but it was worse than that. I had caused it. It was a Nancy's Choice.

If I owned up to it, my mother would have demanded to know why. Nothing I could say would make sense. Maybe she would have punished me with more mental cruelty—silent treatments and enemas. The silent treatment for weeks. But to tell her J. Worthington Foulfellow was Daddy, who was trying to rape me and I could have gotten pregnant—could I do it? A time would come where I would threaten him once I learned my mother was told by her psychiatrist to keep Daddy out of my bed. But when you hear that any witness to violence is a victim of violence, think hard. It radiates out like radiation itself—poisoning mentally, physically, and spiritually.

Scary Tales: What Women Must Know

Great Sacred Females are the true Original Protectresses of the planet's children, animals, infrastructures, female laws, boys into manhood, and most of all—each other. For when women protect themselves and each other, it is possible to change the disordered planet back to Nature's original intentions: Femocracy.

Had I come from a family with a modicum of child empathy, or child sacredness—the horrors that befell me would never have stood a chance to occur. Had my grandmother kept me safe from her sociopathic son, I would have known there held a safe place for me. My mother had not yet been diagnosed as borderline (yet to be diagnosed during the fifties and sixties), or her cruelty behind closed doors might have been checked and stopped.

Had my grandmother done the right thing under Femality's laws, she would have surrendered her son to the authorities. Jailed, institutionalized—whatever would keep this monster from feeding off children's sacred bodies and souls. Grandma, to keep him away from the public eye, kept him busy with painting and carpentry of her apartment houses and her home in which my family lived for four years. Had she turned him over to the authorities, his homemade prey would have been safe from his taloned clutches.

Women on both sides of my biological family were either passive or submissive and accepted their victimization by their husbands, fathers, and the Forefather Death Culture, or Matriarchal bullies. No, I do not find anything positive about a Matriarchy, because an Archy is a system that institutionalizes a female's wild instinctive spirit.

Bye-bye, Patriarchy.

Farewell, Matriarchy.

Adieu, Oligarchy, Monarchy, Polyarchy.

The only "arch" for me is "type.'

Memories returning...

I dream I am his therapist, as he blubbers in my in lap on Grandma's chaise lounge. "I've lost her, I've lost her," he bemoans Mommy's breakdown. Suddenly, she appears. Grandma Mary, Matron of the Keys. Under the archway, hands on hips. Intervenes, pointing to the old school clock above us. "Time's up!" That was the message of the dream; when she could, she tried to end my father's sick behavior. Too rotten she did not her eldest son's.

To be a child of the Dark Force's Death Culture is a death sentence. We, who may be abandoned by our own parents, unsupervised in the cloistered walls of any Authoritarian Male Devised system dubbed as religion, schools, entertainment, medicine, sports, ad nauseum, fall victim to the evil adults who set up these systems/institutions for the purpose of getting away with child abuse.

In short, we are the prey these systems are designed for by adult predators, mostly male, sometimes female. When my daughter was in a taekwondo class, I watched from the sidelines. Her instructor was touching her too often, unnecessarily. When he asked for her to stay after, I pulled her out of that school in a flash. She was a preteen, his actions inappropriate and excessive. It was the '80s and there was no one to give recourse. These were the days when child abuse was perpetuated by putting down, dismissing any parent's complaints. It put me in mind of my high school gym class, watching the female coach touching the prettiest and most vulnerable girl in our class. Her hands' behavior, touching her on the spine, was a flashing red light. I marched my seventeen-year-old self to the girls VP and issued a complaint. Nothing would be done to take action with this teacher, perhaps a slap on the wrist or not—but she remained in that trusted position. I feel for any girl who was subjected to her invasive, predatory moves and pray they sought therapy for some healing peace of mind.

I attended a school where it was known that once a boy graduated (age fourteen), he got to go to the gatherings of a certain male teacher's home. Decades later, it hit me this had all the earmarks of child predation. What adult teacher keeps company with young teen boys? The tragic part was parents of these boys allowed it, trusted the teacher, and may have even considered it some honor. Like Michael Jackson, they would rue the day they left their boys alone and in overnights with him. These are events I was witness to and as an adult in RDFT, acted on. There was never a mother or father present in my life. But in adulthood, I would take action, watching my daughters like a hawk.

Pedophilia, Cartoons, Films, and Demonizing Women and Children

Do you remember *The Exorcist? Rosemary's Baby?* This demonization of women and girls sticks and metastasizes in our Female Brains over a lifetime. *The Bad Seed* scared me out of my wits. I was too young to see it, but all the grownups weaponized it against us, saying, "What are you, a bad seed?"

Watching any and all cartoons from the 1920s and forward sent shivers down every kid's spine. It has been said these cartoons were designed to fill time for adults' feature films. Whatever, children of all generations saw them—*Silly Symphonies, Fantasia,* and *Betty Boop* and more were female-phobic, child-phobic, and animal-phobic. The men who produced, wrote, and directed them used these moving pictures to terrorize the public with horrific images of Violence.

How do we as women overtake this Male-Run, Male-dominated sphere, Maleocracy (dubbed Democracy) and take arms to lead from our Great Female Leadership Brain? By thinking and listening to our bodies. It's ancient uterine wisdom, ovarian instinct. And how then do we accomplish this? We've been terrorized out of our Great Sacred Female BodyPsyche. We take the bold step to find, celebrate our Femality by Rebecoming our Authentic Female Selves. Phoetics offers a way forward by revisiting backward and seeing our story as our Authenticity. That's where our Female Power resides.

In interacting with an RDFT and on my own, I tapped into the truths festering inside me for decades. The more I convened with my childhood photos, the more my pen took on a life of its own. A bold release of toxic truths, which had been metastasizing in my PsycheBody.

The Bottom Line

We have to change, and that change begins with each of us, reclaiming our own Authentic Female Sacred Self. Return to your childhood photos, see what they want to say. Get a reading group going and try out some of the questions suggested. If you can, book a Phoetic's workshop or private session. In any event, reflect deeply with women you trust and be the Nancy Drew of sleuthing your original Authenticity. It works.

7

A COTERIE OF MEMOIRES

"La Senorita Nancy y Don Diego de la Vega"
Music: *Recuerdos de la Alhambra* by Francisco Tárrega

Nancy watched with most narrowed female eyes as Annette Funicello alighted from the carriage to the out-of-this-world-dazzling smile and bow of Guy Williams—whom in Nancy's imagination reminded her of her own father. The two were the same age, except the difference was the twinkle in Don Diego's eyes was not the same twinkle as her father's. The twinkle in Don Diego de la Vega's eyes was kind, self-effacing, almost Scottish in mirth; while her father's held not a twinkle but a glint—and a glint that was scary. This she could not admit to herself, for such an admission would have caused her to lose her wits, and that she was forsworn never to do.

Now that particular Sunday eve proved fortuitous. After the lightning bolts of Z clouds slashed across the screen and Tornado pawed the heavens, after she was certain her nosey little brother was staying at a friend's, Nancy had, for the very first and only time, *Zorro* all to herself. Yet in watching Annette with Don Diego, Nancy suddenly envied with an envy she had never known. And while she was only eight, and Annette was much older, Nancy was seasoned, wizened, and she knew it. More savvy and sophisticated than Annette would ever be, and she herself knew that she was the one who should have alighted from that carriage. Thus, their conversation would have really ensued:

"Ah, Senorita Nancy, a thousand welcomes to our humble Hacienda de la Vega. It is indeed an honor to have you here, at long last."

And Nancy, being forthright and utterly female arranging her black mantilla (black, it was always black) to allow the rolls of her Andalusian brunette tresses to plop upon her shoulders, turned a direct gaze upon him (unlike Annette's downcast one) responding in kind: "Gracias, Don Diego," (or did she say "Señor Zorro' as she could never quite make up her mind because they both knew who he was.) Should she play it for dramatic tension? It varied depending on her mood. He alighted her from the carriage. Not the same as when Calam's frontier fringed gloves encircled Kate's velvet waist, but then again, that was the Female Way, and Don Diego was, after all, not a woman.

The following scene found them settled on the patio, overlooking the beautiful Santa Ynez Valley as the Santa Ana winds softly stole in. The de La Vega winery and vineyards glistened in the somber early twilight; the swallows had flown back to Argentina, and the only sounds were the mesquite and eucalyptus leaves wafting like crepe paper streamers in the May Festival.

In the presence of his trusted manservant, Bernardo ('Nardo' he always called him with great affection), Don Diego proposed something she had been waiting to hear all her life…

"La Senorita Nancy, would you consider living here with my father, Don Alejandro, and myself? We could play our Goyas together, and you could conjure up the caresses of Ladye Santa Ana's breezes in La Noche, with your Andalusian heel drops and the curled fingertips were born clicking.

Nancy breathed in the heavily sage-scented dusk, pursed her lips, snapped shut her fan (the one with the black lace on the edges and the pink and black silk fringe dangling from its holder), and sighed at such an impossibility. She knew her father would find out and come after them, so as this was imaginary, she confided this to Don Diego, and he, in his customary fashion, lifted a quizzical brow as he leaned forward.

"Your father, Senorita, he is an excellent swordsman?"

Nancy thought hard. A rough-legged hawk soared in slow, hypnotic circles over the dark green looping vines in the distance.

"Ahh. No, no, Don Diego," she answered, the tip of her Castilian tongue clicking behind her front teeth.

"He is no doubt an expert marksman with a bow and arrow, a Flintlock?"

Nancy's glance was swiveled to the left as a monarch butterfly flapped its wings on a passionflower and settled softly home.

"Why no, not at all," she revealed in all honesty.

"Then it is settled. Have no fear, querida senorita ..." he leant back, crossing boot to knee, hands thrown open in all Don Diego candor.

"For as we both know," he looked deep into her eyes as she deeply met his glance, "no one can take *El Zorro*. You are safe in La Hacienda de La Vega... and all lands beyond." And with that, waved away the unsafe, ugly world in one courtly gesture.

Claro que si, thought Nancy. She would love to visit and often. The two of them arranged that in the early to late autumn, spring, and midsummer she would stay in her own special la Cámara and her father would never know. And never, ever find her.

Now, as the hour was getting late, Don Diego began to confide the obvious—it had to be said, and he was never one to stand on ceremony. "We know, Senorita Nancy, that Annette does not really know how to play the guitar, she just pretends." (Was that a subtle nod in Nancy's dark eyes?) "*Tambien*, we both of us agree how well you play *Malaguena*. Annette does not understand our ways. And you—who are so at one with Her breezes—are as much a part of this land as are we.' Nancy bowed her head. She knew where he was leading ...

Then, he remembered for her, that visit to Mission San Gabriel with her class and teacher and the patrons of the mission who believed she was just another child seeing through a child's eyes the high cathedral with its flickering warm votives, the arched lathe, and plastered passageways threaded over with darkly twisted bougainvillea; the Indians' rough, subhuman sleeping quarters.

And she, holding hands with Chris, she, in her midnight-blue velvet caballero jacket, and cocked flamenco hat escorted—wrapped in female love as they found their way to the counter in that timeless gift shop, where Chris bought the periwinkle iced-blue Saint Christopher with money her mother had given her. Blue as her eyes, it was. At the very end of the counter above their eye level, because they were only eight, nestled a dainty basket of glass vials. Around each neck sported an apricot satin ribbon; within each vial, the orange blossom water that each girl was given for a penny or free.

All this she remembered while Don Diego watched her listening to the winds, watched as her female eyes now, for the very first time, became downcast and rightly so, as twilight painted orange swathes, darkening violet into its final cobalt. He knew when to come round to her chair and waited for her to grasp her skirts and push away from the table. Wrought iron scraped the pavers. Nardo would clear the table with his customary bow of silence.

Diego, extending an embroidered caballero arm, Nancy's bare hand came to rest upon it as the monarch had rested on the passionflower. They walked slowly, evincingly as he escorted her back, over the dusty path that led past the gardens, dangling bougainvillea right up to the darkly oiled double mahogany doors of La Hacienda de la Vega.

The Monarch in All Hallow's Eve colors lead the way, crisscrossing before them, leading in a long-forgotten Female Code only Nancy knew.

THERE IS A SCHOOL...
Theme Music: Joaquín Rodrigo—Adagio from Concierto de Aranjuez

There is a school in a valley in a basin in a suburb. It exists in and out of time. On SoCal mornings when all the mothers lay abed, don nurses' whites, teach piano, market and clean, spank babies, dye hair; and all the fathers do the drone dance and sacred children suck and gnaw erasers on pencil tops, shoot spitballs in this sea-level spot of child synchronicity, a certain thematic tune begins to wrap in neat, careful, purposeful meshing all around its perimeters….Rodrigo's *Concierto de Aranjuez.*

Yesterday they learned of tugboats, locks, and harbors where the StarKist tuna cannery stinks in San Pedro. Tomorrow they will dance in sacred tartan spirit, "Road to the Isles" on the same tar that remembers from whence they came. In a classroom she will watch the powdery relief map mixed by the teacher, poured into frothy peaks and valleys as it hardens.

This Sacred Girl sits taller than the peaks and mountain ranges, looking down upon the green and brown tempera basins and forests while her sacred cronies struggle with the clay she effortlessly shapes—a Dire wolf here, a Giant Sloth there. She is the one they turn to, and she does all she can, because she sees what others do not. She rolls and molds and fashions, in the soft damp pliable gray oval between her tender palms as the strains of music weaves and meshes around her.

'Tis a sacred time.

Far from bear-slaying Bowie knives. Far from gunshots, gunpowder. Far from Flintlock rifles and Davey Crockett, 'king of the wild frontier,' one more mother bear killer. Far from more mind numbing Paul Bunyan and Pecos Bill fable. Farthest away of the place where girls were always dying like Clementine. Far, far, far away from ghost towns she must visit in Buena Park and in real life find how to survive—one more Great Sacred Girl trapped in a Death Culture consciousness.

No matter. She is an accomplished actress of incomparable measure. At the sacred age of eight she is fully risen and masters all with aplomb and grace, as Rodrigo remembers for her who she is. This morning in the school that resides in the valley in the basin in the suburbs, in and out of time, *Rodrigo* plays in her fingertips as she fashions one more dire wolf for the boy who patiently awaits his treasure when teacher is not looking. He does not hear the French horn's ache, does not smell the wild guitars, does not remember the rustling Bougainvillea whirlpool, knows not of a sacred hand of the one who is home to her. He can only smile as she gently smooths out the snout and winds the tail around her pinky.

She is well acquainted with the real wolves. She gives the dainty whiskers one last pencil stroke and places it in his eager upturned palms as he turns on his heel to boast to all his classmates, while Rodrigo is all a-weave inside her. And she will live to remember this sacred time. Live to tell of the real wolves, the ghost town, the mothers, the daughters, the teachers, and the certain school in the basin in the valley in the suburbs. When no woman receives her. No woman hears her. Yet Rodrigo does and will await her fateful Adagio return…another day, another time, another place.

And so, on this SoCal morning, while her mother lays abed and her father pretends he has gone to work and her brother plays elsewhere and the Wolves for a fleeting moment, are at bay, she smiles across the sea of classroom faces over the tempera peaks and valleys of the very land that holds them together; smiles into the blue eyes of her auburn haired Bougainvillea companion, remembering how they were at Mission San Gabriel when all the teachers were looking and did not see them engulfed in the goldengleam of FemaleLove.

Because like all the mothers, the grandmothers, the aunts, the teachers, the nurses, the women: they no longer see through Female Eyes. And though she does not know it, she will teach them how. Another day, another time, another place.

THERE IS A SCHOOL
Theme Music: Joaquín Rodrigo—Adagio from Concierto de Aranjuez

There is a school in a valley in a basin in a suburb. It exists in and out of time. On SoCal mornings when all the mothers lay abed, don nurses' whites, teach piano, market and clean, spank babies, dye hair; and all the fathers do the drone dance and sacred children suck and gnaw erasers on pencil tops, shoot spitballs in this sea-level spot of child synchronicity, a certain thematic tune begins to wrap in neat, careful, purposeful meshing all around the perimeters.

Yesterday they learned of tugboats, locks, and harbors where the Star Kist tuna cannery stinks in San Pedro. Tomorrow they will dance in sacred tartan spirit, "Road to the Isles" on the same tar that remembers from whence they came. In a classroom she will watch the relief map mixed by the teacher, poured into frothy peaks and valleys as it hardens. This Sacred Girl sits taller than the peaks and mountain ranges, looking down upon the green and brown tempera basins and forests while her sacred cronies struggle with the clay she effortlessly shapes—a Dire wolf here, a giant sloth there. She is the one they turn to, and she does all she can, because she sees what others do not. She rolls and molds and fashions, in the soft damp pliable gray oval between her tender palms as certain music weaves and meshes around her. It is a sacred time. Away from Davey

Crockett. Away from rifles. Away from ghost towns. She will deal with the rifles at the Cumberland Gap, continue to fall into catatonic stupors over one more Paul Bunyan fable, one more moronic Pecos Bill. No matter. She is an accomplished actress of incomparable measure. At the sacred age of eight she is fully risen and masters all with aplomb and grace, as Rodrigo remembers for her who she is. This morning in the school that resides in the valley in the basin in the suburbs, in and out of time, *Rodrigo* plays in her fingertips as she fashions one more dire wolf for the boy who patiently awaits his treasure when teacher is not looking. He does not hear the French horn's ache, does not smell the wild guitars, does not remember the rustling Bougainvillea whirlpool, knows not of a sacred hand of the one who is home to her. He can only smile as she gently smooths out the snout and winds the tail around her pinky.

Nancy is well acquainted with the real wolves. She gives the dainty whiskers one last pencil stroke and places it in his eager upturned palms as he turns on his heel to boast to all his classmates, while Rodrigo is all a-weave inside her. And she will live to remember this sacred time. Live to tell of the real wolves, the ghost town, the mothers, the daughters, the teachers, and the certain school in the basin in the valley in the suburbs. When no woman receives her. No woman hears her. Yet Rodrigo does and will await her fateful Adagio return another day, another time, another place.

And so, on this SoCal morning, while her mother lays abed and her father pretends he's gone to work and her brother plays elsewhere and the Wolves are, for a fleeting moment, at bay, she smiles across the sea of classroom faces over the tempera peaks and valleys of the very land that holds them together; smiles into the blue eyes of her auburn haired Bougainvillea companion, remembering how they were at Mission San Gabriel when all the teachers were looking and did not see them engulfed in the golden gleam of FemaleLove. Because like all the mothers, the grandmothers, the aunts, the teachers, the nurses, the women: they no longer see through Female Eyes. And though she does not know it, she will teach them how. Another day, another time, another place.

"There Is an Elderly Man"
Musical Theme: *Waltz No. 2, Dmitri Shostakovich*

There is an elderly man who resembles Nikita Khrushchev, but not really. He is at his morning ritual, reading the green *Herald Examiner* with his magnifying glass, sipping Lipton's in quick Russian slurps as his granddaughter looks on. She is not a moppet. She is not a live doll. She is a sweet, beautiful, sincere girl of four who wears the pinafores her grandmother buys at Helen Fenton's on Wilshire, and if they don't itch, she likes them, and if they do, they must be returned. She wonders what it is like to read. Her grandpa is munching his French bread he brought home from his morning constitution (walk) to the bakery. A few crumbs fall because it is so fresh, and that's what French bread does. That's the way the cookie crumbles, she thinks as he sips from Grandma's white china cup with the maroon band. In a moment he will scoop apricot preserves of his own making, and drink them down with his tea, Russian-style.

Their tète a tète is one way. Nancy is boosted up the only way children could be in those days—on a pile of sticky yellow telephone books. Sometimes she is a squirmer, sometimes she becomes fascinated with something and drifts through Otherworld's portal. She does not know the word Otherworld, but if she lived in Female Culture (she comes from Planet Female), she would be learning about it by this age. Four—the Age of Authenticity—has its own time-value. She lives mostly between two diametrically opposite suspensions. Time splits for her. Dimensions are her saviors from the hells she never asked for.

At four she is a maven of discerning fight, flight, or freeze. And freeze is the graduate course she has mastered, summa cum laude. She believes it is her own invention. Luckily the doctor warned Grandma Mary to, " keep the children away from her mother."

"I will not be held accountable, Mrs. Llewellyn. She is a very sick woman." Her mother is one of others Nancy knows as a Danger Zone. There is her mother's oldest brother, Uncle Al who threatens, "You'll never see Grandma again if you cry and tell." Kidnapped, and abandoned at the tire store back lot, after he tortures her and then pretends nothing happened.

There is her father, and floating out of her body leaving Daddy peeking in that Vincent Price scary way from under the sheets, playing a game she will never understand. When the room is still, and everyone has gone, when the blinds in the late afternoon make the room a film noir and he plays it like Bogie and Bacall, she transcends with the White Rock Fairy from the black cherry soda bottle, and they hide in Grandpa's humongous sunflowers' eyes. They, too, scare her, but she trusts this fairy. They snuggle here a lot. There is a damned good reason Nancy tries to hide in the bathroom when the children are ordered to play hide and seek. For that is the theme of her Dark Childhood: Hiding from Child-Seeking Monsters.

Under Nancy's Sacred Archetype...

When Nancy was left by herself, she was at home—shimmying and hoisting her little body up to her mini-arch—second from the front door. The whole house was unique—not just for Southern California but for that block. No one else had an entry, breezeway, and patio quite like it. Very much cloistered, it was built back in 1926. Now twenty-six years hence. Awaiting her sacred arrival.

Egg-shaped, lathe, and plaster, just the perfect size for a little girl her age, as if Ladye Fate had it designed and waiting for her since its inception. The breezeway that led up to the front door had four arches, where in the old black and whites, her mother and Aunt Sally posed summer gowns and bathing suits à la Betty Grable, hibiscuses pinned in their dark Ann Rutherford poufy hair.

Nancy's arch was second from the front door. The pavers were gray, slate, and maroon, well-sealed. There even was an Art Deco chandelier tinkling in the breezes when the Santa Anas started gently kicking up. This breezeway was entered through the porte-cochère, and down to the patio, more courtyard than patio. Bordered by the living room's hallway double doors and flanked on the other side by Grandpa's study with the American Flag that came unfurled on the right holidays. Nancy's big cousin Ellen remembered when a large fishpond used to live there; in Nancy's day there was nothing but a rough granite birdbath, dry as a bone with bird shit and the occasional shriveled banana leaf, blackened in death.

Doctors made house calls then. With their black bags. Nancy thought it was more like a Gladstone Bag. She remembers and recognizes all things British, Scottish, and Irish. When she turns six and seven it will all be in her body when she dances "Home to the Isles" in the May Festival, she will come fully home to herself. For now, it is just another morning like *Heidi* and The Grandfather. She will be Heidi during their simple old European *petite déjeuner* with his triangle cheese and pictures of ancient ships on each soft puddle of unsalted butter.

Later, when Grandma bathes the chandelier's crystals in Palmolive, Nancy will finally get to help. Nancy is not like Pollyanna—she does not see the world through Pollyanna eyes. But like Pollyanna, she appreciates a good crystal prism. These, like the drop earrings on Loretta Young, are good enough. Not like the Bellamy's but will do nicely.

Regrettably, there was no spider monkey to let in the window by the old upright in the living room. And alas, no Arthur Treacher to tap dance with. But if the spider monkey came in and started hurtling wet crystals all over the floor, she would not want Grandma to slip and fall on her back and slide while the audience laughs. Pratfalls were not funny. The movies always forget that it is a real body with skin and bones and nerves that get broken and scratched. She wonders why no one seems to care about the faller's pain, while in real life they couldn't even get up.

Nancy's sacred little white arch was where she hid and did all her choreographing, staging, flying (on the iron gate), and tap dancing from Shirley's routines. The sprinkler rod was her cane to sway upon, with "Broadway Melody." Darla's "The Love Bug Will Get You if You Don't Watch Out" was not among her favorites. She *had to have syncopation*. If only she had a staircase to practice on like in the Little Colonel's up and down song with the man in coattails, who moved like he invented it! Ah... da-da-dum! Tap-tap-tap! And now do this, tap-tap-tap-tap! She could hear it in her head and rock, rock, rock to it. Twist, twist, swish!

Once, Uncle Al yanked her by the arm for tapping twists called sugars dragging her to the tool table. "You think you're so smart wiggling around! I'll show you what happens to little girls who wiggle their fannies ..."

The Unmolested Hours

It wasn't always like that, but like all Great Sacred Girls, Nancy learned to appreciate the Unmolested Hours, when Grandma came out wiping her hands on her apron like Mrs. Bridges the cook in Upstairs Downstairs, half scared, half angry. "*Nancy, vere haf you beeeen? I am calling and calling. Come, let us make eat.*"

It was the Mickey Mouse Club again, waiting to see what would happen when Donald Duck came down from his last trampoline bounce. She did not like the show and feared she looked like Annette. She did not know why. Annette was much older and super popular. She also was learning not to like her name. One future day she would learn it was a city outside of Paris. And she would come to adore a woman who had the same name on TV's The Beverly Hillbillies. Some made fun of and most of all, she would consider herself in that pantheon of rare, tough, fearless, savvy young girls who kept company with only girls (chums) of her true namesake: Nancy Drew. The greatest of all Great Sacred Girls! "I Love You, Nancy Drew—Bess and George and Hannah too!" For now, she only saw her name reflected back as the Sunday comic strip girl: pushy, smart, with porcupine hair in that red triangle skirt. Nancy would never have a friend named Sluggo. Her brother loved to slug. Boys were always slugging girls. The day Richard R. (who became an LA councilman) caught her off guard and slugged her arm as they left on the school steps, she was terrified to go back the next day. He never did it again (more hiding), but she learned even the most seemingly mild-mannered boys could be unpredictable terrorists. Boys were mean men in training. And so, she kept looking for the place with only girls.

The Windsor Women (and 'that Margaret!')

Nancy's mother was jealous and threatened by every woman in the world. When Nancy grew older she would accuse her, "You're just like Sally! Selfish to the core! Sally got her own wedding gown. Harriet's was not good enough for her, no, but I had to wear it. Sally got a washing machine first!"

One morning while changing mother's bedsheets with Gram, Nancy thought these Windsor women were overseas relatives. Her mother and Queen Elizabeth echoed each other: on horses, in scarves, married in similar gowns in 1947, each with a sister. The difference was Nancy's mommy was the younger one. It was more than plucked eyebrows and permed hair. "That Margaret" was a woman her mother spoke of as if she were Aunt Sally. There was that time where her mother kept arguing about "that Margaret." She was a lot like the ugly sister Drizella, in Disney's *Cinderella*. Tossing one Photoplay over another, she huffed, "The very idea of running around with a playboy! *That Margaret* gets whatever she wants." Nancy believed Grandma knew these Windsor women too, yet held no more interest after a few non-gossipy groans. However, it was partly true. Nancy intuited all about the Great Female Family. It was just that the Windsor women felt more familiar than all the aunts and grandmas of her own family.

There was no woman to teach her about Mother Blood, the mitochondrial memories in our Second X. No one had to teach her about Femality, and the Female Brain (See: The Great Female Leadership Brain) was the Great Leadership Brain.)

No one enlightened her about The Great Sacred Girl as the root of all things. What gems carried within she would have to dig out by herself. Grandma used to muse they must have started in Spain because of the light olive skin and dark eyes. She declared, "Maybe we fled the Inquisition and fled north."' But Nancy's roots remembered Spain, and the Andalusian caves, and castanets and Scotland and the Horse People, the Iceni. She danced to many a tune at each May Festival with customary gusto (it was so rare when they got to dance). But the only one that thumped and glided through her tartan heart was the pipes, and fiddle lamenting "Home to the Isles." Nancy Llewellyn, right hand on hip, left to the heavens, knee bent, ballerina flat pointed, her crepe paper tam streamers rippling by the Santa Anas and could Highland Fling it with the best of them.

PART TWO

FEMALITY

PART
TWO

1

WHO AM I?

I am the crack of a Spanish fan,
the black echo of a castanet,
the shadow of a fringed shawl.
I am the admiring glance
of a butch to a femme,
and I am the femme's sidelong glance.
Yes ... no ... maybe ...
I come from a place
where violins begin
as sidewalk accordions fold up,
and spider monkeys are tucked in
for the night.
It is a *tierra Baja* place
underground,
under subway,
under Mother's sacred space,
where cave dances
are born.
I am ...
the twist of a beribboned wrist,
the cut of a French cuff,
the pause before a tango,
and the suspension after.
I am the Violet Spectrum,
A black satin pump,
The spindle of a well-turned heel.
I can take my femme to whatever ecstasy she desires
And then turn around
and surrender to
her long-lost moves
until I give her back
that tuxedoed moan

and get up and do it
again, again.
otra vez, une fois de plus ...

I come from a place
Uterine Born,
Female Cosmic,
where children come
first
second
and third.
I come from English Ivy
whiter than white Celtic sighs,
blacker than black African sheen,
and I give Tartan its hues.
Queen Boadica[7] tosses me in her tresses
Vita and Violet[8] are my progeny,
And I roll in on every wave of labor.
Who am I
I am Female Consciousness.
Older than old,
Ever renewing,
I am no 'ism'
I am an 'ity'

Synchronicity,
Authenticity,
Sacrality,
Reality,
Female Centricity.
So call me Femality.
And call me.

---

[7] Boadica, Queen of the Iceni, fought against the Roman invaders, daughters by her side. Burned Londinium (London) to the ground. Her bronze chariot statue is at Westminster Bridge, London.
[8] Vita Sackville West and Violet Keppel Trefusis. Famous love affair in 1918. *Portrait of a Marriage*, by her son Nigel Nicolson, was a 1990 Miniseries starring Janet McTeer and Catherine Harrison.

2

DREAM: DELIVERING
THE MESSAGE

I float in on steady, determined, sacred, white satin slippers. My simple robed gown flows into white cathedral light slanting from high clerestory windows. I am not on trial. The women in the distant bully pulpit are at cross purposes, what they always stir up—forever bickering. These women do not listen and cannot hear. They hear no evil, see no evil. Gaslight Speake. Women of a ⁹colander character the Dark Force snakes through. Their credo: Pretend! *Everyone must pretend nothing is wrong to not upset the status quo. Don't rock the boat. Keep us happy.* They want everyone to pretend nothing is wrong. *We are all happy campers. That is their drill.* Their jabbering subsides as they catch my presence. Their silence is confrontational and combative. No matter. Intuitively, my fingertips arise to meet high in front of me in the Old Female Code.

THE MESSAGE:

Me: "Never. *Never, never, never bow down to the Male Altar.*"

(I anticipate their old dark energy of Blind Innocence Denial mutterings of, "She's back. The Troublemaker.")

They: *But, but ...* they sputter...*The Great God Almighty! He knew!*

Me: He did not. He could not. *He was not in the right body to know any Female PsycheBody Spirituality.*

---

⁹ colander character-a perforated soul; a character easily entered and accessed by The Dark Force.

175

My calm fuels their fury.

They: *Liar! Traitor! You've always been The Troublemaker!*

I am no martyr, no Joan of Arc, Julian of Norwich, nor Hildegard of Bingen. I am here to do my Ladye Folke's bidding.

My hands arise one last time...

Me: Stay in your Female Body. (With a loving pat to my uterus) 'Here is where La Creatura resides, where all creation begins. You must think through your body, where our Female Inborn Truth resides.

My words gin up their already simmering fury.

They do not fight against me.

They fight amongst each other.

The scene morphs to a darker hilly place, paint balls flying in an old Dark Force Female frenzy. Total chaos. They will never change. No matter. I fulfilled my task.

Message Delivered

Dream Conclusion: Think Through Your Uterine Body-Brain (see image below)

WOMB WISDOM: THINK THROUGH YOUR UTERINE BODY

Sculpture- Priene, 5ᵗʰ Century

"Under patriarchal religion maleness is made—invented, mass produced; while femaleness is unmade—devolved, made extinct."

"For over two thousand years Western publicized women have been undergoing conditioning out of our natural powers and wisdom. We grow up learning to disregard the effects of our own rhythms which are cyclic like the moon's, the tides, and seasons. *We learn the habits of ignoring them, denying them, trying to forget, or overcome them...*"

—Monica Sjoo and Barbara Mor, *The Great Cosmic Mother*

3

WHAT IS FEMALITY?

What is Femality?

It is Female Consciousness. When I began my journey to find my story, the more I searched, the more questions cropped up. There was no one word to use when encompassing the whole of Female Consciousness, that it is the root of all things. So I named it Femality. Healing from child sexual abuse, incest—the first book Pat had me read *and do the workbook* (which I loathed but thankfully completed and saved) was *The Courage to Heal* by Laura Davis and Ellen Bass. If ever there was a groundbreaking work, a breaking the silence around children being abused especially by family—it was this award-winning healing salve for Adult Survivors of Child Sexual Abuse.

I had no idea it was Femality that was driving me on to this first book and then all the next, but it became a "calling" thing. What prompted these two brave women to put out there the very first book about incest and child sexual abuse-healing was for me a synchronistic steppingstone. It was the first time I found women who tapped into who we are, what we must do, and inspired by that I kept searching for the next book with that female focus. Time went by; I did the work. We went over it in therapy and in journaling, and my memory started to poke at my psyche. Traumas I had to hide and lock away thirty-five years were ready and waiting. As I gained the courage to blood-let all the toxicity that I had slugged around to age forty-one, it encouraged me to seek out more women who wrote about Femality.

The Great Cosmic Mother: (A must-read)

Then I hit upon the grand dame and most comprehensive of all Femality books: *The Great Cosmic Mother* by Monica Sjoo and Barbara Mor. It was the greatest blessing I had been looking for all my life. That first page nearly knocked me over with a feather.

> "In the Beginning, We Were All Created Female." This jaw-dropping moment was followed by, "In the beginning there was a great female sea …" Blinking over and over I could hardly believe what I was staring at, wide-eyed, and in print.

What? What? What? Was this real? At long last—Female Sanity Found! Where I come from. Mind-blowing that there were rare women who knew what I always knew in my marrow and *had the temerity to tell the Female Truth and publish it.* A brave shout-out to a world that in the 1980s showed such uncommon courage.

Sjoo and Mor took their work of truths deadly seriously, as Character, Calling, and Sacred Duty to women, girls, children, and the males who would deserve the truth. These uncommonly brave and brilliant women compiled a masterpiece of Female Sanity. While there are followers, it is a grain of sand in what should be on all the world's shore. Needless to say, few are the countries where women and girls have a voice—and that falls to us who do.

I discovered *The Great Cosmic Mother* in the early '90s. Today, more than forty years later, the world crumbling and pulsating with unbearable throbbing violence, Female Sanity is catching on, especially in the wake of the #MeToo Movement and the slow, ugly, unconscionable death and agonizing atrophy of Nature's Female Planet.

In *Women Who Run with The Wolves,* Clarissa Pinkola Estes tells us women are searching for a culture that will enable them to free their own true nature. She describes this yearning as below:

When one brave woman takes her work deadly seriously, tells her story, revealing who she is/we really are, other women follow, inspired to publish their own. (I know. This has been my process for more than thirty years, in the spirit of awakening, to inspire and support all women via the girls within them, for the girls yet unborn, the ones living in the Sacred State of Girlbeing now, and those in the future.)

Sjoo and Mor alone saved my sanity. From that remarkable book, I was able to excavate, dig, dig, dig, and connect what I call the Female Dots. What all these women authors have in common was seeing through Female Eyes with the character that could realize their calling. I could hand-pick in their indexing, notes; I was finally home, gained a far-reaching understanding, as well as drilling down to all that has been stolen from girls and women.

I was so alone as a girl. There were things I knew, things I brought with me from my female spirit origins in order to unpack once I arrived, yet the nitty-gritty was we all were flailing, and I knew why. Trying to live who we were in the Sacred State of Girlbeing, under the Death Culture. The world we arrived in was an artificial, falsely presented one. One ginormous and age-long gaslighting. The overreaching delusion of a natural Male Centric world, calling our home Mother Earth out of one side of their mouths and bowing down to male-created fantasies of what their brains wanted to be their punitive, female-phobic gods.

"In the beginning was a very female sea." "We all begin as Female." As I read these first golden truths, finally it was out there, and all we had been indoctrinated with were lies. *We* created *them*—not the other way around. I knew this in my motherblood mitochondrial X, but it appeared the rest of the world knew not, cared not, or just pretended not. The unbearable? *Women should have known.* Bad enough my own mother was female braindead—I could not expect it from her. Yet I would gather into my female embrace women like Sjoo, Mor, Rachel Carson, Maryja Gimbutas, Audre Lourde, Adrienne Rich, Muriel Rukeyser, Andrea Dworkin, Kathie Carlson, and others.

Female is the root, the beginning of all things. Ours is a Female *Uterverse*. The arrogance of the male mindset persuaded to coopt Female-knowing (PsycheBody) and female-discovered was a backhanded slap in the face. They could know nothing about Female, yet dictated everything to our psyche and body—and was evil. And I was living it. We all were.

Sjoo and Mor carried, knew, and told the Female Truth: *In the beginning we created them, not the other way around.* Gaslighting was going on long before gas lights were invented. To be fair, women are no different when it comes to lying, cheating, and flipping their secrets inside out. It is just that we do it on a different scale and with a different agenda. Ours is rare. Dark Force Females exist just as Dark Force Males. Evil knows no gender, yet it recognizes a colander character, a perforated soul.

This still cannot change the Female Truth: We all begin Female. And when the great self-propagating (gynandrous) female sea had to find a new way to reproduce on land—Female Nature came up with a short-lived solution. "A phallus male to perform special tasks and then die away ..."

This is no theory but scientific fact you can read further about it in Dr. Melvin Konner's, *Women after All.* A man with a cast-iron sense of his own Male Masculine energies. He writes about how we females—the original and first sex created the male for land procreation only. To inseminate and then die. He muses how a female insect may "look back with a leery eye," as if to reflect, why did we create this sub-creature, only to have introduced a monster we could not control? (Interpretation mine.)

It reminded me of a session I had twenty years ago:

Me: What happened? Males are the cause of obsessive domination, and wars are boy-games. How did it backfire on us?

Therapist: I guess it didn't work.

So, with Femality as the root of all things, why do we not live and thrive in a Female Centric world? Why is Mother Earth on the wane?

Since when do the queens abdicate to the drones?

A funny thing happened when the great Stephen Hawking of Black Hole genius was asked if there was anything he still had not figured out. His answer: "Women."

The Place With Only Girls-Starting My Journey

Scene: In my father's '53 two toned Chevy

Red and white, white sidewalls with three steel-scooped-out holes on the fins, I plot how I am going to ask The Big Question. Something in me knew it was big, or might be—that was in my female psyche. So under the porte-cochere I sat choking on my father's pipe smoke, trying to gulp whatever air I could reach. Pointless, as this was LA and the air was as toxic as his stinking tobacco saturated car.

Me: Daddy, is there a place with only girls?

Him: (Poking tobacco back into his Old King Cole bowl with his thumb) No.

In the background, Vince Scully drones on about Farmer John's All Beef Wieners (I know.) All I remember is I kept imploring him because all I wanted was to find Home. My home. That female-run, female-centric sphere. Of course, what ensued was the usual drill: he obsessed with the poking of pipe cleaners, find his rumpled yellow envelope of rinds, while I kept praying there existed this place. It had to.

Me: Daddy. Where is the place with only girls?

Him: Gone.

Me: Where?

Him: An island.

Me: Can I go there? Just to see?

Him: Nope.

Blowing out the stem of his pipe I thought of Old King Cole, not knowing his only pathetic reference was Sappho and the Isle of Lesbos. Lesbians. The male mindset's idea of women who got it on with each other, thereby rejecting them as fully blown cosmic earthly beings.

Forty years later I found myself telling my therapist, what My question was: where is the land of Female Consciousness? Find me Femality. Find me Queenie's world. I don't want to live here anymore. There must be something that fits girls."

In the fifties it became obvious. A terrible sinking feeling dashed with every hope—that this was not to be. Like all girls I was stuck with moms, teachers, women in general and the fools, female-braindead ones in my biological family who neither questioned nor felt the burning rage against the artificial mechanistic-male-centric world we were consigned to.

There were countries where they had no freedom to escape, but we were different. Weren't we? The hellish part was that I was the only one who seemed to see it all through Female Eyes.

What hurt the most was coming into my teens and early twenties and the shocking misogynist, racist behavior of hypocritical women of the "women's movement" who treated women as "other," meaning not of their middle- to upper-class, color, or sexual orientation. That was so insane I found myself enraged at Betty Friedan. I was only in my early twenties, but to call Real Deal Females a Lavender Menace—when they were the RDFs who worshipped at the altar of Femality's Truths, Our Great Sacred Female PsycheBody was unconscionable. How dare they in their ivory college towers segregate any woman from their Female Lib movement? Is that what we needed? More of the same, just from the greedy, meanspirited, ego-driven women who would never know better. Character. Character. Character turns a Female Brain into a submissive Dark Force Female.

Years went on, and in the 1980s and '90s I met their betters. Muriel Rukeyser. Audre Lorde in *Warrior* sharing her story with her signature boldness and female spirit. Adrienne Rich and her oft-quoted "wildly unmothered" courage to name what it was that drove us all to madness or suicide or both. Those were my peeps, but by the turn of this century, some were gone. They were of my mother's generation and the irony must be shared.

My mother tried to drill into me: "Never trust a woman. In fact, the only woman you can ever trust is your own mother."

The tragic truth was the opposite. Small wonder I had to keep it close to my heart. Would never show my cards to her or anyone else, but that is another Female Tale.

Femality: root of all things is the fact-based premise of this book's theme.

Femality leads us to write the book you always wanted to read, yes? No one will tell you it may take the rest of your life or a few decades, or just a few years. Still, *at least you will know who you are.* Without knowing, meeting, becoming acquainted with the Original You who arrived here, you merely just exist. *To be or not to be. That is always the question.*

Femality is Female Reality. Femality's Foundation: Children come first, second, and third. Honor Thy Child. The Great Sacred Child. It teaches adults as parents, teachers, caretakers that we must first earn the respect and reverence from their children, honoring them first. That is the proper order. The Great Sacred Girl is the root of all things. She alone represents the Primacy of Femality: No female, no life.

Chapter 3 Women's Bodies Link the Personal to the Cosmic

Women have a privileged cosmic connection because of their bodily rhythmic cycles of menstruation and pregnancy. Kristeva believes that sensing this link between the personal and the cosmic can lead to what she calls jouissance, a term we might express as joy ecstasy and perhaps serenity. When women are fully in touch with the experience of their own bodies, they can reclaim the full power within and use that power ... to reveal the mystery it is to transform themselves and our culture. French feminist, Julia Kristeva in The Once & Future Goddess pages 306-7

Literary critic Alice Jardine picks up on this sacred truth...

When women allow themselves to think about their own intuitive feel for Time rather than accepting the linear, departure and arrival time sense of the modern male organized world. What they discover is something much older. Because menstruation cycles link them more closely to natural cycles than men, women hold a key to the past that men do not have. (The Once & Future Goddess Page 306.)

This exclusively female vantage point enables women to touch these two forms of time consciousness—that men as non-menstruating creatures can discern only with greater difficulty." Jardine concludes, "This is the infinite, unbounded and all-encompassing tie the mystics try always unsuccessfully, to describe. (Italics added. Gadon 1987, 288–9. (italics added)

Finally, someone tells it like it is. What I felt something was not right The Place with Only Girls. As young as four, my female leadership brain already knew and intuited what is best expressed below:

> "A woman's body is sacred not to some distant deity or to an institutionalized religion—but to herself. A woman's right to control her body, her sexuality, and her reproduction is basic to the recovery of woman's full humanity.
>
> Womens' wombs are their power centers, not just symbolically but in physical fact. When we say we act from our guts, from our deepest instincts this is what we are speaking of. *The power of our womb has been stolen from us.*" (Gadon, Reemergence of the Goddess; Pages 288-9. 1987). (*Italics added*)

The Great Female Leadership Brain

We Must Think through Our Bodies—But First, We Must Be Fully In Them

"I am really asking whether women cannot begin, at last, to think through the body, to connect what has been so cruelly disorganized—our great mental capacities, hardly used; our highly developed tactile sense; our genius for close observation; our complicated, pain-enduring, multi-pleasured physicality."

Adrienne Rich, the great feminist visionary writer and influencer lived in a different time and still hit upon the nitty-gritty of the Two Primary Female Essentials we are missing. Our Uterine Psyches—forever on the defensive focused on rape and unwanted impregnation, pregnancy wanted with all the highs and lows over nine long months, the challenges giving birth, the way this precludes a decent livelihood, when the gifted skills we carry are seldom accepted as invaluable, let alone leading the domestic scene—all the eras before Rich became a mother of sons in the fifties continues today. It is baked into the Death Culture and new generation are helping to change it but need more answers and guidance. Those answers and guidance reside within us.

While our times they are a-changin', it will take many decades to guide males to find their comfortable place in this sphere—divorced from the Patriarchal Toxins of the Breadwinner, the Warrior, the Rescuer, the Womanizer, etc. If we care about males, we will take care of Authenticity. It is up to us, our task to return their due, to feel important by Femality, we must return to our Uterine Psyche.

On Thinking through our Sacred Uterine PsycheBody

If you kid yourself that you are fully in your sacred female body, think again. No one can be one hundred percent. This is not a safe sphere. As long as the Male Brain-Body rules the planet.

In his landmark book, *Women after All*, Melvin Konner MD puts it succinctly. A father of daughters, and secure in his own male masculinity, he sends us a chilling, critical warning. "We must give up the illusion that men and women are the same ... *we cannot develop daughters into the roles for which they are destined ... unless they fully understand males and how males are different.*" (italics added.) Casting a broad beam of truth-to-consciousness, confirms that, "Males' two traits are *violence and driven sexuality,*" yet in fairness stresses that, "The excesses of male violence would never have been needed, were it not for the fact of *other* males' violence."

"As for male sexuality ... detached from relationships and affection ... intertwined with violence, make it a force that *women should respect and fear.*" Lest the reader infer that women should allow that force to control them, he clarifies that, "On the contrary, *they* must control *it,* and that starts with *wary understanding.*" (Italics added.)

Konner's warning to women is to be aware. Wake up. For you and your daughters. Abandon the Male Altar, and heed this warning. It will stand you in good stead and save your life and the girls and boys in your orbit.

Intersection of Rich's and Konner's Insights

Rich's and Konner's higher knowledge intersect on the plane of Female Rights and the impact of Male existence. Rich's, from having lived the Sacred State of Female Being under the Death Culture; Konner's from rarified perceptions and truths from a male whose Character supersedes/transcends his Male Brain.

What does this mean, then? I take it to mean that to think through our body, a gargantuan task as it's never safe to be fully in our body, we must not give up. I believe facing Konner's *wary understanding* is the only way to conquer, return, and deliver this destructive testosterone sphere, back to its Original, Natural, Authentic Female Centrality.

This piggybacks on the child who covers her eyes, thinking you won't see her. Isms. Isms are prisms of hidden darkness. Isms rely upon conformity, group attraction as opposed to individual thinking, all those institutions of nationalities, religions, and male-driven written and enforced laws, the mandates dictating what we superior females can and cannot do with our own sacred bodies. This has been the hardest, most challenging chapter because it required synthesizing these two realities. We cannot take control of our bodies while our bodies walk the tightrope of FFF (fight, flight, or freeze).

What may feel like a catch 22 must become a triumph. And that means to return to our sacred female PsycheBody via the only way possible: Real Deal Female Therapists, the choice adjunct process of EMDR (moving PTSD out of the Trauma Zone and processing it into consciousness memory, ridding ourselves of the constant triggers and intrusions), and Phoetics—the route back to original Authenticity. Phoetics opens the paths in the crystalline tunnels of The Great Sacred Girlbeings we were—before we were indoctrinated, gaslit, brainwashed by those who obey the Death

Culture (consciously or subconsciously), physically, emotionally and most of all, spiritually.

Spiritually is always the answer. Phoetics is its guide.

If your spirit desires to Rebecome its original Authenticity, Phoetics help you tap into the super strength and Female Power that you arrived with and within. The particular elation that comes after sessions—whether it is a session where all the others bring you to this epiphany elation, or begins at the beginning—you will remember who you really were, the you so misaligned by family, community, and Death Culture. When we do this, we return fully to our Female Bodies. When we return to our Female Bodies, we return to each other, Rebecome our Authentic Female Selves, bonded, trusting, living in Femality's sacred MotherDaughter Love rebecoming the Great Sacred Female Family. Then the world of Female Centricity gains momentum and takes flight.

Adrienne Rich understood what had to happen yet did not possess the answers to how we got there. I remain indebted to her words, which buttress, bolster my platform of Phoetics for Female Centricity. She understood the critical, key first step to changing this decaying world: "We need to imagine a world in which every woman is the presiding genius of her own body. In such a world, women will truly create life, bring forth not only children (if we choose) but the visions, and the thinking necessary to sustain, console, and alter human existence—a new relationship to the universe. Sexuality, politics, intelligence, power, motherhood, work, community, intimacy, will develop new meanings; thinking itself will be transformed. This is where we must begin."

In rightful conclusion, she wraps it up with a platinum bow: "Imagine a world in which every woman is the presiding genius of her own body. I am convinced that "there are ways of thinking that we don't yet know about ... *I know of no woman—virgin, mother, lesbian, married, celibate— whether she earns her keep as a housewife, a cocktail waitress, or a scanner of brain waves—for whom the body is not a fundamental problem: its clouded meanings, its fertility, its desire, its so-called frigidity, its bloody speech, its silences, its changes and mutilations, its rapes and ripening. There is for the first time today a possibility of converting our physicality into both knowledge and power. Physical motherhood is merely one dimension of our being." (Italics added).*

Thank you, Adrienne Rich. We have already begun and will never give in, never give up.

4

AGES AND STAGES OF FEMALITY & THE GREAT FEMALE LEADERSHIP BRAIN

PART TWO: THE GREAT FEMALE LEADERSHIP BRAIN & FEMALITY

The Great Female Leadership Brain

In 2006 I finally found a book dedicated solely to the female brain. Ecstatic. It connected so many long lost Female Dots. Louann Brizendine, M.D. took the time to value, address and share with us and the rest of the world how and why females do what we do, and how we see the world through a female perspective brain.

Throughout her book she offers facts, reasons, definitions, observations of how the female brain develops en utero, from birth through childhood. I wanted to know why I felt so odd around boys, and there were the answers and explanations about what makes the Female Brain so different from the Male Brain. And the weirdness I went through in trying for forge relationships:

Why was it we spoke a foreign language? Why did they slug you out of the blue? Why were things more peaceful and creative with girls and why do I –the introvert—feel more at home with one girl, better than a large group? Earlier in therapy I learned from the original *Please Understand Me book*[1] that although I was an actress and could feel at home in front of any audience, in character or giving a speech—I was an introvert. Most actors are. We draw our energies one on one. As a female with a female brain, it quadrupled.

The Female Brain² filled in so many blanks that desperately needed sharing with all women. Especially since our authentic female self is the original mammalian brain-body. Here is what I learned. Certain scientific facts come from the biological truths of our original double XX. Because we do not lose the second X—that is the key. In a nutshell, she relates:

"It's not as if we all start off with the same brain structure. They (female and male) are different by nature." Already, I am exhaling. Finally validated. "What if the communication center …and emotional memory center is bigger than the other? What if one brain develops a greater ability read cues in people than another? You would have a person whose reality dictated that communication, connection, emotional sensitivity, and responsiveness were the primary values. This person would prize these qualities about all others and be baffled by another…with a brain that didn't grasp the importance of these qualities." And then, the female truth I intuited since birth: "In essence, you would have someone with a female brain."

Not found in any book. Not taught in school. Not passed down by grandmother to mother to daughter throughout the ages. Blank spaces with the scientific facts from the first eighteen weeks of a female's development all the way through early childhood. I especially enjoyed learning how girls interact, (play, negotiate, communicate) as compared to boys brains and why.

Certainly it explained an incident that happened in first grade when I was walking out of school. In the middle of chatting, the boy[10] walking beside me, slugged me in the arm. What was so unreal about it was the shock of it all. I shook like a leaf. Petrified when I got home, scared to go back to school, was told by my mother "Boys do that when they like you." What floored me was this kid was not a known bully. Just a neutral guy. What had happened? Sixty years later I found the answers in Dr. B's book, and it all made sense.

---

[10] He became a city councilman

THE KEY DIFFERENCE IN THE FEMALE AND MALE BRAIN

In the 8th week of gestation, the XX female brain changes to male by the androgen switch flooding the fetus brain with testosterone. The second X shrink losing one leg and becomes a Y. This will determine a males behavior as opposed the female's. Boys are cheated out of the empathy factor and the very way they communicate is diametrically different from girls.

"Until eight weeks old every fetal brain looks the same—female is nature's default gender setting. A huge testosterone surge beginning in the eighth week will turn this unisex brain by killing off some cells in the communication centers and growing more cells in the sex and aggression centers. If the testosterone surge doesn't happen, the female brain continues to grow unperturbed. The fetal girl's brain cells sprout more connections in the communication centers and areas that process emotion."

Finally. I had an answer. Small wonder I found it so frustrating to connect, be heard and seen by boys the same way girls did. Not only did girls hear and see you, you both were not the 'other.' That did not guarantee any girl would understand me speaking in metaphors, but there were less moments of blank faces, and disinterest. Again, Dr. B validated my female experiences at an early age, saying that, "This girl will grow up to be more talkative than her brother. *These communication centers define out innate biological destiny and coloring the lens of each through which each of us views and engages in the world.*" (Italics added.)

I have come to understand that boys deserve our authentic, fully integrated selves as much as girls, because when we know how we roll, only then can we teach, role model, appreciate and support the boys we come in contact with, leaving new perceptions the rest of their lives. And the same goes for males of all ages, because it is never too late to forge better relationships between women and men.

1. Please Understand Me, David Keirsey and Marilyn Bates 1978
2. The Female Brain, Louann Brizendine, M.D 2006

Birth to four: You are born with a character; it is chosen a gift from the Fates, your Guardians, upon your birth. The child tries to live in the world she is born into and the world she has come from. Age four: The Age of Authenticity. We tap into using our Nondominant and Dominant hands.

Ages and Stages of Sacred Female Consciousness : From Seven to Nine, We Turn on a Dime

Age seven: Female Masculine energies arise. Body starts to leave earliest childhood, first loss of teeth, becoming more angular and cautiously spontaneous. The Death Culture looms in our family of origin, and the outer worlds of school, social media, books, and movies.

Age eight: Female Feminine energies rise to consecrate our sacred Masculine energies.

Age nine: The Sacred Union of Female Masculine and Female Feminine Energies. The natural urge to Female Wholeness is activated. Like a double helix, a centrifugal force, in harmonic tandem. Girls reenact this Cosmic Female Reunion in countless ways. Females are born with this knowledge. We may not know it consciously. Nevertheless, we perform these rituals as a precursor to Female Wholeness. Integration is always moving in our subconscious.

Nine: The Number of Femality

Nine months to carry a baby. Nine planets thus far in the solar system. Nine is three times three. Three is the oldest number of magic, of transformation. Three wishes. In *The Wizard of Oz*, Dorothy must click her heels three times to return home. Three times three is nine—the Number of Transformation. The Triple Goddess: Maiden-Mother-Crone symbolizes Birth-Death-Regeneration. Nine in ancient Chinese is the Ultimate Power Number (three times three).

A Personal Share: I was born on the ninth day of October, in the ninth month in the pre-patriarchal, female calendar with thirteen.

How We Roll—Female Body and Soul

The Body Female—Earthly and Cosmic. Connected to the Moon Pulse of Tides and Moon phases. We are Cyclic from Day One.

Our Spirit Ancestresses

Biology is not destiny. We are brainwashed, trapped in the Family Fallacy (or perhaps *phalacy*)? What the Death Culture uses to trap you in its spirit-poisoned Isms.

Your story is not about your family, though many may serve as the dark background that emphasizes and pops out the light of your true Authentic Self.

Image Is the Female Principal

Image is our first language. Subjective. Poetic. Truth. Dream language (i.e., symbols).

Image is subjective, in the eye of the beholder.

Text comes from another region of our Great Leadership Brain.

Only women know; no one can erase an image from any mind, let alone the Great Female Mind.

Eight-Year-Old Girls Make Honey, and Women Are Starved for It

Eight-year-old girls make honey. They do this in divine ecstatic female dance. They do this unattended. They do this automatically, intrinsically, innately. Eight-year-old girls know who they are and what to do. They do Female. They dance. Female Dance is the mitochondrial key that unlocks self-knowing. Music adores us; our bodies follow suit. No Dark Force can break our spell.

It is a girls-only, girls' holy rite. Our enzymatic ecstasy. I cannot put it any better. I lived it. I dance to it still. It is the Female Life Force: Femality.

This dance is like the Waggle Dance of female honey worker bees. When I danced with Chris, buzzing on the threshold of pure Female Otherworld, it was the early sixties when we rock-and-rolled to raw, female vibes. Female brain vibes only girls know how to harness into honey. I was hovering between life and death; one leg up to Snow White's glass coffin, while the other bebopped with her. I'd take the lead in my black flats and sway her in a back lead. Lead-follow, follow-lead. Her follow was my salvation. We were fortuitous.

Del Shannon ruled the airwaves with "Runaway"

Lead follow. Lead follow. My S-curve to her S-curve. Every sway, the female bee-waggle in one eternal swirl, the Infinite Figure Eight until honey overflowed through our hexagonal hearts. Instinctively we knew how to nourish, empower, enlighten our female spirits. We knew what and how to do what our mothers and their mothers' mothers may have done at our age, but now were wearied, gaslit by the Death Culture's edict to permanently separate us from each other:

"Girls outgrow girls. Move on. Forget. Forget about her. Forget and let go."

I never could.

Women Are Starved for Each Other Physically, Emotionally, and Spiritually

Women want more than anything to remember how. When I dance with a woman, eight-year-old eyes meet mine, and when we finish, honey flows.

She wants more. It has been so long ... doing the creative work of Female Dance is more than literal dance. Honey-making is for a lifetime. Female Dance is the surrender to our original authentic selves, seizing upon its ferocity to change worlds. My task is to guide women and teach them to guide each other back to the natural course MotherDaughtering.

Women are starving for each other, for the honey, for those times when we knew who we were left in harmonic bliss to savor our female identity.

This world is crashing, unravelling.

We must take the reins and teach men and boys who they are.

There is a way back, a way out of this madness.

We must guide girls back to the storied honey we had stolen from us and all women.

Remember. Hold on. Hold fast.

Honey-making is every girl's rightful inheritance.

Be a bee. A female bee.

Queen. Female Worker. Both.

"Bee" in eight-year-old ecstasy.

It's just a dance away.

Waggle on …

The Great Sacred Girl & The Bee Goddess

5

THE GREAT FEMALE FAMILY (TGFF)

Nothing has ever been written about the Great Female Family because no woman has ever truly understood who we really are. TGFF is who we are, where we hail from, and the direct link to our unique *Female* authenticity and identity. In our *Female* bones, we know that if we were to tap back into our true *Female* identity, we would have to own our own power. And with that power in full force, a long-lost power paradigm shift would occur. The world would be back on its original great *Female* Axis. We would become intimately, irrevocably acquainted with our Sacred Female BodySpirit. And it's knowing that males would gain and receive life guidance from us: real *Female* guidance, universe information, deeper vaster knowledge, and greater sustenance—intellectually, emotionally, physically, and spiritually ... to understand who they are and how to live, full stop. We would have return to our Great Leadership Female Brain, via thinking through our sacred body. On some psychic-cellular level we have always known this; males have always known we know it (and cower under the irrational fear of the magnificence of our awesome female body power), that one day we will awaken and act upon it. Well, rise and shine. That day is here.

Female Is Creation

Female is the center of the universe. Wise males possessed of a brain and body will intuit, honor, and pine for our guidance, have every right to. By women choosing—consciously or subconsciously—to sever ourselves from our female body power, we continue to sell short the good men of this world and the boys who deserve better.

The Great *Female* Family does not yet actively, consciously exist on this planet. We go through the natural-cosmic motions but without awareness. It's how our brains are wired. Empathy. Negotiation. Connection on the deepest uterine levels. And all under the heading: Children first. The problem lies in not understanding, protecting, clearing out the toxins and much more of our own Great Leadership Female Brain.

Small wonder polar icecaps are melting at alarming rates, the near extinction of the Y chromosome—the very unnaturalness of the world's deteriorating conditions to date—all are soul-sickening metaphors of when women sever themselves from their Sacred Female Bodies and therefore each other. I chose to tell all I know about the Great *Female* Family.

I will state unequivocally, unabashedly, and proudly that women are born to be together. Women are born loving their sacred bodies and each other. At age eight, we submerge ourselves in the intoxicating, ecstatic divinity of *Female* Love. This is the Great *Female* Force at the center of the universe. And we must turn around and return or this world will be no more. It is only that if we do as did our own female guardians, who abdicated their sacred duty of guardianship, *Female* fealty, *Female* love, that we cripple, disfigure emotionally, psychically, and spiritually the girls who turn to us for their sacred rights to be honored and cultivated. It is only thinking through our bodies, staying in our bodies, that we can validate, reflect, revere, and bow down to their sacred identity. For that is what every girl represents, what the Great Female Family is: *Female* Worship. And all the goddess returns and attempts to return, all the sacred rites to menstruation that women have so lovingly and powerfully tapped into, all the sacred witch covens and cults, all the "fuck this shit about pay discrepancies, maternity leaves" will never amount to anything until we return to the Authentic *Female* Self we once were and abandoned along the way to adulthood. That brilliant, spontaneous, and truth seeking girl awaits our sacred return.

What will you do? None of all the wonderful, sacred, powerful, insightful, brave, courageous efforts we make as women will ever make the Difference needed to save this place. Not until we come back to our Own Grounding:

The Great *Female* Family. That is the center of the Uterverse and must become the only place of *Female* Allegiance if we are to leave this place with a clear conscience to any and all future *Female* descendants.

And give us the ability to fulfill our duties to guide, support and enlighten the males we love.

6

WHAT DO YOU SEE?

Le feu

(To view in color, find online)

This exquisitely elegant painting from the Art Deco era portrays two archetypal women who embody the idealized images of Female Beauty in that day. The one, in a black tailored evening suit and cropped hair tenderly supports her lover's head, as her lover leans back, propped up on her elbow on a black-suited thigh. *Together they form an image of pure Female* Balance, which keeps the eye roving. The other, in an outrageously lowcut evening frock, drowsy opera bead dangling, delicately brushes a pale pink rose upon her lover's cheek. It is Femality in imaged form. Everything about it resonates ButchFemme. The background of Female Eros, a nude mermaid arching her back as she clings to an urn. Fireworks symbolic of what happens when female souls unite. The alchemy of Femality.

So what do you see?

Perfection. Arresting to the *Female eye.* Who are you in the picture? Are you one of them, or each?. Are you the both, creating the image that projects the magic? Questions worth exploring ... yet I see more that's going on beneath the canvas's surface and into the eternal primacy of Femalehood.

What I See

The union of our two sacred energies: The *Female* Masculine and *Female* Feminine. What the Death Culture chisels away from childhood until we are split down the middle—each side foreign to the other because we have been brainwashed, gaslit. This image is a sacred one, for this is healing to the Female Eye and resonates the primacy of female relationship ... MotherDaughtering. The principal essence of Female Love.

What is going on here *is a cradling.* The way an enraptured mother cradles her daughter, and the daughter, feeling the touch, reciprocates the love brushing a baby pink rose, brushed against her cheek, saying, "I am here for you." There are double Xs hidden throughout the artist did not consciously intend, but as always, *Female* Truth managed to slip through the bristles. Mindful of the artist, Barbier, was male, one may travel to cosmic truths if one is in that energy zone.

Tenderness personified, and despite its name, Le Feu (the fire), the choices of newborn peach and pastel aqua keep projecting a softness, even with ballerina pink fireworks raining down. I use this as the epitome of illustrating what our *Female* primacy is, and it does not change. (Online for colorized image).

Warning: If you see only through The Genital Eye of the Death Culture, you will see two lesbians from another era, or same-sex love as it is called today. When you see through the genital eye, the Female Eye is blinded by the cataracts of the Patriarchy. The male mindset. Would true Female Eros describe the rapture of *Female* Love? Whether a mother, daughter, or lover, the eros and rapture make our imaginations take flight—home. To *Female Centricity*.

As these women project the gentleness of maternity, strength of motherhood and daughterhood bond, it really is Eros and the primacy of who we are, how we love and women who know well about it.

In Adrienne Rich's book, *Of Woman Born*, Susan Silvermarie explains the exquisite, preciousness of this *Female* Phenomena.

"In loving another woman, I discovered the deep urge to be a mother to and to find a mother in my lover. At first I feared the discovery. Everything around me told me it was evil ... but gradually I came to have faith in my own needs and desires. Now I treasure and trust the drama of two loving women in each can become mother and each can become child."

I remember when I came across this woman's life experience feeling a pain I had no name for. Unbearable and obscure. If only I knew just how deeply it went and what it all meant. I would have to wait years for the ecstatic, warming, sacred sharing, and it was my task to discern its ancient truths.

ButchFemme, Embracing them

The most masculine woman is infinitely more feminine than an effeminate man.

—Harold Nicolson, husband of Vita Sackville West

We are all of us a unique combination of ButchFemme energies. These complementary energies are the essence of *Female*—and arise between ages seven and nine to sacred union. I have tried my level best to come up with new words for these energies but as yet, these do suffice. The key understanding being they are of Female Origin. Under the Death Culture, male mindsets are both intimidated by the Great Sacred Female with whom we resonate—and mistaking Female Masculine energies as *maleness*.

Nothing is further from reality. The male ego, which sees through genital eyes (the rare exceptions come from Character and Calling) and cannot have a clue as to who we are, how we roll, and what the ButchFemme paradigm is that lives within and between us. We are blessed. As I do not reside in a male body with a male brain—I cannot speak their truths but that will come through their own efforts. It would be wrong to arrogate my opinion on a reality I do not live.

What I do know is that I am blessed to be Female, to carry both energies, and even though I have been told life-long "You are the epitome of femininity," I have worked harder to face and embrace my own masculine side. It was cheating me out of something essential—not to take joy in it. The joke I used to tell was lamenting that even my masculine side was too feminine. Since then, I have the comfort I fought so hard for, in meeting that element my own brand and style. (A blazer, boots, slacks, and Fedora do help in a pinch.) Contrary to what gaslighting wants us to accept, the Feminine is Active Receptivity. The Masculine is active, in the world and comfortable with ambition, whatever its particular style/brand happens to be. Together they work in tandem. What causes confusion in our understanding is that these are not two different women—they exist as twin energies in every female. When female couples connect—it can range from ecstatic, to blessed, to anything is possible. Female relationships are MotherDaughtering, and like the ever-spinning yin and yang principal.

I grew up and down in the rigidly polarized 1950s and 60s. Women wore skirts, and it was a tacit thing that they wore them, the tighter and shorter the better, for the Male Gaze. Men wore the pants. The famous Edwardian saying, "When hats were of enormous size, and hips were hips and thighs were thighs." The post war era had a radical change and women could choose to wear suits and ties and flout it especially the aristocracy. However, the vaudeville stages and nightclubs, boîtes of Paris and Harlem had crossdressing female entertainers. Bessie Smith, in her tuxedos, Josephine Baker in tailored top hat and tails.

And the inimitable Lillie Elsie.

Force of Female Nature, Miss Lily Elsie

She could go from high femme in *The Merry Widow*, sashaying the stages of Europe in gowns by Lucille—feathered, flowered hats bigger than a battleship, to the wholeness embodying the ButchFemme cavalier in every female in *The New Aladdin*, with Adrienne Augarde,1907.

Female Masculine energies caused me so much consternation that at eighteen, I took advantage of free counselling and saw a psychiatrist at UCLA. The funny thing was, they assigned me a woman and I asked to be switched to a man. I shake my head today knowing full well why. How to put it? if you want to go deeply into Femality, you connect with another safe, smart, and mentally stable female. But I avoided those cosmic depths like the plague until I was forty.

My mother was not just female phobic. She was butch phobic, of which I now understand was her fear of transparency of her own masculine side and secret desire for FemaleLove.

The first image I ever encountered of the great female masculine (besides Lady Liberty) was on a billboard high above Kerr's Sporting Goods in Beverly Hills. Synchronicity gifted me with the famous publicity shot of Doris Day as Calamity Jane in the 1953 musical. There she posed, arms thrown out (singing "Once I had a secret love"), that wide-legged stance in buckskin and fringe and I was transfixed. All of three, I was obsessed with the blonde pulled-back ponytail, leather clasp that became a fashion fad through the '50s. My ballet teacher at the park, Mrs. Rowan, wore her hair that way. That image of Day in those early years—you can readily see in Margarethe Cammermeyer in a softball uniform. I did not know that my mother had a deep-seated fear of masculine women, but she made it known as the years went by.

Fast forward to catching *Calamity Jane* in black and white on TV as a young teen. When I got the courage to watch my female fantasy (the whole film, but that is another book), I caught a scene that gave me more validation, thrills, and happiness than any other.

Calamity Jane Musical, 1953

SCENE: "That Ain't All She Ain't"

Calamity and Bill Hickock are bellied-up to the bar in the Golden Garter Saloon, awaiting the debut of a real live burlesque performer. Little does anyone suspect that the person booked turned out to be a man, and the owner forces him to dress in drag or he'll be run out of town. The band strikes up. The wild galoots pound on tables and silence falls as Francis, petrified, wobbles on stage in heels in a green satin gown, bad wig, and long black gloves. He starts to sing, and all the men—drunk, or drunk on seeing a real-live burlesque queen—go crazy. What follows is an all-time moment of Femality. The men see a female, however unattractive. But Calamity—in her buckskins and fringe, sees through female eyes. Only a Real Deal Female can spot an imposter a mile away.

Bill Hickock: She ain't that pretty.

Calamity: That ain't *all* she ain't.

Through Female Eyes: The Inner Butch defends and
That ain't all she ain't   supports The Inner Femme

For all her buckskin, wild-woman attire, gunslinging, and pretending to be as tough as any man—Doris Day perfectly cast as the woman who sees through female eyes. Those who resonate a transparent masculine side there often exude a tender, loving maternal side, qualities we imagine as feminine … and we imagine correctly. Not what is perceived through the genital eye under the Death Culture—but true, natural Female feminine.

Contrary to how we have been gaslit, this Femality fiercely protective, receptive, and actively receptive. Think of the mamma bear and you will get the two of these natural female energies fast at work, protecting and shielding, feeding her cubs. Better still, The Great Mastadonian Mama, Leader of the Herd, Great Mother Ancestress of today's sacred Female Elephants and their precious calves.

The character Nancy Drew has it to the max. Her two chums (BFFS) Bess and George represent the natural Female Masculine and Female Feminine. Although her mystery novels were a product of the 1920s, '30s, and '40s, the woman who penned them was quite a feminist—by the life she lived. Millicent Wirt supported herself and her invalid husband as a staff writer at Ohio's *The Blaze* until ninety-one years of age. And birthed these encouraging positive image under the skeleton plots of her publisher, Edward Strathmeyer. She was paid a pittance because she was female labor considering her creations of what I call souls alive on the page. When a limited tribute-version came out in the 2000s, they began with a fascinating take from three generations of women who had grown up with Wirt's versions-visions from 1928–59. What struck me was the one from an African American woman who shared while Nancy was white and middle class, she still reaped the energies from Nancy's accepting character: that young women were smart, savvy, and could be as good or better than any theretofore male detectives. I concur. We as girls in the last century had precious little role models in fiction, save Pippi Longstocking who was the ultimate Great Sacred Girl-Sovereign

Pippi Longstocking, by Astrid Lindgren. Young girl, living sovereign with her father away at sea, with her horse she could lift with one hand and a monkey named Mr. Nilsson. Pippi, along with other adult Sovereign female characters, were all that kept me going and going insane and hopeless. Nancy—while it never hit me we had the same sacred name—was the first life preserver, and I laughed off her so-called boyfriend, Ned. Somewhere I read Mr. Strathmeyer told Mildred to add him in as filler because he was getting feedback that Nancy needed a guy to heterosexualize her to the readers who were suspicious.

Today this is laughable yet not. It is typical of how we are inculcated, indoctrinated about females who prefer female company are anti-male. Back then, I was deflated and pissed to find something that did not jive. There was a real paper doll filler feeling when he first shows up, and the stories where he assists in her discoveries do not ring true. George—her "soft butch" chum—is her true masculine side who serves to be up for anything to find the answers to who the bad guys and gals are.

There Is no Such Thing As a Lesbian—We Are All Born Women's Women

> Through its acceptance and with the emergence of a new lesbian sensibility, we have the opportunity to rethink the meaning of a uniquely female sexual identity. Women who express their erotic and sexual desires for other women have a privileged access, a special knowledge of the female body. Can we bend our minds? Perhaps that is what we have to do.
> —Elinor Gadon, *The Once and Future Goddess*

I used to wonder, what would I say if I were asked, "Are you gay?" My internal answer was always, *I am beyond gay.* It took me decades to decipher what I meant, but I knew it was spot on. Ages ago, all the pejorative 1950s and '60s images of Women's Women—those who lived at Female Ground Zero—jumbled and tumbled in my confused and tortured child's and teens psyche. I could not find a way to come to terms with what it meant. The demonization was the worst, but that is another writing.

I loved My Own from day one, but the culture(s) that sprung up around them scared me. Attracted to those who played softball and yet unable to relate to sports which meant competition, yet today I see that competition was not limited to sports. It was the very idea of any competition—in music, art, dance, anything that brought someone joy—was anathema to me. To dance like no one or everyone is watching was me. I was not intimidated by female athletes—quite the opposite—was entranced because I am an INFJ. The personality and temperament predominantly introverted, intuitive, feeling, judging (as in work before play) does not understand nor value winners because that makes losers, and we don't want anyone to feel like a loser. I would beg a close friend to please explain to me what rooting for teams was—define it, describe it. In the end, I was left as I will always be. Don't make anyone out a loser, don't pull the last musical chair out from under anyone. Period.

So without knowing it, that factored in subconsciously. These women moved in their subcultures and social groups and made true but self-deprecating jokes about their "incestuous pools" (i.e., everyone has slept with everyone). But I do not accept other's impressions. It is unwise and unhealthy. Still, this world of only females called to me when I was four and my pursuit of *the place with only girls* was lifelong.

Wise. Observant. Watchful for girls who bullied, putting them in the lowest common denominator with a boys' bully potential. Not all boys were bullies either. I was no fool. My mother was dangerous, and I carried no illusions that females—certain females—could be mean-spirited, cruel, and downright dangerous. My mother tried to hammer into me, "Never trust a woman ... in fact, the only one you can trust is your own mother," when the unbearable truth was the only one I could never trust was my own mother. She could talk until doomsday, which followed her like Pig-Pen's dirt cloud. No one but no one could make me accept what I knew in my very marrow. She and her jealousy could not keep me away from women, whom I admired any more than away from the stage. The one thing I knew no matter how suicidal I got: My *Can't Touch These* cards of those sacred souls and places to which I belonged. As I matured, I chose not to pursue being trapped in the biz, once I saw the reality of what and all a female would subject herself to, and even the smallest community theatre I encountered would have its own heady toxicity cliques.

Female Primacy is my altar. Yet women who self-identified as lesbian and/or gay did not know what the hell I was talking about. It was crushing. Devastating. Forced by Ladye Fate, I was to first live a very long time. Next, study and be ready to interact with those who accepted the Death Culture label of lesbian to finally grasp that all women are Women's Women. There is no such thing as what we are gaslit by the Patriarchy as their label lesbian. We are all born as Women's Women, meaning we belong first and foremost to each other, governing the world, and that men are an option. That is the Female Natural. Males see primarily through the genital eye and of course, sexualize and objectify us. Small wonder they came up with this word. Think about it.

They could only take it from that which they will never understand. Their brains are not our brains. And Female Love, the kind Sappho wrote of so prolifically and beauteously is not about "getting it on" with another female. She was exiled to the Isle of Lesbos by her own parents under the Death Culture of those "forward-thinking" Socratic patriarchs, whose vases, urns, and frescos celebrated adult males sexually abusing enslaved innocent, defenseless boys. And what did they come up with over the centuries of female phobia, born of envy and rage? They slapped a label on any female no matter what age, like any specimen, lab rat, a butterfly pinned to a felt display: "Species: Lesbian." She who loves her own kind, ergo rejecting us, the Normal Preferential Male Supremacy.

I honor any woman of any generation who cherishes this label as a positive identity. These are different times. Young women of older generations, their mothers, and grandmothers, who fought for their rights and the courageous act of Visibility. I am not so young to not recall the Dark Ages Inquisition PSAs on TV that warned mothers about their daughters who preferred the company of their own kind and not boys. You can search on the internet, and while today they could strike one as pathetic, like an SNL spoof, I remember when these were the dark-shadowed reality. When these female-phobic propaganda were very real. I could not dare approach and interact with my Calamity Jane-Doris Day-Margarethe Cammermeyer heart's desire. Besides that, my mother rejected what I thought they might—who I was, what I looked like. Untouchable. All together it proved a hell many girls of borderline moms in that era and other eras suffered.

These PSAs, deliberately shot in shadowy home settings, replete with the *man*datory menacing, male narrator warns mothers to be watchful if their teenage daughters take an interest in other girls. Chilling today as it was for me back then, the message was always "girls who love other girls are abnormal" and you must cut them off at the path of perversity. More than ever, it was depicted—this mother-daughter scene, in a bedroom like *Father Knows Best* meets *The Twilight Zone*.

Let me state for posterity for younger and future generations of females, that was the reality. The big brother of Orwell's *1984* was used to terrorize women and girls to keep away from each other—or else. Women and girls were made taboo to other women and girls. In school, if you were caught holding hands, linking arms—you were ostracized by all. At home, disowned by your families and friends. Since I already rejected my family, my fear was being thrown into jail or harassed by dangerous someone. Besides, the time was not right, for reasons of my path and all I would glean in the decades to come.

It was up to my conscience and trusting my inner sense of "something isn't right." Like the goodly Miss Clavel of *Madeline*, always sat upright, and "In the middle of the night, turned on the light and said something is not right." She does this because Madeline is suffering with a burst appendix in the floor below. She is securely bonded with her girls. Empathy rules that old house in Paris all covered with vines, but today I know—my soul comes from the same. Whatever was going on in this world, I wanted no part of it, being on survival from day one. But I never accepted that my coveted altar was the diametric opposite by the pornographic and pulp fiction books about Patriarchy labeled as lesbians.

What was wrong with women's visions then remains today. Take a good look at these covers and the words they use to titillate males. It is always about one pretty woman, dominated by another pretty woman, with a man (as the victim) in the background. I won't address the titles, but women who want women are characterized as Predatory.

When you are stuck with being a visionary, time is not of the essence but can be on your side if you believe all you are, where you hail from, and stick with it.

The Woman Identified Woman, 1970

Recently I came across the expression "Woman Identified Woman," coined in a testament from forerunners of the Women's Movement in 1970. They called themselves Radicalesbians and were totally right in what they expressed, but had no female language to reflect their wisdom adequately and accurately. They knew exactly what they were talking about and clearly saw through Female Eyes. They included Artemis March, Lois Hart, Rita Mae Brown, Ellen Shumsky, Cynthia Funk, and Barbara XX. While Betty

Friedan, President of NOW, badmouthed them with the female phobic slur Lavender Menace.

This puts one in mind of what Secretary of State Madelyn Albright warned at a luncheon: "There is a special place in hell for women who don't help other women." That is a Woman's Woman, married, partnered or not, with a woman or man. Any woman who makes a face about women's intimacy is self-rejecting of her own body.

The irony was, they understood in some ancient way what was the Female Truth. That all women are a Woman's Woman or born with the potential for becoming a Woman Identified Woman. However, under Patriarchy a real (i.e Normal) woman is deemed and defined to join the Male Brigade, by marriage, by national allegiance, by religious and social rules. Any woman who rejects all these institutional teachings and enforcements for her own life (refuses to conform to the Patriarchal Death Culture by betraying her own Female Consciousness), is labelled as Other.

My close friend—herself a Woman Identified Woman since the sixties, treasures the term lesbian because it invokes the Strong, Independent, and Woman Loving Woman she has always been. What it invokes for her does not invoke the same for me. I have shared with her how this pejorative label came about, and she gets it. Yet it remains in her heart of hearts, and I honor her.

What those "Radical Lesbian" women trusted spoke from their second X mitochondria's Glowing Female Cells ...

The sad part is that as these brave and brilliant women who signed an equivalent to their own Death Warrant *had no such female language with which to convey their consciousness. Not the way it needed.* There is no such thing as a lesbian is also true, but they accepted that label because it was the only way to express women who worship at the Female Altar. Often, I say that I live at the bottom of the pelvic floor. There is no such thing as gay for a woman or a man—because I come from a place of female consciousness, hence the female brain, hence nature's default. Ergo, the world—Nature, Mother Earth, this Sphere is not naturally male-centric.

If you buy into that, you can never be an authentic female being, your true self. This artificial male-centric world we all have suffered under for millennia is the reason Mother Earth is dying an unnecessary, tragic, meanspirited, horrific death. Which should be unacceptable under a Female Centric World. Women must once and for all refuse to allow it by becoming their RDF (Real Deal Female) selves and taking over via the power of FemaleLove and Authenticity.

So I will state once and for all: To be female is to love each other first, foremost, and teach the world, especially the males we carry, birth, love, protect and guide.

The male mindset label 'lesbian' is used strictly to divide and therefore conquer us. It comes through the genital eye of the Death Culture. And not come from the Great Female Leadership Brain, nor how it sees through the Female Eye.

We, the Great Sacred Female, as Nature's Default, belong first to and with each other. In order to better heal the wounded chasm—what has forever kept us apart, served as divisive and alienated. We must return to our Authentic Female Selves, tell, and publish our stories, build a world of Female Centricity, lest it be nuked by the male-run Death Culture institutions across Mother Earth's body— by patriarchs, oligarchs, monarchs, prime ministers, presidents, et al.

In the second wave of the Women's Movement, women still behaved the way they were trained by their patriarchal parents, grandparents, and sticky schoolbooks. Those white and middle class were racist, and worst of all—female-phobic. (This demands a book all its own.)

Women's contributions redacted—our accomplishments stolen by the Death Culture.

I recall flipping through history books at school, scanning and scouring for girls and women. Where were the women?

Decades later it was taught in colleges that Countess Ada Lovelace discovered algorithms, but was that in the science book? An English mathematician and daughter of the poet Lord Byron, she was the one who wrote the first algorithm for a machine in the 1800s. Her notes were hidden until the 1950s, and today she is recognized as the first computer programmer. The early programming language Ada is named for her.

In 1961, Mary Jane Sherfey MD discovered her Inductor Theory. She posited that "all mammalian embryos, male and female, are anatomically female during the early stages of fetal life." So why did this not reflect in medical literature? The males who dominated the field did not want it to be true and so locked it away. Nonetheless, their time was up with the publication of her book, *The Nature, and Evolution of Female Sexuality.* *One more redaction, exposed for the Female Truth beneath.*

Rosalind Franklin discovered DNA, but Watson and Crick stole all the credit. Worst of all, slave owners like President Thomas Jefferson falsely imprisoned (enslaved) Sally Hemmings in a brick basement like a kennel and kept her literally barefoot and pregnant. That ain't my hero—*that is the enemy.* But that's for another book. Not my forefather, not anyone's.

Gay? I see it for what it is. Divide and conquer women from each other, and from their sacred authentic power collectively, and individually. (Femocracy and Femality). All about the Female Brain and those who stayed faithful to it.

In her later writings, Adrienne Rich hit upon the nitty-gritty—that the primacy of all women's love for each other is not Sisterhood but MotherDaughtering. That is why I could not join them. They omitted the Great Sacred Girl; they omitted the Great Sacred Child.

They forgot to put the child first, which led her to speak about how women must learn to think through their bodies. I call it our Uterine Brain. Bucranium genius. That's who we are. Because I adore who we are and how we are made and love—as a Great Female Family and as individuals, mothers, daughters, friends, and lovers—there cannot be a concept such as gay. To use that is unacceptable, erroneous, and unnatural. The ancients were a Female-based groupings, the only reason for survival. We are the norm, the core of Life, and keep it going.

> "The Woman-Identified Woman" argued, "The primacy of women relating to women, of women creating a new consciousness of and with each other which is at the heart of women's liberation, and the basis for the cultural revolution." At the following NOW conference, held in New York City in September 1971, the Congress adopted a resolution acknowledging the rights of lesbians as a "legitimate concern for feminism." *(https://en.wikipedia. org/wiki/The_Woman-Identified_Woman#:~:text=%22The%20 Woman%2DIdentified%20Woman%22,by%20the%20 Radicalesbians%20in%201970.)*

Through Female Eyes: The Primacy of Female Tango

The *Female* Body speaks in *Female* Code. Every tanguera's (tango dancer's) body speaks in its own female code in its natural unique style.

Diana Cortès calls it 'The Echo in the Other,' (covered extensively in the upcoming Chapter 7). The Leader-Mother takes on the strong, gentle suggesting role. It is as if a mom is saying to her daughter, remember when I taught you this? Or it can be, opa! You followed so well! Opa! Since the nature and counterintuitive thing about Argentine tango is to never anticipate the lead; the excitement is the "ride." And then it reverses, where the Follower Daughter takes the lead, and the great bond of sacred attachment—empathy, connection—is played out.

Most women (not all) who learn the Lead start out as a Follower, and so it is common to watch them switch places throughout a dance. There is a feminine-masculinity flow that cannot be replicated with a male. Since *Female* is Nature's Default, and MotherDaughter lives out that primacy in those roles throughout a woman's life, all of this *Female* Cosmic magic is lighting up the dance—while at the same time, it is earthy, earthly, and deep into the Uterine psyche caves.

7

DIANA CORTÈS INTERVIEW

'I like to find an echo in the other ... and an accomplice response to the movements I propose.'

—*Diana Cortès, Tanguera*

How totally divine do these words express and capture the truth and accuracy of the nature of Femality? This sentiment—active, profound, and confident—comes from a woman who is a born teacher, student, and performer—in tango, in loving, in life.

When I first caught sight of Diana Cortès leading her female partner in *Tormenta*, my jaw dropped. Watching her was like hearing k.d. lang sing for the very first time. In a tailored silver suit, long dark braid down her back, her dove-gray shoes moved with the Sovereignty only women of the most powerful Female Spirit carry. The performance was pure, unadulterated FemaleLove and Divinity.

Her partner, in black velvet elegance, was the perfect foil-complement to Cortès lead; the divine *Female* Feminine in perfect harmony with the divine Female Masculine. Never have I seen such a symbolic grace and honor between two women on the dance floor. They moved in and out of shadows, though slanted cathedral light, in a filmy chiaroscuro Female Otherworld. There are close-up stills from these performances that show Cortès in close embrace, captured in sacred bliss, eyes shut, face beatific.

Hers Is the Face of Femality

Other videos of Cortès dancing the Follower role of equal star quality ... the High Femme in slits up to here, who leaves a spellbound glamor in her wake. Yet—this new Leader-side emerges almost unrecognizable. The walk. The shoes. The subdued condensed power. Many women choose to learn the lead even if they aren't teachers, but this was rare. My own teacher agreed.

Cortès was something rare.

So I asked her *what drew her to taking the lead role (Rol Conductor) and stay with it?*

She was as clear and crisp in her answers as in her polished gancho strikes, (leg hooks):

Diana on the Lead Role (Conductor):

> "I began to have a fascination and a special taste playing the leading role. I realized that I could play more with my creative part. I developed differently and I liked it and I

like being able to hug giving away a little of this love that gives me the fact of dancing tango. I like to share this happiness that I have felt many times. *And then, there was a moment that I consider* Fundamental *in why I continue to learn the leading role."*

Yes. I had wondered what it was like for a woman to lead, how she was received by other women. In today's same-sex Female Tango there is no machismo. The old patriarchal male domination-female submission does not play out. This was my reason for quitting tango so many times. No matter how quickly I picked it up, it felt stilted, all in the head. I could not feel normal. This rigidity of roles and the "right way" to execute a step just syphoned the sheer joy of *Female* Spirit right out of it.

She agreed and went on to explain:

> "Dancing with different women was the best school to understand how I could grow in my role as Follower. Sometimes I danced with teachers or *milongueras* [female tango dancers] who made me understand from their dance how I could look for a certain type of relaxation in my body. *I was embraced by women who clearly indicated a distance to me, and I knew that this was not what I wanted to receive or give."*

And there it was. The "touch starved, touch-phobia" thing. The female family disconnect; fearful yet starved for *Female* Love, *Female* Touch and Reconnection. Still, there was a positive balance, women who were comfortable in their own skin, receptive, giving, and generous as she.

> "I was embraced by women who saw in me a being passionate about tango and hugged me with my heart and guts and that was always a magical sensation. I like to take care of the other when I dance on a track, in a milonga, and be able to draw music by building two."

To take care of the other is the natural maternal instinct, which Cortès has bigtime. As we learned in the previous chapter, the primary relationship between women is that of mother and daughter. If ever we needed proof positive of *how natural females roll*, it is Diana Cortès' heart-gut-felt resolve. She refuses to accept anything or anyone not authentic and generous as she. We can learn from her way of Sacred Female Being. Cortès never forgot to *be* who she is; centered, unapologetically Female.

As we learned in Chapter 2, the Female Brain is all about connection, intimacy, one-on-one, give and take. All of which explains why Cortès loves to lead. The *echo of the other* is that old Female Connection we danced as girls together in ecstatic joy. We should all be inspired as Cortès practices, continuing our unbroken Female dance, for mental, physical, and especially spiritual health. Women like Diana are role models in significant and primary ways. They not only make it okay for two women to dance, touch, sway, twirl, stomp together in full public view—they create the spellbinding beauty long-forgotten by women and men alike. It is that *Female* Dance we did in wild abandon when we were eight that keeps us whole, balanced, harmonically powerful, and *real to ourselves and each other*.

The music calls us to it. We enter through the Portal of Female Otherworld, dancing a language girls are always fluent in: The dance of FemaleLove, Female Authenticity and *finding the echo in the other*. Diana Cortès holds a lifetime pass.

Tango Links:
Diana Cortès y Cinthia Diaz Cinthia Diaz Tango:
https://youtu.be/PMY07YiND8c
Yohana Ardila y Diana Cortés en
Milonga Solidaria--
https:/ /youtu.be/O6FEUj SnysI

8

MOTHERDAUGHTER PARTICIPATION MYSTIQUE

The Ache I Felt Watching Female Tango

It would take a full year of trusting a woman to lead and teach what I knew was always in the most intimate of my spirit cells, a brave willingness to allow my sacred female BodyPsyche to just notice it and follow. To finally have the courage to see what I had been seeing all along. This was more than an epiphany—it was a life-altering realization. Psyche whispered, "This is what your sacred unmothered daughter saw, felt, and recognized from the start."

The MotherDaughter Participation Mystique

The MotheringDaughtering Ache (not to be misunderstood as *constant craving* or *mother wounding*) was so archetypally agonizing, so female fundamental in its primacy that it doubled me over. I watched. I couldn't. I watched. I couldn't. The want of that Sacred Female Intimate Connection—music, rhythm, cadence, touch—the MotheringDaughtering participation mystique, was a subconscious inborn knowledge. From the Gift of Femality: every girl's right.

Starved for its ride all my life, and the shame of the starvation that piggybacks on it, cut like a knife under the ribs, down to my solar plexus. That left out stabbing shame—but left out of what? After this brave acknowledgement, I watched the videos and caught the way the women walked toward each other. As in a marriage march, it was a betrothal of Womanhood. A conferring of blessing in their hands' touches.

The placement of Cortès's hand on her partner's back—confident, knowing, respectful, an honoring I had been waiting to see forever. And the moments where her partner gently lifts Cortès's long hair from her shoulder, letting it snuggle over her hand on her shoulder—was the loving mothering gesture what women seldom get as girls, daughters, or lovers. And then the other film, with Diaz and Cortès, dancing in and out of the chiaroscuro shadows. This was truest female intimacy. And then it finally transmitted, transcended to consciousness. This was the truth of who we are, uterus to uterus.

Brainwashed from birth through the Genital Eye. This is right out of the Death Culture's playbook: control what we feel, how we act on those feelings. There are those whose natures and characters cannot submit to this and continue to see through the Eye of the Heart. For us born of the *Female* PsycheBody, we are born seeing though the *Female* Eyes.

In Female Dance, Female Tango, the dancers make their magic with every step dictated by the music it is a fluid and spontaneous feed that tap into the erotic *Female* otherworld, female energies, with humor and passion. This is something so innate and rudimentary to our female core. You cannot see this through the genital eye. Feminist scholars have called this genital eye "the male gaze," and they are spot on. It originates from the male brain—though not exclusive to males.

This Mothering and Daughtering dance is a participation mystique we have denied ourselves. Why? If you see only through the Genital Eye, you will miss the root of what's really going on. Women as Lead and Follow (often switching during the dance), their particular styles of close embrace are masterpieces of this MotheringDaughtering dynamic.

The Great Female Dance can be anything. Freestyle. Two step. Lindy hop, shag, waltz, tribal together, one on one, you name it. But nowhere have I yet to witness the Full Female dynamic in poetic motion than when women tango. I am ashamed to admit that it took me until I actually danced it for a year and all the living I did as well as my interview with

Diana Cortès and some processing due to the stay-at-home process that allowed me to see what I had been seeing.

When I first caught sight of tanguera Marina Ventarron in her black tails, slacks, and patent-leather dancing slippers leading Ana Morisot, it shook me so hard I could not live with it but had to. What was going on here? My erotic truth? I could deal with that. But something else.

That something else was a "Visibly Invisible." It was not until I found Cortès and Ardilla's performance of *Tormenta* that it was taken to a whole different level. Still, I ached. I ached and felt despair. It prompted me to call around and find a female tango teacher—impossible back when I danced in the '90s. I took a chance and struck gold—I found Lauren Woods, Mistress Lauren—my nickname she giggles over, any student's wish-upon-a-star teacher. Gets exactly what is going on with me, head-wise via my body at any given moment. For a year I went through different stages of consciousness but never associated it to the MotherDaughter dynamic

Cortès (as I would learn in the interview in the previous chapter) had recently switched to the Lead, and to say her lead is jaw-dropping barely does it justice. I showed the videos to Lauren and she confirmed, saying how most women usually lead in circles, but Diana's was more linear and that made it very, very rare. I got up the nerve to contact Diana and asked if she would care to be interviewed on her experience of Leader with women as Followers. She was all for it. Quite a struggle in the translating back and forth—my Spanish is not advanced, and she does not speak English.

Still, I ended up with an interview every woman should read. And besides, all women are dancers in their own exquisite way.

Bottom Line: Female Tango is the very visual metaphor of MotherDaughtering energies that enrich and teach all that was redacted from our Female Primacy. The only way to watch it is through *Female* Eyes.

9

THE MOST ALLURING CREATURES ON THE PLANET

The most alluring creature on the planet is both planetary, earthly, and resonates cosmic aura from within. She dazzles, as she dazzled me the first time I caught wind of her calling to me through the Santa Anas, back when billboards advertised films of Southern California's autumnal version of fall, when the weather cycles were more constant and Ladye Santa Ana would steal in and wrap her loving arms around my small shoulders.

Had I never been in Beverly Hills in front of Kerr's Sporting Goods, I might not have been pulled toward the thrall of this alluring creature's magnetic force, plastered high on a brick wall in buckskin-fringed Femality. At three years old, I was stupefied. I have never seen Woman like this. Whether in books, old movies, new magazines, real life, this was not the definition in art form of Female.

Women wore full skirts, sheath dresses, pencil skirts, pedal pushers, Audrey Hepburn black leggings in black and ballet flats, pumps, stilettos, Keds to go with the capris, or with off-the-shoulder Calypso blouses, bubbles (bouffant hair), hoop earrings, ropes of beads, layered pearls, and long hair for a ponytail with pixie bangs. Those with short-cropped blonde DAs always wore full makeup and played secretaries or housewives like June Cleaver (of *Leave It to Beaver*) to "feminize" them.

Earliest female annunciation—1953 Beverly Hills Billboard

High atop a billboard was projecting something beyond goddess. There she stood, in all her buckskin, fringed Otherworldly-ness: Doris Day as Calamity Jane in the musical film of the same name. And there I stood, chin to the heavens at the corner of Wilshire and Rodeo, my mouth agape. This was the first woman I actually recognized, as someone I was supposed to remember and never forget the rest of my life.

Sporting suede leggings, Cuban heel boots, a matching jacket, fringe flung wide from her triumphant arms. The song she was belting out would win the Academy Award that year. And what I could not have consciously known was that other girls and women recognized her too—*in the way* I recognized her. She was from the Female Sphere. The *Uterverse. This was holy. The spirit of Femality. Of the Great Sacred Girl.*

Had I been all alone, I would have dropped to my bare knees, but I knew the drill and soon enough my father, who had been chasing my little brother on the rampage for a Bowie knife, came out of the store and spit on the pavement.

The whole damned world was his spittoon. Once again, I was back with him in This World, the one I never fit into. But I could not stop thinking of the woman with her arms thrown out, her spellbinding energies that called, "Come home, come back to us."

The women in question, those alluring creatures I am talking about are not male fantasies. They surpass erotic fantasies while at the same time, fulfill them for those who see through the eye of Female Myth. To see through Female Eyes under a male-ridden Death Culture is indeed a lonely existence. That is why books like this are beyond rare—perhaps the women who do see the way I do—are not writers, but I do know they are painters, musicians, and highly creative. My self-educated guess is that what they do see is a deep uterine feeling they have not words for or else they would put it out there. In many ways, that is why I had to write this book—because while my early childhood intersects with these images—it was too lonely to bear.

The woman on the billboard alongside Kerr's brick building was Doris Day as Calamity Jane. All I saw was Home. I was young enough not to intellectualize or critique what many have noticed in the true romance of the women in the scenario—unintended subplot, but if you see through Real Deal eyes, you will get it right away.

Point is, while Day was my first take on The Great Sacred-Sovereign Female, there were those I would catch a glimpse of in the early days of television on my grandparent's green glass Zenith in old movies and new sitcoms in my own life. She is so monumental in this film, and the film itself in terms of Femality, Patriarchy, and what happens when Ladye Irony takes ahold, it requires a full book or at least a long chapter in my next one, *Femocracy, Femality, and The Death Culture.*

The best way I can convey these alluring creatures and all they embody is to illustrate their inner energies, that you may allow your female psyche meander its serpentine flow.

Following, you will meet or reacquaint yourself with two of my favorites. These women possess an eros of Unflappability, Active Listening (reminding me of the fictional Miss Clavel in *Madeline*), the Powerful Female with the Transparent Female Masculine Energies, balanced by a gossamer more subtle Female Feminine Side. In short, they are so visibly integrated that onscreen, larger than life, are the archetype of the Earthly-Cosmic Woman that holds me in their thrall. There are others, but that will appear in the next upcoming book.

For now, read on for your pure delight to perhaps discover for the first time this dazzling actress, what studios called and cast as a famous "character actress" in the 1930s and '40s, from the inimitable Edna May Oliver and following in her footsteps in the 1950s and '60s, the unforgettable, entrancing Nancy Kulp of *The Beverly Hillbillies.*

The Powerful Woman with the Naturally Transparent Masculine Side

Edna May Oliver: A Force of Female Nature

I first caught sight of this magical figure in *A Tale of Two Cities*. We were studying it, and the 1933 film was availed to us. Wow. She played Miss Pross (Prossie to Sidney Carton), nurse-companion to Lucy Manette, a young woman whom she had always cared for like a great Mastadonian Mama. To watch her in action was like I had never known such a Female creature existed. Even though she was no taller than five foot seven, she always appeared larger than life on screen. A force to be reckoned with, for all the right reasons Her equine energy melted the silver off the screen—certain she overpowered her scenes with Ronald Colman, a screen idol, no mean feat.

What stands out forever in my female psyche was her ferocity at protecting her charge—a mother polar bear protecting her female youngster. The viewer could intuit that by the way she behaved there was no way her opponent of evil would leave alive—if it took both their lives, so be it. But she was too formidable to abandon Lucy by her own death, and when all is done, we are applauding in our hearts when Miss Pross wins the battle, grabs Lucy, and takes her to safety, no matter what it takes to escape La Guillotine. The best part I had forgotten, because we only got to view it once. Sixty years later on YouTube, there it was. When the bloodthirsty, rabid Madame du Farge threatens her with pistol and knife, Pross barring the door she has locked Lucy safely behind, drops her voice two octaves, juts out that with her Death Knell warning, that exquisite equine chin: "I am an *Englishwoman!*"

My heart of hearts—the British Isles in all its fantasy and myth—burst alive. American women have their own heroine. Worldly women are heroic around the world of the Death Culture. And of course, Sidney Carton is presented as the hero of heroes, going to the guillotine in place of Lucy's innocent husband, "'tis a far, far better thing …"

But the scene of MotherDaughter love (FemaleLove) was what grabbed my heart. That there existed women who would risk their lives for other women, that there were mothers who would fight to the death to save their daughters from a brutal death—was my wish upon a star. I did not know this on a totally conscious level, but the rare times a woman appeared on the screen acting the role of her heroine—I melted. In those days it was a fairy tale. Today I know it is real. There are women who bar the doors from abusers. Who take on an identity such as, "I am The Great Sacred Female, don't even think about it.

Edna May embodied that woman, as did the Statue of Liberty. I never saw her as Lady Liberty. If you sheared her hair, gave her a T-shirt and jeans, she was the masculine and feminine energies in perfect balance. Leave it to another mindset to come up with this image. The French were not American. Gender was fluid, at least to artistries.

And Edna May had it in spades.

My fourth-grade teacher, Miss Henry, carried this archetype of the elderly school matron, with snowy white hair pulled up in a Katherine Hepburn topknot, a true character from a previous era, black neck ribbons, white ruffled blouses, and since this was before pantyhose, hose with visible seams, slingback, slightly open-toed pumps. Everything about her said Prim Teacher, 1930. All that was missing were spectacles.

I do not remember her as the best teacher except for the stellar fact that she showed up, every day, at her age (late seventies?). That in and of itself was a quality at number one of my list of coping, functioning women. Other than all the details I can share about Mrs. A., who came after Miss Henry, I remember the woman. Showing her age a bit, hands a little shaky, and the day as she was powdering her nose as her generation did, her compact flew out of her hands into shards of face power all over the brown vinyl floor. Oh, boy, did the kids take advantage of the meanness and bullying in their back pockets, this incident, laughing and poking fun and imitating—instead of helping her. My heart was just breaking for her helplessness and worse, not even helping. I was more terrified of my peers mocking me than anything else.

Looking sixty years back, Miss Henry had my respect as much as Oliver because I know what it takes to take on mean-spirited souls every day and showing up the next day and the next.

Oliver and Henry kind of meld together in that Miss Pross showed up for her charge, and Mrs. Henry showed up to teach up the mind numbing his-story and planets to her charges. Subjects that numbed me out so heavily I dissociated out the window. Perhaps that is why I felt so protective of my teacher, bending to the floor at such a doddering age (whereas Oliver seemed steel-spined and ageless) but *you could depend on them*. I wanted to be there for my teacher because she seemed humiliated and rather flustered. Maybe her hands shook from shingles or arthritis, making the compact easy to drop. I so wish I had done more. Perhaps it wounded me more than she.

Rarely were we treated to this side until playing a tough, rifle-toting warmhearted widow in *Drums Along the Mohawk*, for which she received an Academy Award nomination. "Although some have described her as plain or 'horse-faced,' Edna May Oliver's comedic talents lent a beautiful droll warmth to her characters. She was usually called upon to play less glamorous roles such as a spinsters, but she played them with such soul, wit, and depth that to this day she remains one of the best loved of Hollywood's character actresses" (https://www.imdb.com/name/nm0646829/).

In oft-told interviews she is asked why—since she had such an operatic singing voice and was a professional pianist, she didn't go for musicals or other roles. (Note: she played the supporting role of Nurse in *Romeo and Juliet*, hardly a comedy.)

She responded: "What? With a horse face like mine? What else can I do but play comedy? Oh yes, I am grateful in a way for this face now that I've gotten used to it. I know it's brought me to this success. It's given me the chance to work and make money … but all the same I am a woman, and what woman doesn't long to be beautiful?" (https://www.imdb.com/name/nm0646829/quotes/.)

Oliver lived in a time and place (Hollywood Patriarchal Starlet culture) that even today would put her face on an Old Maid card. What I shall never see is that she was beyond beautiful because of her depth, breadth, and wit. A female of extraordinary power to buck the system her own way and take care of herself as well. She had the inner strength to make fun with the Red Queen in *Alice in Wonderland,* as well as bristly Aunt March in *Little Women,* still projecting allure both in myth and human. Oliver was my kind of Myth. My kind of Female. Perhaps the screen will invite her energies back, only this time, in the alluring creature that she, and those like her, remain eternally.

This woman is a rarified type no longer in film existence. But if you cross fingers, she may cross your archetypal path leading Children's and/or Animal Rights Organizations, Environmental Protection; running Women's Shelters, etc. This woman represents the Sovereign Female. The Powerful Female with the Naturally Transparent Masculine side. As a girl she is the fictional self-sufficient strong superhero Pippi Longstocking. Living alone. No mother. Her father sailing the Seven Seas. She belongs to herself.

Oliver found other roles she shined in. "Her magnetism brings about her own film series, the *Penguin* mysteries. The series was successful thanks to Edna May's stingers and her chemistry with James Gleason, who plays Inspector Oscar Piper in the series. The contrast between Edna May's perfect English accent and Gleason's New York "tanks" and "moidah" is supremely entertaining, as are the flirtations between them." (https://aurorasginjoint.com/2023/01/07/edna-may-oliver-she-had-a-long-face-and-she-stuck-it-where-she-wanted/.)

These rarified unexpected flirtations are something to savor, as her tough exterior is for a moment—visibly nearly girlish—before she switches back to the unflappable detective.

Finally it brings us to the unfair, ignorant, and insulting diatribes against this sacred, alluring Female Archetype: The Spinster falsely portrayed as man-starved as on the Old Maid Cards.

Our loss, these Female archetypes have faded from the culture. What we must do is bring them back as they truly were: Alluring Creatures for all time. A descendent of the second and sixth president his son, John Quincy Adams. Edna May was born and died on her fifty-ninth birthday, November 9.

Following in her footsteps in the '50s and '60s, appeared the unforgettable, entrancing Nancy Kulp of *The Beverly Hillbillies*

Touchstone to The Place with Only Girls—Nancy Kulp

My feelings were so mixed and confused. Here I was a teen, in a trance over Miss Jane Hathaway, a creature whose magic proved iridescent but was supposed to be comical, even zany. How could the two be one in the same? I did not find it funny in the least in that episode where she is put alongside Miss Ellie, forced to wear a 1920s bathing costume, black horn-rimmed glasses while Miss Ellie is the buxom blonde, making Miss Hathaway as an object a mockery.

As Miss Jane, Kulp was no fool and no jester. She provided the same wit and wisdom as did her forebearer, Edna May Oliver. I resented the all-male writers-producers-directors pulling off the oldest female insult in the world. Taking a poised, classy, erudite, elegant, beautiful woman—who outclasses everyone around her—as much a buffoon as they tried. They failed. But it did not stop me from my personal fury.

I knew an alluring creature when I saw one, and the exquisite equine was a prize. What happened was what they never expected as she out-Kulped them. An expert at comedy, she stole every scene. Yet, it was this image at times, that infuriated me. As an actor, we do what we have to do. It is a job and we need to eat. However, it was not the insult anyone might see, save one who saw through Female Eyes.

It's funny how certain archetypes will turn as magic keys to our past, those truths we could not have understood as a child, yet we intuited. Children are the most intuitive of creatures, especially before ten and live in Archetypal City. I remembered every teacher from kindergarten through sixth grade. Yet there was one I did not even have a vague image of until I sent to the LA Unified School District for my report cards. What I received came as a blessed tsunami of a shock.

There in my second grade teacher's long, easy script read the words, "Thinks she is ugly and black. Wants to be pretty like Chris and Jan. Really quite a sweet and beautiful child. Reflects attitudes at home. Mother seeing a psychiatrist."

It was like a priceless Faberge egg dropped into my hands. All the lies my mother drilled into me about what a happy childhood I had. And the interview with this teacher came back to me too. Where we sat. The day each kid was given their own interview. Yet she had the guts and temerity to scribe it on the card in permanent India ink. Pretty gutsy for those days, for any day. And then in my fifties, I had this dream:

Dream: Mrs. Blakewell

I had moved to Columbus, Ohio, and was at a ladies' nightclub when I saw her. Mrs. Blakewell. There she was. My second grade teacher, now in her sixties or seventies. I had remembered her as exactly Nancy Kulp. They were interchangeable. Who I had seen first? I was only four when I caught Kulp in *Love That Bob*.

Mrs. Blakewell, don't you remember me?

Yet she does not remember me. I am a grown woman now. Sixty years gone. But I know her. And she and Kulp were one in the same.

"Thinks she is ugly and black …"

The *black* part came from my step-grandfather, Joe, a mean-spirited cuss who hurtled insults to any child in front of family. He, the archetypal gnome, he began spurting "Just look at her. Black as the ace of spades!" He soaked me with kerosene and lit me on fire. He turned me into a charcoal briquette. My father, coward that he was, just laughed with everyone else. When my mother heard about it later, she shot out, "I've seen *his* grandchildren. He *wishes* they looked like you!"

Black was not a person of color. Yet was it? Whenever I saw a person of deepest black, I wondered who had blackened them with shame? The irony was, the older I got each summer my light olive skin tanned the way these women would have sold their firstborn for. It was a big coveted deal in that era. Tan meant signified wealthy and desirable. Country clubs and no office job. Kept by a man or married to a rich one. Very Jackie Kennedy. Envious moms whose bodies sunburned peeled like Elmer's glue would assault me with their passive-aggressive, "My, my, look who was in Palm Springs!" The painful truth they never knew was my family never took us anywhere. Even with Disneyland in our backyard, I never saw it until I was twelve. Sometimes their jealousy would escalate into passive-aggressive tropes: "*So, dear, what nationality are you?*"

The fact that this teacher had the guts to write the truth, verbatim, to tell the female truth. I wrote to the school's unified district for those back-office notes. Reports neither we nor our parents would ever see. That I might see it fifty years later was a gift she never could have imagined. This second grade teacher who interviewed me have resembled Nancy Kulp, one of my Nancy heroines. (See: The Most Alluring creatures on the planet).

There I was, years hence, *The Beverly Hillbillies* came on and I watched Kulp every week, riveted. Miss Jane, 'Competency Incorporated,' strode in skirts as slender as her pencils, sporting pearls she would never clutch, addressing her bumbling boss the bank's president as 'Chief' when the TV audience caught the irony. The real deal 'chief' was Miss Jane.

Nancy Kulp was classic and an original at the same time. A born New Englander, she could do that lockjaw-Bryn Mawr-speak better than Joanna Barnes and make you feel you were watching a fairy tale and not some stupid sitcom. When I was able to flip through the early fifties, predating *The Beverly Hillbillies*, I caught *Love That Bob* episodes on YouTube. I watched as she did the same version of a man-starved nerd, Pamela Livingston. Birdwatcher. In Bermuda shorts and funny hat, binoculars strung around her neck. She was the foil for all the glamourous throngs of starlets who came gliding and wiggling in and out of his photography 'studio.' The perfect excuse for titillation of the male gaze, and his shoots of them in early fifties one-piece swimsuits and strapless push-up dresses. The perfect contrast to Kulp's nerdy character who—while she pretended to salivate for Bob, was ridiculous. Only the male teams behind these idiotic themes imagined a woman who looked like her would be man-hungry.

She was in the first *Parent Trap* (1961) around the same time, playing as a camp counselor. No matter how hard I tried to wish she'd come back to the screen, I knew she only had bit parts or supporting roles at best. I just wanted to be Haley Mills and meet this lovely counselor who never shows up in real life. (Except perhaps as one's first grade teacher?)

If you look at some of her younger pictures, she is positively drop-dead divine, with a capital D. If there is such a thing as bedroom eyes, then Kulp had boudoir ones. My best friend bore an uncanny resemblance to Kulp's younger version and could mimic her until I fell over on the floor. Truly she brought her to life just by me begging, "Do Jane!" Sadly, as with Oliver, Kulp never knew just how classically desirable a woman she was, because of the male-run Patriarchy-Death Culture, gaslighting women, aka Hollywood Inc.

Rarely did she give interviews. When the inevitable question would assault her: "Are you gay?," she would reply: "Well … birds of a feather."

This Woman's Woman respectfully agrees.

Nancy Kulp, Actress & Advocate

PART THREE

PHOETICS

> Stories set the inner life into motion … cut for us fine,
> wide doors in previously blank walls, opening that lead to
> the dreamland, that lead to love and learning … that lead
> us back to our own real lives as knowing, wildish women.
> —Clarissa Pinkola Estes, *Women Who Run with the Wolves*

I never knew when I first configured the Phoetics Process, what an eager reception awaited.

I joined a women's entrepreneurs networking group and ended up getting my own radio show on Bexley Public Radio. Guests would come in on Saturday mornings and I would take them through a simpler, modified version of Phoetics. They told their friends, and many chose private sessions and workshops. Bottom line, they all told me that, hey if you can get Ohioans to do this, California will be a piece of cake.

Once I returned to my home state, I did hold several successful workshops and privates—but there came a time where women kept begging me "I want to read your book!" They were more than right. I was thinking, *You want to read my book? I want to read it!*

It was glaringly obvious that to move forward, I had to understand the full scope of Phoetics, how it was seeded, how it worked its magic that women and men could Rebecome their Authentic Selves. It took many years for this comprehensive, brave book of bold Female Truths, how we are impacted as Great Sacred Girls under the Death Culture and information about the Dark Force, Dark Force Females and Males—and scraping away the redactions of our individual sacred stories. What the Death Culture does to us, gaslighting from the get-go. We do not stand a chance of embracing our Authenticity when it is constantly being torqued, twisted, obliterated by the fiction of our parents' projections of their own falsified identities.

Today, I have finally woven this into one multifaceted, never-before-shared nor written book, to comfort women and men and assure them they are hardly alone in their struggle of not being able to be authentic. That I know is the most sacred gift we are packed with—and why I created Phoetics in the first place. My upbringing was bizarre, twisted, anti-female, and toxic, but no more or less than any other girls and boys under this Death Culture sphere.

The rare souls you will meet via their sacred Phoetics, their uncommon courage to agree to have them published gives and sustains my hope for a changed, Female Central World. Women seemed to convene unknowingly, but well-meaning women know we must further this 'women come together and change the world.' Or they work hard to protect, defend, and celebrate girls, leaving their inner Great Sacred Girl aside. That is why I could not see myself marching in the Feminist movements of the past—and after reading so many books, the few that wrote of Female Equality just did not reach my deepest gnosis. My female soul's core.

It boiled down to: When you do not rebecome your Authentic Female Self (the Sacred Girl who never got a chance to use her voice), you leave out the key that opens the portal to True Femality. I live for the day women will do the work and play of Phoetics, to enable us to then come together and switch the axis from Male Rule and False Supremacy to the Great Female Leadership Brain in our creation of a new world of Female Centrality.

When we discover our true Sovereignty and refuse to abdicate our roles of teaching males with loving guidance the males that is our duty and their right, how life it supposed to be lived. Femality is the core, always has been.

The Art of Rebecoming: Seeded in Phoetics

Rebecome. Rebecoming. I first came across this word in Elinor Gadon's *The Once and Future Goddess: A Sweeping Visual Chronicle of the Sacred Female and Her Reemergence in the Cult.* She uses the preface "re" for many words throughout because our Female Cycling Natures require change, growth, and transcendence. For the sake of our sacred Authenticity, we must Reimage and Reconstruct to Reclaim our Authentic Stories.

This is what I teach.

Rebecoming is what Phoetics is all about. We want to rediscover our original authentic selves, the way we were in nanoseconds of childhood. We long for spontaneity, the freedom of silliness. Inclusive in all this: We want our story. It is our birthright, birth-write, and not the one our family wrote for us. We are starved for our sacred story *as only we know it*, as only the authentic child in the photograph is more than overdue to share.

She never abandoned us. We abandoned her, parts of her that the Death Culture threatened, and destroyed. Phoetics allows us to reenter the scenes we lived in and find those shards of self so vital, the primacy of our True Identity. How we arrived from the Female Otherworld we still had at least one foot in at four, the age of authenticity.

In *The Soul's Code*, Hillman reminds us what no one ever is taught by Stupid Adults (SAs). His plea for children is thankfully for us—brutally frank. Paraphrasing here, a child's state of being struggles to find her place, where she fits, if she fits in this strange sphere. A child is "living two lives at once": the soul they were born with and the strangers they were born to. His book does indeed speak for and champion the sacred child.

At that critical time in my healing my precious early self with new female spirit growth, his words portended all I needed to find. I read more than anything Alice Miller, though she did shamelessly acknowledge how adults gave the pretense of cherishing children while treating them quite the opposite. Stupid Adults make for Hypocrisy, an altar of Phobia. And why not? The child has no Death Culture filters, speaks the blooming obvious, just like in *The Emperor's New Clothes*. "He is naked!" While Stupid Adults keep silent. *Out of the mouths of babes* does not come from nowhere.

Phoetics taps into those babes' nonverbal truths. That is Femality's nature. The Female PsycheBody, as our brain and body are symbiotic. They work together. When we stop thinking and paying attention to our body's messaging, we discover our bodies' wisdom and survival antennae. Because the Death Culture has severed us from both mind and body we are not operating at Female Full Capacity. Hardly so. When our Phoetics kicks in, the switch of Authenticity is flipped on.

Phoetics was not seeded in Columbus, Ohio. It was, however, watered, rooted, and lovingly cultivated by the great women I was blessed to encounter and teach, create, guide, and celebrate The Great Sacred Girl within us and through their trust. They trusted me, I trusted them and together we surrendered to the blessings and power of Phoetics. It was Female Central. It blossomed from the female nature of their curiosity, desire and daring—to rebecome their authentic selves no matter what it took, as far or as short as each chose. Using my absolute "knowing" of what women were wanting, what they were and were not comfortable with, using what I would have appreciated and trusted, I would begin every workshop and private session with the cardinal understanding that, "This is a sacred and safe space. Everything is about your individual comfort and choice. If you do not choose to sing, or dance—that is respected. If you find you must leave, no justifications. You changed your mind? Welcome back. Come and go well, with the blessings of the Great Sacred Girl."

It is essential for all people to have autonomy. We may live in a Female-centric-made world—that is, Female is Nature is Us—but we are harnessed, duped, and imprisoned by a Dark Force's Death Cultures. Where it is never safe to show feelings. To express emotions, opinions. And that 'cult'ure is left outside the door. When you visit the Female Centric Phoetic sphere, all is optional. That simple.

We especially as women are always saying, "I'm sorry, but ..." and justifying why we make a choice when it is our personal business. Even with the HIPAA laws on our side, we might have a boss or manager who just wants to know why we ask for time off. And that is how we are duped and inculcated from Day One. I notice on one of my favorite programs, that characters, men as well as women, begin a question, response, or thought with, "I'm sorry ..." This is like, "My bad. Shame on me." "I beg your pardon" would better suffice—just a few shades off our self-blaming.

The Violet Root

The very purpose of Phoetics is to watch how the foreign-induced shame evaporates as we observe other women's responses that validate "been there, done that" and "That's not shameful. You were right to do/think/ act on that." Female Validation is the finest elixir I know. Expressed from the Violet Root, it is literally a spiritual, physical, spa-like soothing balm like no other. When I am validated by another woman or girl—I know I can relax. They are right. I am OK. We are OK. So the very dynamics of Phoetics are truly Female Rooted. Every moment, poem, blessing, joke, song, harmony, dance move, quiet sit—arise from this Violet Root. It is what you feel on your haunches. I use that to get women to return to the root of their female consciousness. Where you first feel cramps. Where you deliver. The birthplace.

If you have ever done EMDR, you come away knowing that no matter epiphany or not—the process keeps going. You may have a dream. You may see an old image. A song plays in your car that totally connects to your session.

Phoetics is a process.

A female process, which is also customized for males.

Women are earthly-cosmic, dynamically cyclic, as nature's embodiment. So connecting the cyclic to Rebecoming makes sense. Cycles are Birth, Life, Death, Rebirth, Life, Death, and so forth. It would only make sense that to rebecome who we once were *en totale*—before the Death Culture stole pieces of us, shattered our wholeness—it would mean to return to where we left those self-pieces or elements or energies or all.

Sounds a little *Hansel and Gretel*—finding the breadcrumbs of lost self to get back home, except Home is Me. I never remember leaving breadcrumbs of self along the way, but that is what the Death Culture succeeds in its agenda to obliterate and lobotomize all of us as Great Sacred Girls. Stop us in our natural Future Woman Tracks. We enter Womanhood broken, shattered, confused, and tentative. For me, it took a good twenty-five years from age forty to put myself back together again. Clarissa Estes (*Women Who Run with the Wolves*) reminds, we are members of the [1]Scar Clan.

What is true is that the destructive, sly, sinister nature of the Dark Force is that it kills, little by little—every moment that would have been your spontaneous self. With each and every hesitation, there goes another crumb except, they aren't crumbs in the forest. They are pieces of self, shattered. Scattered. Tattered. Once I had a bad dream about holding a kitten and pieces fall off out the car. My RDFT told me it was pieces of the feminine self. She was right, and that was twenty years ago. Dreams, as in art and myth, represent Feminine-Masculine Female energies.

You are hardly alone. It happens to all girls. Whatever happened to you, that sapped your spontaneity, can be retrieved, revived, and Rebecome those essential pieces of you stronger than ever. The more you lose those first ten years, the more there is to take joy in. Phoetics pats you on the head, on the back and pleasures your heart because those your sacred childhood photographs have waited to be blessed for so long. Upon your return, your sacred touch upon them—transcends them to the present.

"They ask for so little, only that they be remembered" (paraphrased from Hillman's *The Soul Cycle).* When we show them we care and how precious they mean to our life's story, that we are open and listening when ever did—the Great Sacred Girl is right where you left her. Your Sacred Rebecoming and Reunion begins through Phoetics.

Phoetics: Distillation of the Authentic Essence of Childhood Memories

What's the connection between your childhood photos and your body? It's simple. The body remembers what the mind forgets. Alice Miller reminds, "The body never lies." Similar to the old expression, "The camera doesn't lie." When earliest films began, they were referred to as "moving pictures." This process takes place in the psyche when interacting with an old child photograph and leads to the moving pictures and episodes we know as dreams. Our childhood memories and photos are tattooed, illustrated on our sacred PsycheBody.

Just like when you are healing from abuse, your body's memories from that abuse is always there. A masseuse, a lover, anyone may press, pinch, caress just plain absentmindedly touch a spot that holds a traumatic event.

Or a pleasurable one. Bottom line—Phoetics hooks up with our body and psyche via photographs and other processes included in the sessions and workshop. The body remembers. Indeed.

> There is nothing that keeps on giving like a childhood photograph. Every time you revisit, it gifts you. Blessing. And blessing goes both ways. We are blessed by visiting and listening to what our sacred childhood photos must bequeath. All they ask in kind is that we don't forget them. They await our return to honor their presence and all they preserve for us.

I could never forget my childhood photos. They were the only proof of my existence to myself. As my intensity waned so was my essence diluted. I cared little for the few photos that came after. Everything stops at eight. For a girl. That is why Phoetics is so rare—it is intentional. To tickle our psyches back to whom we once were. Phoetics. Authenticity. They mean the same thing. Our bodies preserve whom we arrive as; our essence, our soul, just as the camera captures and film development preserves its truth in Time.

How Do You Treat Your Childhood Photographs?

The way you keep or do not keep childhood photographs speaks volumes. Do you know where they are and keep them jumbled in dusty decaying boxes, out of sight, out of mind? If the frames and albums have dissipated, it is not only highly symbolic of your relationship with your inner daughter or son, but also literal. Some of my clients are set about to find theirs with an aunt, some never find them. Still, if you remember one, Phoetics is available. I once did a whole radio show interview with a man who remembered his place across from a nunnery, and the more he described, the more Phoetics blessed.

The question begs, if you don't have them—why? Did your mother offer them, and you declined? Many clients find the search and journey of finding them—an aunt, a childhood friend—becomes part of their life's journey, life altering: Part and parcel of the Phoetics journey.

Mine were offered by my mother in my early thirties. "Take whatever you want," was said as "Take my wife, please." She didn't care anyway but perhaps she knew. I will never know, but she told me to take the picture I called The Portrait 1917, of my grandparents. My mother told me to take it, but I could not. There is built-in integrity in every photo. Though I neither loved nor respected her, it did not spiritually belong to me until she passed on.

"Why don't you just take it? You're the only one who loved it." I have it today, but that's because I came into it when it was time. And used it often in Motherblood, MotherDaughter Workshops.

Unexpected Surprises: Amazing Hopeful Outcomes

Many most-dreaded childhood photos turn out to be our True Power Photos.

My most dreaded photo turned out to be the Power Photo. It would take me into the very roots and matrix of Phoetics. And as I related to my therapist and journaled, I related how and why I loathed and feared it. Shame. Shame trickles down from so many of our childhood photos. So many of mine reek of awkwardness from the secrets I had to keep. The sheer discomfort of having to be in my own body, all the "not enough" that bled from both the culture and family that oozed the malignancy of the culture were right there. I saw. The average eye would not. I was an outstanding actress. But this one, the Power Photo I learned, was the opposite of the shame I kept seeing in the telltale dark circles under my eyes. My father abuses me, and I dissociate and then go to school sleep deprived.

The point to remember is this: Your body remembers what you believe your mind forgets. However, just because your mind does not consciously remember events, your body does not repress. Any touch can bring back a flood of feelings. You cannot do Phoetics without returning safely in your sacred body, but there are degrees. Maybe one day you can go deeply, and the next session, just below the surface. Women do not live fully in their bodies because we all know it is not safe. We are always on alert. The trick is to unlearn the numbness, while retaining our necessary fight, flight, or freeze. Sounds impossible, but it can be done. Degree by degree. That is how we heal. As women, as females it is the wisest protocol to follow. I have done it and will for the rest of my days and nights. There is no better choice. You find moments where you wonder, where did that good feeling come from? That signals you are healing. Phoetics is a healing process and like our bodies and memories know how to do, a distillation.

For that is the beauty of what ageing gifts us: The finest vintages from The Aged Distilled PsycheBody.

¹The Scar Clan comes from CP Estes' 'Women Who Run with the Wolves,' refers to all of us who have been abused and healed from it. Hence, transcendence as scar clan. (Pages 374, 386, 460)

Woman, Know Thy Story—Conclusion

He who has the story, has the power. She who has no story, not even her own, has no power.
—Rebecca Solnit, "The Storykiller and His Sentence"

Solnit's exquisitely wrought exposé about Harvey Weinstein, relative to the toxic, male-dominated stories produced in the film industry: male directors, producers, agents, power brokers, writers is all about how Story is Power and Storyholders of dark energies wield power over the Light of Truth. Our Truth. Female Truth. I would say instead, and more pointedly: "She who has not her own story, has no power."

Power is Voice and Voice comes from Sovereignty of Self. Female Self. Your story is the most fundamental way to Rebecome Visible to yourself. Woman, want to know thyself? Know thy story.

Your story—which you may adore, embrace, venerate, resent, revile, or hold at bay for all the pain and beauty beneath the pain, retains your essence *or Character and Calling.* James Hillman suggests that we go into therapy to find our story—to make sense of our life. And women's stories, as told through the long lens of adult objectivity –are the building blocks of Female Culture and Centricity. Our collective and individual Female Spirit is its mortar, which embeds that culture immutable.

Stories are medicine. Male stories carry healing male medicine; Female stories carry healing female medicine—the most potent (again, why we find ourselves in such suffering today). When I was a girl searched for female tales, stories of another girl's lives told by them or in a library book—nothing existed. I never bought into the crap they pushed on us. Nearly every last story was about a boy, a man, a male animal told through the male mindset or women writers who did write from the Female PsycheBody. Where were the real stories of girls'? I felt some gargantuan betrayal was afoot that would take me a half century to deduce. And today I understand what and why it was.

The Dark Force Stole Our Stories.

The darker your story, the more reluctant you will be to retrieve it. I was. *And that is precisely what The Dark Force counts upon.* It has the skivvy on every woman's story. Your fear seals its fate. Yet it doesn't have to stay that way. That is the reason we as women, as girls suffer, resulting in why the world is nearing extinction.

No female stories, no female connection.

No female connection, no Female Centrality, no Female Culture.

No Female Culture, no creation. No creation, no life.

So Much More Than a Few Good Men—What We Owe To Boys And Men

Whenever I find myself down the rabbit hole of males making war on all sacred beings, I remind myself to wait for the next inspiring story. That is what keeps me hopeful. There are so much more than a few great sacred men and as Great Sacred Females, we have an earthly-cosmic duty to them. Not only do we let ourselves and children down, but we have also abandoned those males who deserve our teaching, guidance, support, and healing. Not only is it the right thing to do, but it is also existential to the planet-sphere's survival.

As we Rebecome our Authentic Female Selves, we take up our responsibility to the males who need *their* new world consciousness. Males deserve the gift of Phoetics. Those with the uncommon courage to started asking for sessions, it was an easy alternative in the process, substituted for the male's Body and Soul.

It taught me that no matter how lethal testosterone has been and continues to be, we cannot give up. Cannot give up on males any more than walk away from our duty to our Authentic Selves. Our kids depend upon us. Like grabbing your oxygen mask before you assist the child, adult next to you. Saving our sacred Authenticity, ourselves means saving men from Toxicity of The Death Culture. Younger generations question that toxicity and it is reflected in commercials: men doing the laundry, feeding their babes, children, and those great men who take up humanitarian needs. To name a couple who individually and collectively make the difference in lives, such as Doctors without Borders, and José Andrés, who feeds the world with his foundation, The José Andrés Group. Such blessings. Gives me great pause to grow into a more enlightened woman.

That really is what keeps me going. Whenever I catch a Dark Force Female colluding with the Death Culture, women against women, putting males ahead of themselves, it is hard to describe the inner explosion that erupts in me. Men—we expect to collude with patriarchal Death Culture. *Yet women should know better.* Many are born cowardly Dark Force Females. All we can do is dive deeply into our Phoetics Authentic Truths and connect with women and men who make the bold choice and follow through. That is how we shift this world back on its Female Balance. The earth's wobble depends on it.

What is Phoetics?

Phoetics˚ is a highly intuitive, spiritual self-awareness counseling technique designed to return a woman to her true story and authentic self.

Phoetics˚ draws deeply from ancient female consciousness as it guides and teaches how to interact with the imaged truths captured in childhood photos that preserve her true story using the five ways women connect: Mind, Body, Soul, Spirit, and Image.

Phoetics˚ safely guides a woman back into her female body

When a woman is fully present in her female body, her psyche opens

When her psyche opens, she receives from her sacred inner daughter her poetic truths

When she knows her poetic truths, she knows her story

When she knows her story she is bonded with her sacred daughter

When she is bonded with her sacred daughter she feels empathy

When she feels empathy she lives fully present in Female Consciousness

Phoetics˚ is Female Consciousness and every soul's birthright-rite.

Every soul is entitled to know and own her authentic story. To tell it to herself and to share it with any soul she chooses.

Birth of Phoetics©

Phoetics both created and grew out of my notes called Nancy's Truths

I wrote the majority of my archetypal childhood memoirs, and sketched the charcoal portraits with both my dominant and non-dominant hands using the earliest photos of myself, mother, father, brother, uncle, grandmother, and cousin.

In August 2009, I met a woman dedicated to helping women get a head start in launching a business. Synchronicity she was also named Nancy, born in the early 1950s. And like many of my clients, is a twin sister. After an intense three hours sharing my Nancy's truths I start to leave and shake her hand. She stops me, *Wait, wait!* Before I know it she has split open a plastic page of her thick baby blue wallet. *There it is. Her prized possession. A faded old black and white photograph of her father with her twin sister on one side and Nancy on the other, a beaming two year old.* She is looking back at me with the same beam. This is her deepest treasure. Her father said she could take anything and this is what she always wanted. I am stunned. *She is showing me who she is, her deepest female self and story.*

As I stumble onto the street, all I can hear in my head is: *It's the photographs; it's always about the photographs.*

Two months later, I sit with another wise woman soul who wants to help me launch *Nancy's Truth*. I have read excerpts to her, shown the charcoal sketches. She asks how did I do it? *What?* I ask. *How did I write such powerful prose, poetry, narrative, and portraits*? I stop and think. *From the photographs*, I shrug, *what else?*

Teach it. A veteran writer, teacher, creatrix and wise woman, she wastes no time, no words. *Women want their own myths. Women want their own mysteries. Women want their own stories. Women need new and better ways to find them. Figure out what it is you do. And teach it.*

When one woman shows up with a message, I listen.

When two women show up with the same message, I act upon it.

In less than a month **Phoetics**™ is born.

Introduction to Phoetics®

The Art of Rebecoming

Rebecome. I first came across this word in Elinor W. Gadon's, The Once and Future Goddess: A Sweeping Visual Chronicle of the Sacred Female and Her Reemergence in the Cult. She uses the preface "re" throughout the pages, because its premise is *the necessity to change: reimage, reconstruct, and return to our original selves.*

This is what I teach.

Rebecoming is what Phoetics is all about. Your original authentic self. We want to rediscover our original authentic selves, the way we were in nanoseconds of childhood, we long for spontaneity, the freedom of silliness. Inclusive in all this : We want our story. It is our birthright, birth-write, and not the one our family wrote for us. We are desperate for our sacred story, as only we know it, as only the child in the photograph can share with us.

Phoetics taps into The Female PsycheBody. Our Brain (Psyche) and Body are symbiotic—they work together. Because the Death Culture has severed us from both brain and body we do not operate anywhere near at Full Female Capacity.

*

If you were to ask if I started out with any notion of all that lives within this first book, I would be speechless. Nonplussed. All I ever wanted to do was act and dance. I discovered many other talents. I could draw portraits and easily, women and girls. Then again, I was sketching their portraits via female spirit from the day I arrived and it intensified the more my brain and female consciousness constellated.

Was I looking for larger- than-life statues of girls as power figures? No, not then. In a world that does not run on Female Centricity you learn not to keep looking for 'that which doth not exist.' In simple words, seek what is not valued and ye shall not find. I can well imagine in more ways than one what it was like for girls who were not blue eyed blonds to not be offered dolls of any other complexions, non-Barbie or baby bodies, hair that matched or echoed their own, not to mention any differenced that changed their bodies as a result of accident or nature/biology.

However I never stopped seeking what I considered 'the place with only girls.' I was doing the natural female thing—seeking Female Centricity. A world that matched Mother Nature: run, created, and fully powered by The Great Female Psyche (Brain). Of course that 'world' would make sense, be fair and I could finally relax. Even with troublesome girls, there would be grown up women who were real deal females (RDFs) that would know what to do to keep the rest of us safe—because they remained within their original, authentic sacred female-leadership selves. The bad eggs, rotten apples…in a Female Centric World would be handled from the Great Female Leadership Brain's solutions, but one thing I knew in my bones: it was where *I* belonged. *Me.* Where was the place with only girls? Small wonder indeed that I wanted to live next door to Miss Clavel's bedchamber, and not with all the rest of the girls like Madeline, but as me, Nancy Lee who was far savvier and street smart about never, ever saying 'pooh-pooh' to any tiger in the zoo. Bars and cages can fall open, too.

THE PLACE WITH ONLY GIRLS, MY FEMALE CENTRIC HOME

If I chose to step out of the sphere and interact with any boys, it was *my choice.* No one would push me. No one would even dare. Because I would never have to return to a world that was so darkly barbaric, I found it unbearable to keep waking up in it. Worse, it appeared like the rest of the world and the one that orbited round me seemed perfectly okay about it. Either people did not notice or if they did, did not protest. Nothing. Certainly never the men or boys and tragically, like a sucker punch to my solar plexus—the women. The *women.* The ones who were supposed to know better. They went about what they called 'life' and 'doing' but their 'being' was the sticky wicket. *My being* was: great, quiet, reverent, sacred, and Forever Female. I have since rediscovered what I carried with me and have now Become The Great Sacred Girl living within her Sense of Being.

It is a Female Sensibility. I call it Femality. Female Reality. For Female consciousness. Femality.

The Art of Phoetics created from Femality

Phoetics was not seeded in Columbus, Ohio. It was however, watered, rooted, lovingly cultivated by the great women I was blessed to encounter and teach, create, guide, and celebrate The Great Sacred Girl within us and through their trust. They trusted me and surrendered to the blessings and power of Phoetics. It was Female Central. It blossomed from the female hubris of their curiosity, desire and daring—to rebecome their authentic selves—no matter what it took, as far or as short as they each chose to be taken.

Using my absolute 'knowing' of what women were wanting, what they were and were not comfortable with, using what I would have appreciated and trusted, I would begin every workshop and private session with the cardinal understanding that, "This is a sacred and safe space. Everything is about your individual comfort and choice. If you do not choose to sing, or dance—that is respected. If you find you must leave, no justifications. Go well, with the blessings of The Great Sacred Girl."

It is essential for all people to have autonomy. We may live in a Female Centric-made world—that is, Female is Nature is Us—but we are harnessed, duped, and imprisoned by a dark force's death cultures. Where it is never safe to show feelings. To express emotions, opinions. And that 'cult'ure is left outside the door. When you visit the Female Centric Phoetic Sphere, all is optional. That simple.

We especially apologize all the time. Always saying, "I'm sorry, but..." and justifying why we make a choice when it is our personal business. Even with the HIPPA laws on our side, we might have a boss or manager who just wants to know 'Why' we ask for time off. And that is how we are duped and inculcated from Day One. I notice on one of my favorite programs, that characters, men as well as women begin a question, response, thought with, "I'm sorry...." This is like, 'My bad. A shame-shame on me' Perhaps, "I beg your pardon' would better suffice—just a few shades off our self-blaming

The very nitty gritty purpose of Phoetics is to watch how the foreign induced 'shame' evaporates, as we observe other women's responses that either validate, 'been there done that' and/or that's not shameful. You were right to do/think/that." Female Validation is the finest elixir I know. Crushed from the Violet Root, it is literally a spa-like soothing balm like no other. When I am validated by another woman or girl—I know I can relax. They are right. I am Okay. We are Okay.

So the very dynamics of Phoetics are truly Female Rooted. Every moment, poem, blessing, joke, song, harmony, dance move, quiet sit—arise from this Violet Root. It is what you feel on your haunches. I use that to get women to return to the root of their female consciousness. Where you first feel cramps. Where you climax. The birthplace. (See: The Bucranium Genius.)

If you have ever done EMDR, you come away knowing that no matter epiphany or not—the process keeps going. You may have a dream. You may see an old image. A song plays in your car that totally connects to your session. Bottom line: *Phoetics is a process.* A female process. We are earthly-cosmic, dynamically cyclic, as nature's embodiment. So connecting the cyclic to Rebecoming makes sense. Cycles are Birth, Life, Death, Rebirth, Life, Death etc. It would only make sense that to rebecome who we once were en totale—before the Death Culture stole pieces of us, shattered our wholeness—it would mean to return to where we left those self-pieces or elements or energies or all. Sounds a little Hansel and Gretel-like—finding the breadcrumbs to get back home, except Home is Me. I never remember leaving breadcrumbs of self along the way, but that is what happens to all of us Great Sacred Girls. For me, it took a good twenty-five years and counting. I am 'put back together again' and as Estes reminds us a member of the Female Scar Clan. (Women Who Run with the Wolves)

What is true is that the sinister nature of the Dark Force is that it kills, little by little—every moment that would have been your spontaneous self. And with each and every hesitation, there goes another crumb except, they aren't crumbs in the forest. They are pieces of self, shattered. Scattered. Tattered. Once had a bad dream about holding a kitten and pieces fall off out the car. My RDFT told me it was 'pieces of self.' She was right and that was twenty years ago. In dreams, as in art and myth, represents Feminine-Female energies.

You are hardly alone. It happens to all girls. Whatever happened to you, that sapped your spontaneity can be retrieved, revived and Rebecome those essential pieces of you stronger than ever. The more you lost those first ten years, the more there is to take joy in. Phoetics pats you on the head, on the back and pleasures your heart because those your sacred childhood photographs have waited to be blessed for so long.

Upon your return, your sacred touch upon them—transcends them to the present.

"They ask for so little, only that they be remembered."

When we show them we care and how precious they mean to our life's story, that we are open and listening when ever did—the Great Sacred Girl is right where you left her. Your Sacred Rebecoming - Reunion begins through Phoetics.

*Paraphrased from TSC, James Hillman

PHOETICS: How It Works and Processes

Engaging with your childhood photos brings you back to the 'me' left behind, the me that livens your first, true sense of self and what orbited around you. It is a circular, cyclic dynamic.

Interacting with your childhood photos fire up old neurons lain dormant in the trauma zone of your brain, which hide away the bad but the good goes with it. Children—the younger they are, the more ego-centric and magic-mythical orientated. After all, they still have one foot in the Otherworld they come from. "They are trying to live two lives at once, the one they were born with and the one of the place and among the people they were born into," reminds James Hillman. (*The Soul's Code*)

These are the two worlds that make our story, our own. Unique and special to that 'me'—peeking out from the corners of our psyche, in delightful surprise and blessed that we, in adult form, have chosen to rescue, protect and bond securely with their authentic self. In essence, the me that was abandoned by biological, adoptive and Death Culture 'family.'

In this new neuron firing, new synapses create brand new realities, perspectives filling in the blanks with adult objectivity, the very thing needed for Integration of self. This galvanizes what spins out our story— archetypally, mythically, cosmically, and earthly. Timelessness is the key that pops opens the portal to Phoetics, hidden behind the steel vaults of Patriarchy's Fort Knox-like Death Culture. Finding our authentic self is a bit like entering through double glass security doors into the sacred space of safe deposit boxes. It is both real and dreamlike.

What spoke to me in any chosen book; myth, autobiography, female consciousness, goddess cultures, Female Primacy of Mother-Daughter Love (cosmic and earthly), and self-help books about family 'racquets,' dark secrets of societal shame, Abuse of You Name It....Children, Women, Animals, Maleness, and their short changed biology, how the truth flows through our non-dominant writing hand* worked together with my writing in a back and forth flow. Serpentinian. The Female Cyclic Moonpulse always taking me where I need to go.

I had been fighting sanity and hanging onto staying alive under the Death Culture permeating everywhere, everything, everyone—language, image, and punishment of just being born female. There were incidents that I could not make sense of, shook me to the musical core in intimate gatherings, paralyzed frozen from Peer Gynt and The Mountain King, just like Betty Boop in her ice block, the ghostly Cab Calloway clown, whipsnaking above her death ride; to the woman in the French film caught in an so-called 'Apachè dance' a euphemism-excuse to batter and pummel a woman who 'begs for more', an adult dance for any public entertainment. In a snuff movie in the 1930s-her partner throws her brutally through a window where another man awaits to stab her to death. Another Mack-the Knife. For Halloween my mother dressed me up as a female Apachè dancer, complete with French beret, hair pinned back on one side, black leotard, mini skirt, and the signature scarf around my neck. She was so excited. Didn't I know what Apachè dancing was? Yes. I saw in children's cartoons. When the rooster throttles the hen.

Where the hell was I?

Phoetics sparks a stream of consciousness that is both free flowing yet under your adult objective control. To wit—you are safely able to return to all that was uniquely your story's scenarios and imagery –all of which require full-on Integration. You get to finally make sense of the senseless and the lies we are hoodwinked with—the skeletons in mom and dad's closets, all the way back every generation.

This is the blessing and beauty of Phoetics. We are blessed as we bless our own images, cell by cell, frame by frame, digit by digit. All this happened over 19 linear years; the therapy sessions, journalling, books on Female Consciousness, connecting the Female Dots whilst unravelling the mares nests of Patriarchy's Death Culture.

In 2009 I began to share my Nancy's Truths binder of memoires, female glossary, photos and their portrait sketches, and goddess overlays to women healers, protectresses of sacred children, and one highly experienced writer-editor. Separately, each came back with the same thing:

Figure out what you do and teach it to women and the men who love them.

Are you a Phoetics Soul?

Are you starved for something you cannot name?
Are you secretly furious when your family writes your story for you?
Are you a woman who misses something she cannot name only
to awaken in long-lost tears and laughter you cannot name?
Are you a woman who remembers being
nine but can't sustain the feeling?
Are you a woman who can't remember being nine yet wish you could?

Are you a woman with daughters between seven and nine and
wish you could relate at a deeper, more authentic level?
Are you a woman who fears your daughters are secretly
being robbed of something you cannot identify?

Did your mother tear up her photos?
Do you know where your childhood photos are yet never frame them?
Do you *not* know where your childhood photos are and
wonder why you keep putting off finding them?
Do you ever dream of your childhood photos?
When you look at your child photos are you unable to
identify a certain feeling that is your birthright?
When you look at your childhood photo can
you finish, "Once upon a time…."

Are you a woman in traditional therapy and feel stuck
Are you a woman who has tried traditional therapy and feel famished
Are you a woman starved for something no therapy has yet to name?
Are you a woman starved for your truth? Myths? Mysteries?
Are you a woman starved for your true story,
your purpose,
your calling,
your sacred self….
Then You Are A Phoetics Soul

A Phoetics' Woman….
Finds her way back
Unearths her true story
Deciphers false myths
Preserves & honors her real myths
Fathoms, envelopes, cradles her beloved mysteries
Feasts upon female magic of her childhood photos
And tells her story to herself and to any soul who will witness.

CLIENTS' PHOETICS

Amanda Mia Mehalick-"Seeking Source"

I first met Amanda when I was conducting workshops and private sessions at the shop where she worked. Awakenings. She managed their events and was eager to try her own Phoetics session. It proved to be incredibly yet not surprisingly Spiritually Perfection. A Phoetics Biggie.

Amanda is a rare spirit here to grace the planet with her inner beauty and gifts of an intuitive empath. Her first Phoetics shares proof positive there are goddess images in all our girlhood photos, that we are the carriers of that spirit. We are not the echoes. The goddesses are echoing us. It is our original Female Language, The Female Code.

Amanda's first session birthed a rather Amniotic Image. She is just a babe-toddler, emerged in her bath, in what she calls her favorite position and to be in the water. When I first saw it, it tickled the back of my mind. Again, where had I seen this body language in some ancient or pre-ancient sculpture, portrait, votive, cave painting goddess?

The photograph was too old and blurry for publication, so I gave it my usual Styized sketching, and lo and behold, there she appeared! Totally line up with the Sleeping Lady-Goddess of Malta. Five inches long, five thousand years old.

Quite a coup for my beautiful Amanda. With her permission, these two images side by side echo her inner self. To know her is to be astounded by the uncanny similarities. It so matches her spirit.

"Seeking Source"

"Find Yourself in Phoetics®
Your Story Do You Myth It?"

"The concept of Now"

My Phoetics®

"I love naptime in the
tub
I can swim like she
does.
—naught he cue
Through the light
it begins, her
Birth!"

Amanda's Take on Phoetics

"A special recalibration occurs when you have a Phoetics session like this. If you're open to it, a remembering can take place, and through that memory a feeling of wholeness can emerge. I am very grateful for the session with Nancy and value the work she is doing in the World."

Amanda's Contact Information:

amanda@AmandaMiaMehalick.com.
Amandamiamehalick.com.
Instagram: @amandamiamehalick.

Cindy Riggs "They have the courage to beg for more"

There is no one on this earth like Cindy. Catch her Phoetics and see how she writes backward automatically as her spirit self. For readers, she translated and handwrote what she had expressed backward.

Cindy is a rare medium, spiritual consultant, certified hypnotherapist, personal development coach, energy bodyworker, author, and speaker.

The sum total of her extraordinary Phoetics experience can be enjoyed on her website, www.CindyRiggs.com

(Ducks)

I Interaction with Nature
Interaction With Nature

Nancy's Truth.com
My PHOETICS™

…Find your story…

"The dog knows not how I feel as I
Commune with The ducks and learn
Their behavior. They just want To eat-
like me. Always hungry for more
experience. Loving The water - Their
home, Their safety. Courage They
have To beg for more."

270

Lisa's Phoetics "Freya. The Norse Goddess & More"

Lisa, Lisa, Lisa! Another amazing medium, and so much fun to be with. I think my laugh muscles ached after every time spent with her. She gave of her time so much that I could never have pulled Phoetics together without her generosity of spirit and such a true, dependable friend.

Lisa is one of my clients who bequeaths multiple Mythographs. Our *Fun with Phoetics* sessions had us laughing away at the end of a photograph that had always brought frustration.

As you peruse her Phoetics, see how her girlhood images consistently line up with Freya the Norse Goddess and all she symbolizes. Every bullet point is identical to hers. Lisa's Character, Calling, and Authentic inner self.

Lisa-Freya
Norse Goddess
℘

Who Is Freya?
℘

- ❧ Old Goddess culture, Life Giver, Life Taker
- ❧ She is 1 and she is 3 = The Fates/Triple Goddess
- ❧ Powers extend into the realm of death and magic
- ❧ Loves all that is "fey" Elves/Fairies/Angels
- ❧ Her sacred day = Friday
- ❧ Her Sacred Number = 13

How Phoetics Impacted Lisa and Her Healing Journey

"When Nancy first told me she was finally writing her book and asked if I would consider sharing my girlhood photos and experiences of Phoetics, I was so honored and thrilled, I absolutely said yes! Looking back on first meeting Nancy, her presence was so beautiful and her ability to create such a safe place to be vulnerable allowed for tremendous healing to take form. I had no idea so much could come from reading a childhood photo. I had many to choose from, and in each session, (and I had many) I was guided to allow my inner child to choose which one. Photo by photo, session by session, the magic unfolded. Nancy started me on a journey of healing in a way I've never experienced before. With her loving guidance, my girlhood photos spoke of sharing, loving, and guiding me to find my giggles, my light within, and to go with the flow and be free. Absolutely a life changing experience that I will cherish for the rest of my years. Thank you, Nancy; you will forever grace my heart with your gift of Phoetics.

"Nancy, from the bottom of my heart, thank you for giving my little girl a safe place to sing!"

Lisa Noland
Email: EarthAngel913@LisaNoland.com.
www.LisaNoland.com.

Susie Schiering—Her Phoetics Knocked Me off My Feet

The day Susie brought her photographs over and I sifted through for just a nanosecond, I just about fell over. In fact, she had to catch me. There it was, what I'd been seeking all my female life, all my girlhood.

These two best friends, aged eight, reenacting the natural Sacred Union of our Female MasculineFeminine energies. Her accompanying Phoetics express the natural FemaleLove we are all are born with, ending with the natural bond longing, and she ends with, "I miss her."

> On both knees, looking reverently up at her best
> friend enacting the Natural State of Sacred Girl
> Being—-it is the very depiction and image of:

"Between Seven and nine, we turn on a dime.."

Susie expresses her Phoetics session as "Opening my eyes to things I did not realize. Phoetics gave me some clarity about my childhood and the experiences I had. It was great to remember the good times and feelings through my childhood photographs. Also, it helped me to let go of some untruths I had held onto which in turn gave me from the past. Overall, the practice of Phoetics was amazing and added to my growth as a human."

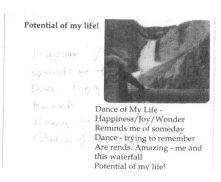

Potential of my life!

Dance of My Life -
Happiness/Joy/Wonder
Reminds me of someday
Dance - trying to remember
Are rends. Amazing - me and
this waterfall
Potential of my life!

https://susieschiering.com.
https://www.linkedin.com/in/susieschiering/.
https://www.facebook.com/fitgreenfab.
https://www.instagram.com/susieschiering/.

Vic in Stroller

Vic's Phoetics "Deeper Levels of Play"

Vic taught me one good lesson. I was giving a presentation at a spiritual bookstore, the Phoenix in Columbus. There was quite an attendance. We always hope this will light up someone's consciousness, but was I shocked when the one soul who contacted me for a private session was male.

What came out of that session blew me away. There he was, in a stroller no more than six months. And Vic started a dialogue with his younger self, who was looking around at all the colors, and trees, and the world itself.

Baby Vic: What is this place?

Adult Vic: It allows for deeper levels of play.

Only his earliest Authentic Self self, so fully present in his first earthly year, could elicit this profound Cosmic-Earthly response.

"Find Yourself in Phoetics®
Your Story Do You Myth It?"

Baby stroller

My Phoetics®

What is this place?

I'm still figuring it out. But I'm leaning towards
"it's a school of experiences". Different caliber,
"denseness in brightness
"It's energy in physical form"
It has a different quality to it that forms
these dimensional things.

These things of different qualities
where did it come from? to have
the idea to do this?

from what I can speak on: it comes from
a Source, that formed the brightness
you see in everything, and yourself.
It's about play in the brightness, that's the
idea part. This quality of dimension allows
for deeper levels of play.

Why I Was Thumbelina

There were books, many illustrations of this disturbing child trafficking tale. In my head, my grandmother was Mrs. Mouse, who took me in and then sold me to Mister Mole to be his "wife." As my grandma read me the story, I looked at her bird-like lips reading our story. How could this not upset her? How could she "sell" me (turn me over to) her many male predators in her family? It was subtle. It was glaringly obvious to me, in neon.

It behooves all of us to reread the child-trafficking, ugly truths lurking within the "time-honored" Children's Classics, to open our eyes to the crimes perpetrated upon children, disguised as children's happily ever after morality tales.

Grandma's Entry & The Great Mother Goddess Tomb

 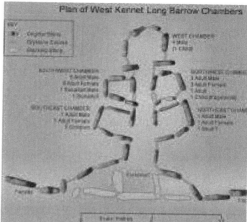

The Great Mother Goddess Tomb

The entire time I lived at my grandma's house, when I was still halfway in Female Otherworld trying to get my footing to assimilate to this strange sphere, something was always there. It was purely subconscious, like on the backburner for when you are ready to flip on the gas flame.

It was only recently when I remembered seeing floor plans from several goddess sites, that I started to draw what I remembered from Grandma's house. After all, it was where I spent the bulk of my time my precious first five and a half years When I compared my drawing to the ones on the Internet, it was astounding. I will let the image speak for itself.

The most incredible thing that jumped out at me was, not only did it fit with many Goddess Womb-Tombs from thirty thousand years ago, it also took the shape of a Queen Bee.

FEMALE GLOSSARY & TERMS: INTRODUCTION

Birthing Female Language

Male supremacy is fused into the language so that every sentence both heralds and affirms it.

—Andrea Dworkin

What a struggle for language and true female expression before my pen hit the paper, fingertips plinked the keyboard, voice hit the recorder. Trying to express my female sensibility, state of being using a male mindset language might have been from another galaxy. Dancing in molasses on crutches. Words I needed to express failed me.

Thank you, Andrea Dworkin, for validating my inevitable frustration. How was I going to express my memoirs, the sacred female truths that blossomed from them without a language that reflected all? I had no choice and began creating a female-based glossary of terms and words.

Meryl Streep and No Female Language

Recently I came across a snippet on YouTube with Streep struggling to express our lack of Female Language.

Words that come from our Female BodyPsyche. At some point, frustrated, like it was racing around her BodyPsyche pell-mell, furious there was no language for Females. Female-rooted. That women need their own language to communicate their thoughts, feelings, perceptions. All the men on stage sat in dead silence. Pregnant silence.

Then, the man furthest to her piped up with, "I think what Meryl is trying to say ..."

He never got to finish. She shrieked, rocked backward in her seat, heels in the air, howling at the irony. Well, Meryl, here is my gift to you and all Women and Girls of the World. Feel free to add your own. That is its purpose.

As time went on, a Female Glossary long-seeded itself within, flowered and blossomed in the wilds of my psyche, embodied, and fed by my Uterine gnosis. A little-known fact: women have indeed out of necessity created their own language when under the slavery of a harem. Now it is time to bring forth for women and girls, teach, make attainable and continue to cultivate, cultivate, harvest, and cultivate more. Our female Psychebodies are shame-soaked from all the words that emanate (e-Man-ate?) from the male brain. And because it is so deeply embedded in our generational subconsciousness, we don't think about it even when it permeates both written and spoken. Male thinking is either/or, all or nothing, and their language reflects it in linear terms. As you read, notice you will come across new words that are not separated by spaces. That is because they are cleaved together in my body, heart, and mind. PsycheBody. MotherDaughtering. That is Female mindfulness. Quite opposite from male, mechanical mindset. Our language reflects how we are wired, plain and simple.

My dearest, most ingenious feminist scholars fall victim to male language because what else to they have? They study, live, write, express themselves indoctrinated by the male-based institutions they attend. Huh uh. You now have a glossary to get you started in your next journals, films, fiction, nonfiction, memoires, biographies, love letters and any which way you create. Dworkin heard, saw, and was ready to parry, thrust, and riposte with one, yet she did not live long enough to create her own. Or perhaps was trapped in the century's old indoctrination like the rest of us. At least she recognized it. Its lethal effect on our well-being, self-expression, like being verbally handcuffed.

In writing about her mother, Adrienne Rich hit upon a conclusion and offered, perhaps women had been wrongly focused on using the term Sisterhood when really they should have chosen Mother and Daughterhood, echoing the primacy energies of the Female Relationship.

When you focus on MotherDaughtering, you return to everything that is us. Rich was a mother of sons and her essay was more from her daughter's point of view. However, she was a wise and brilliant, verbally sensitive woman. Openminded. Open spirited, like her contemporary, the inimitable Audre Lorde. I see that these women and others got just so close to understanding—we can't tell our stories as we feel, see, and perceive them—without the truth from our own female tongues. Silenced. Divided. Conquered by lack of language expression.

Judy Graham tackles gay language in *Another Mother Tongue*. Extraordinarily verbally sensitive, her book is worth a second and third read, especially the root origins she intuits about how these words might have begun. Dyke. Butch. Bull dyke. *Over the dyke with it.* Her take is amazing, on limitless possibilities of what certain words signified in women's status and roles. I agree with her. Language and Female-based language are the essentials of what we have gone without for eons. Emotionally starved for true expression via female verbiage.

No Female Language=No Female Power

Whenever we set out to create, write, speak, or read, another alien mindset intrudes, trespasses, interferes upon who we are, and what we are entitled to as female-owners. Do you often dream of trespassers? Do you have to trespass some old childhood backyard to get back home? My recurring dreams reflect about the frustration of no language that is Female. Sometimes it is the trampling and gate crashing of Male Mindset Language on my sacred grounds. (Dreams about bursting through your bedroom is a whole different kettle of fish, about sexual abuse.) Language holds sway over all beings. Unlike images as subjective, language is used effectively to bend minds.

From nursery rhymes to nationalistic propaganda (Disney's "Who's Afraid of the Big Bad Wolf?" was allegedly commissioned by the government during WW2). Fairy tales, tall tales, and legends are the primary anti-child propaganda and more so, anti-female child dog whistles. No one is free when words forced from an alien mindset are all that is available for self-expression. That is why this is the first text with a language flowing— succinct and image based—from the natural untainted female brain.

The challenge was obvious. Create a natural female flow. That embryonic stream of Female Consciousness, while maintaining a cogent, integrated thought system. Rather than the male, linear "this after that," this new female jargon is more myth-after-that. You may want to copy the Glossary to have beside your first and future readings. I would have preferred it perforated but it was not an option.

My favorite books are those that fall open with their own agenda, own life to points me to the energies I need at that particular moment. You may find variations on a theme cropping up but Madame Memory knows her entrances and exits so similar scenes edit themselves in more than once. Just go with it. I write, speak and must Female-Speake and that means, I may repeat a phrase here or there, in case you did not read the other piece.

Finally … there is no finally.

Femocracy, Femality & Phoetics, Rebecoming our Authentic Sacred Selves, has an eternal life all its own.

This is not so much a book as perhaps an anthology and a series, considering all the gaps and schisms in our pristine authentic PsycheBody, we must catch this first momentum in the creation of Female Language and leave all the Death Culture's in the rearview mirror. It is a wonder that women are in the throes of awaking, whole new generations of latter-day Snow Whites and Sleeping Beauties coming out of their male mindset trance, to awaken with the Kiss of Female Authenticity. After all, Authenticity's Kiss of Death is Family Over-Identification (to be discussed in book two about the Death Culture).

A NEW FEMALE GLOSSARY

Words, Phrases, and Terms

Bodypsyche. The definition of the Female Uterine Brain; how they merge and connect.

bucranium. Refers to the skull of an ox.

bucranium genius. The image of the Sacred Uterus and Fallopian tubes, as in Georgia O'Keefe's paintings of cattle skulls.

butchfemme. Our Sacred Inner Image = The Sacred Female Energies MasculineFeminine merged and balanced.

childbeing. The Sacred State of the Authentic Child.

childhood. The many "hoods" the Death Culture imposes on the Great Sacred Child.

collapsed mother. Clarissa P. Estes's term for a mother who is broken; an unmothered daughter from an unmothered daughter, who cares more about her image (the neighbors) than putting her daughter's needs first.

CSAI. Child Sexual Abuse Incest. In the Great Female Family, all child sexual abuse is incestuous; it's just a matter of degree. When one child is neglected and abused, we are affected and as adults, responsible.

dark force female (DFF). A Dark Force Soul in Female disguise.

death culture, the. Any culture derived from any consciousness other than from the Uterine Root of Femality.

eye of the heart, the. The vision of Imagination, Myth, Mystery; falling in love with the inner essence of a person place or thing.

283

emotional incest. Whenever a parent reverses roles with a child.

female eyes, female vision. The natural inborn vision of the Sacred Female; to see through Female Eyes means to see the Female Truth in all things; it turns down the volume and watches the behavior.

female psychebody. The unbroken symbiosis of female mind and body. BodyPsyche = one in word and spirit.

female being. The authentic state of being fully, securely, & consciously attached to one's female bodypsyche.

femalelove. The Force of Creation. Womb at the center of the universe. Fully present before age ten. Creative attunement fostered in girlhood and cultured for womanhood.

femality. Female plus Reality; Female Consciousness.

female wound. Those wounds particular to the sacred Female BodyPsyche.

female leadership brain, the. The original Female brain zones that carry the Characteristic necessary for Leadership.

Femocracy. Female intuitive sense of Self-Governance & Sovereignty.

genital eye, the. *The Eye of the Death Culture*. Inability to see the Invisibles. Objectifies and reduces all to the third dimension.

girlbeing. The Sacred State of the Authentic Female Child.

girl being, the sacred state of. Quintessential state of how an Authentic cosmic earthly girl rolls/diametrically opposite of Childhood or Girlhood.

isms. Isms are Prisms of darkness— the crystalline colored camouflage of dogma's lure.

mythstery. My word that combines Myth and Mystery.

Nan (from Nancy, Nun, Nonnie). Patriarchal Kryptonite; as in "That's very Nanish."

rebecoming. In Phoetics, we rebecome our Authentic Selves, or the act of Authenticity Reclaimed. In psychological terms, fully integrated.

RDF. Real Deal Female/the woman who leads from her uterus, trusts, and thinks through her body and sees see through Female Eyes.

RDFT. Real Deal Female Therapist and/or Therapy.

unmothered daughter. Any female raised by an unmothered daughter who has not done her work and reconstituted with her sacred inner daughter; all females under Death Culture are unmothered daughters of unmothered daughters.

uterverse. Combines 'universe' with its centrifocal center 'uterus'. **Also, womb at the center of the universe.**

uterine consciousness. To think-create from the Female BodyPsyche. See also Bucranium genius.

violet root. Femality's Core; our needle thin, steel-ramrod spirit nerve, the creative root from our haunches; the violet energies transmitting to and from our Sacred Female Psyche. The highest wavelength, both earthly and cosmic, is fulfilled by the second (double) X.

wildly unmothered. (First coined by Adrienne Rich). The child in us, the small female who grew up in a male-controlled world, still feels, at moments, wildly unmothered.

woman's woman. A woman who identifies with and worships the female bodypsyche; bonds with females emotionally, intellectually, spiritually.

womb at the center of the universe. See: uterverse.

LIST OF ACRONYMS
AND INITIALISMS

CSAI	Child Sexual Abuse/Incest
DFF	Dark Force Female
MDL	MotherDaughter Love
RDF	Real Deal Female
RDFT	Real Deal Female Therapist/Therapy
SSGB	Sacred State of Girlbeing
TDC	The Death Culture
SA	Stupid Adult
TDF	The Dark Force
TGSG	The Great Sacred Girl
US	Uterine Selves
VR	Violet Root
WID	Woman Identified Woman

BIBLIOGRAPHY

Ellen Bass and Laura Davis. *The Courage to Heal: A Guide for Women Survivors of Child Sexual Abuse.* New York: Harper Perennial, 1988.

Bolen, Jean Shinoda. Crossing to Avalon. New York: Crown Publishing Group, 1994.

Brezendine, Luann, MD. *The Female Brain*, reprint edition. New York: Harmony, 2007.

Capacchione, Lucia. *Recovery of Your Inner Child.* New York: Simon & Schuster, 1991.

Carlson, Kathie. *In Her Image: The Unhealed Daughter's Search for her Mother,* 1st edition. "Touch Starved, Touch Phobic." Boulder, Colorado: Shambhala, 1989.

Gadon, Elinor. *The Once and Future Goddess: A Sweeping Visual Chronicle of the Sacred Female and Her Reemergence in the Cult.* New York: Harper One, 1989.

Gimbutas, Marija. *The Goddess.* University of California Press, 2001.

Grahn, Judy. *Another Mother Tongue.* Boston: Beacon Press, 1984.

Herman, Judith. *Father-Daughter Incest* 1st edition. Harvard University Press, 1981.

Hillman, James. *The Soul's Code.* New York: Penguin Books, 1996.

Konner, Melvin. *Women after All: Sex, Evolution, and the End of Male Supremacy.* New York: W.W. Norton, 2015.

Lawson, Christine MD. *Understanding the Borderline Mother*. Lanham, Maryland: Roman & Littlefield, 2000.

Lorde, Audre *Warrior-Mythobiography*. *New York:* W. W. Norton, 2004.

Montagu, Ashley. *The Natural Superiority of Women*. London" Allen and Unwin, 1999.

Nicolson, Nigel. *Portrait of a Marriage: Vita Sackville-West and Harold Nicolson*. University of Chicago Press, 1998.

Pinkola Estes, Clarissa. Women *Who Run with the Wolves*. New York: Random House, 1992.

Rich, Adrienne. *It is Hard for Me to Write about my Mother*. New York: W. W. Norton, 2018.

_____. *Of Woman Born*. New York: W. W. Norton, 2021.

Shapiro, Francine, MD. *EMDR: Eye Movement Desensitization and Reprocessing*. Berlin, Germany: Springer Pub., 1989.

Mary Jane Sherfey MD. *The Nature and Evolution of Female Sexuality*. New York: Vintage Books, 1973.

Siegel, David MD *Parenting from the inside Out*, Penguin Publishing 2013

Sjoo, Monica and Barbara Mor. *The Great Cosmic Mother*. New York: Harper One, 1987.

Soares, M. *Butch Femme*. New York: Crown Publishing Group, 1995.

Solnit, Rebecca. "The Storykiller and His Sentence: Rebecca Solnit on Harvey Weinstein," *Literary Hub*, March 12, 2020. https://lithub.com/the-storykiller-and-his-sentence-rebecca-solnit-on-harvey-weinstein/.

EPILOGUE

"Myth"
by Muriel Rukeyser

Long afterward, Oedipus, old and blinded, walked the roads.

He smelled a familiar smell.

It was the Sphinx.

Oedipus said, "I want to ask one question.

Why didn't I recognize my mother?"

"You gave the wrong answer," said the Sphinx.

"But that was what made everything possible," said Oedipus.

"No," she said.

"When I asked, 'What walks on four legs in the morning, two at noon, and three in the evening,' you answered *Man*.

You didn't say anything about *Woman*."

"When you say Man," said Oedipus, "you include women too. Everyone knows that."

She said, "*That's what you think.*"

(Italics added)

Printed in the United States
by Baker & Taylor Publisher Services